Abiding Hope

Books by Dr. Criswell . . .

Expository Sermons on Revelation, 5 Vols. in 1
Expository Sermons on the Book of Daniel, 4 Vols. in 1
The Holy Spirit in Today's World
The Baptism, Filling and Gifts of the Holy Spirit
Expository Sermons on Galatians
Ephesians — An Exposition
Expository Sermons on James
Expository Sermons on the Epistles of Peter
Isaiah — An Exposition
Acts: An Exposition, Volumes 1, 2, and 3

A DAILY DEVOTIONAL GUIDE

W. A. Criswell

Edited by
Paige Patterson

Scripture quotations are taken from the *King James Version* of the Bible.

ABIDING HOPE: A Daily Devotional Guide

Grand Rapids, Michigan

First printing September, 1981

Library of Congress Cataloging in Publication Data

Criswell, W. A., 1909–
Abiding hope, a daily devotional guide.
1. Devotional calendars—Baptists. I. Patterson, Paige, Editor. II. Title.

BV4811.C69 242'.2 81-13041
ISBN 0-310-43840-3 ACCR2

Printed in the United States of America

To the young men and women
who are training in our
CRISWELL CENTER FOR BIBLICAL STUDIES
here in Dallas, Texas,
for the work of our Lord around the world.

Preface

This volume has been prepared to assist and encourage you in setting aside a portion of each day to spend some time reading the Word, meditating upon it, and offering your prayers to the heavenly Father. The devotional messages have been taken from half a century of ministry and experience.

Dr. Paige Patterson, a gifted theologian and my comrade and yoke-fellow in the work here in Dallas, has directed this project from its inception. There is no way in the world that I can carry on the multitudinous detail of all the responsibilities of pastoring a church and still take time for such an expansive project as this one. I am indebted to Dr. Patterson, the able president of our Center for Biblical Studies, for giving his time and effort to this project. I am also grateful to Mrs. Jo Ellen Burch, who typed the manuscript.

May God grant to you a hunger and thirst for His precious Word and a determination to read and meditate upon it daily. It is my prayer that these devotionals will assist you in the study of the Scriptures.

W. A. Criswell, Pastor
First Baptist Church
Dallas, Texas

Foreword

The daily quiet time is an opportunity for regular spiritual sustenance. Just as it takes food and rest to make your physical body run smoothly, even so it takes the reading of the Scriptures and meditation upon them to maintain spiritual fitness.

The writings of Dr. W. A. Criswell—the beloved pastor of the First Baptist Church and the able chancellor of our Criswell Center for Biblical Studies in Dallas, Texas—have been blessing the hearts of people around the world for many years. Some of those volumes penned by the great pastor-theologian are now out of print, but we have gone back through all of his numerous volumes and extracted portions to be used in this daily devotional guide. (The sources are listed in the back of this book.)

This book is designed to encourage you to read a passage of Scripture daily. Each passage is accompanied by a brief and thought-provoking devotional message, together with a focal verse for the day. We encourage you to mark the focal verses and even to memorize them.

Just reading the Scriptures will give you new purpose in living. The Bible is the only perfect word available to our troubled world. It contains the matchless principles by which every problem can be solved. We trust this collection of devotional thoughts will encourage you to the regular study of God's Word.

Paige Patterson, Editor
Criswell Center for Biblical Studies
Dallas, Texas

Genesis 1:1–28

THE MYSTERY OF THE HUMAN BODY

And God said, Let us make man in our image, after our likeness: and let them have dominion over the fish of the sea, and over the fowl of the air, and over the cattle, and over all the earth, and over every creeping thing that creepeth upon the earth (1:26).

Where can a man buy a cap for his knee
  Or a key to the lock of his hair?
Can his eyes be called an academy
  Because there are pupils there?

What gems are found in the crown of his head?
  Who crosses the bridge of his nose?
Can he use when shingling the roof of his house
  The nails on the end of his toes?

Can the crook on his elbow be sent to jail?
  If so, what can he do?
How does he sharpen his shoulder blades?
  I'm sure I don't know, do you?

Can he sit in the shade of the palms of his hands
  Or beat on the drum of his ear?
Does the calf of his leg eat the corn on his toes?
  If so, why not grow corn on the ear?

As you watch a child grow and become an adult, think of the marvelous mystery of change, rebuilding, and reconstruction. During every minute of every week of every month of every year of the whole life, the entire body is being marvelously rebuilt. Solid bone, piece by piece, is being torn down and reconstructed. Every unit of the eye is being taken apart and rebuilt, yet it never loses a moment of life. The stream is never cut off; the electricity is never shut down. Each little worker comes in, picks up where his predecessor has been working, and carries right on without a moment's hesitation.

We need new brains, but we are never conscious of any change. We need new lungs, but we never lose a breath. We need new stomachs, but we keep on digesting our meals. We need new hearts, but they never cease to beat. All of this marvelous work is being changed piece by piece every moment of every day, and we are never conscious of it at all.

January 2

Genesis 2:1–15

THE HOAX OF EVOLUTION

And the Lord *God took the man, and put him into the garden of Eden to dress it and to keep it (2:15).*

The evolutionists say that life came about accidentally. For example, a great flash of lightning passed through the gaseous vapors that envelop this earth and created a life that fell down into the ocean and began to grow and evolve until finally the man emerged.

That proposal reminds me of a passage I read in the *Reader's Digest,* quoting Professor Edwin Conklin, the great Princeton University biologist: "The probability of life beginning from accident is comparable to the probability of the unabridged dictionary resulting from an explosion in a printing factory."

Not only is the hypothesis or theory of evolution unable to explain any of the differing phenomena we see around us, but another thing must also be earnestly considered. The fixity of the species as we know them is a rebuke to and a repudiation of the theory of evolution!

A species is a solid, unbreakable unit in the organic world. God made it so. There may be varieties in the species. There may be change and development in the species. But the species itself is unbreakable. It has never been demonstrated that the limits of a species have been set aside. That is according to the law of God. The Lord God said that the fowls of the air and the fish of the sea and the living creatures on the earth shall bring forth after their kind. This law has never deviated!

Every life form gives birth to a progeny after its kind. There is no exception to that, neither in geological time, primeval time, historical time, observable time, nor in contemporary time. The fixity of the species is a blind alley up which evolution comes to a dead end!

January 3

Genesis 7:1–24

THE CERTAINTY OF JUDGMENT

And the Lord said unto Noah, Come thou and all thy house into the ark; for thee have I seen righteous before me in this generation (7:1).

History books describe the terrible flood which destroyed Galveston, Texas, in 1900. The federal government sent a warning to the city, saying, "A great storm is coming. Flee for your lives! Find refuge in the mainland. Leave!" At that time, a long iron bridge connected the city with the mainland, and a few people left the city over that bridge. But the majority of the city went outdoors and looked up at the sky. There was not a cloud to be seen. The ocean was calm and serene. The people went back to work and about their business.

The federal government sent them warning from the weather bureau not once or twice, but time and again: "A great storm is coming! Flee for your lives!" The people went out and looked at the sky. It was still blue, and the ocean was calm and peaceful.

Early one morning a woman awakened her husband to tell him the wind was beginning to blow and the rain was beginning to fall. He got up and checked all the windows. The rain became a deluge, and the wind became a hurricane. Great tidal waves swept over the island endlessly. For months rescuers picked up dead bodies. The entire city was destroyed.

There are some things in life that are not optional. Our mandate from the Lord to repent is exactly like that. A time of vast judgment is coming upon this world.

January 4

Genesis 18:1–26

THE FOUNDATION OF ALL VALUES

That be far from thee to do after this manner, to slay the righteous with the wicked: and that the righteous should be as the wicked, that be far from thee: Shall not the Judge of all the earth do right? (18:25).

Once on a tour I traveled through Hungary, Poland, Russia, Rumania, Czechoslovakia, and East Germany. The people in those godless, communist, atheistic countries own nothing. There can be no communist government in a land where the churches preach the gospel in power and the people turn in faith to the Lord. When people turn away from God, they lose the great values that are dear to their hearts.

An illustration of this truth can be found in America. Many years ago an affluent atheist decided to build a town in Montana. When he built it, he said, "There is to be no church or no preacher in it." His city had a population of five thousand people.

He soon found that he had plenty of women but not a decent one among them. They were harlots and prostitutes. The men who flocked to the town loved to gamble, drink, and fight. No family with children wanted to move into the city.

After five years of that experiment, the bottom fell out of his little city, and he delivered a manifesto through the newspapers and in handbills:

> To Whom It May Concern: God knows that there is no such person as God, and my motto has always been, "To hell with religion." But for some fool reason, which no man can fathom, I have found by experience we cannot do business in this country on any other basis than that silly bit of sentiment which we stamp on our coins, "In God We Trust." Therefore, infernal foolishness though it all is, I have sent out for a parson and we are going to build a church.

The church is the very foundation of all the values we hold dear to our hearts. Even all of our material and secular *values* are based upon the spiritual values that are taught in the Bible.

January 5

Exodus 2:1–25

THESE ARE MY PEOPLE

And it came to pass in those days, when Moses was grown, that he went out unto his brethren, and looked on their burdens: and he spied an Egyptian smiting a Hebrew, one of his brethren (2:11).

Faith is a wonderful and precious devotion. Moses identified himself with God's people, even renouncing the throne of the pharaohs to be numbered among those poor, outcast Jewish slaves.

Let me illustrate this from an experience in my own life. I was in Kharkov, a great city in Russia, where the Russians build their tanks and industrial complexes. The Soviet government often takes the church and places it out on the edge of town behind a wall in order to persecute it and hide it away. I wanted to visit the Baptist church in Kharkov on the edge of town. When we went through the door in the wall that hid the church, the pastor and his congregation walked toward us. Walking by my side was the Intourist escort, the state-assigned guide of the Russian government. As we faced the approaching pastor and his people, the guide said to me, "Look at them! Look how poor they are; look how ignorant they are! Such trash!" He spoke in contempt of the people.

I turned to him and said, "But these are my people. I am one of them, and I want to be numbered as one of them. Poor, ignorant, trash? They are God's people; they are my brothers and sisters; they belong to me; and I belong to them. My life is cast with them."

That is what it is to be a Christian, and that is saving faith. By faith, Moses, turning down the allurements and pleasures of Egypt, chose rather to stand with the people of God.

January 6

Exodus 10:1–20

HOW TO PLEASE THE DEVIL

And Moses said, We will go with our young and with our old, with our sons and with our daughters, with our flocks and with our herds will we go; for we must hold a feast unto the Lord *(10:9).*

Satan hates family religion. He does not like it when the whole family goes to church. In our church we have a special entrance in the educational building for children. On any Sunday you can see fathers or mothers, or both, drive down, stop at that entrance, open the car door, leave their little boy or girl, and drive off. When the Sunday school hour is finished, they drive by that same entrance and pick up their children.

When I see that, I think in my heart, "Now, that pleases the devil very much." He likes that. He has whispered into the home of those parents, "If you feel that you must do something about the church services, it is all right to take the little boy. But just take him; don't go with him." The devil knows that when the little boy grows up to be a man, he will not continue to attend church services. He is going to Sunday school just as long as his parents make him. But some day, when he is grown and can do as he pleases, then he will cut out that church business just as his father-model did before him.

Oh, for the spirit of the great noncompromisers! "Not so," says Moses. "We are all going. Every son, every daughter, every father, every mother. The Lord loves family religion. The Lord God has called us all. And all of us are going."

January 7

Exodus 15:1–27

THE GOD OF HEALING

For I am the Lord *that healeth thee (15:26).*

Only God can heal, and all healing is divine healing. If there is healing, God does it. Doctors can operate, cut, saw, sew, prescribe, and diagnose, but only God can heal.

It may not be in God's will for healing to occur in a given case, but we have every scriptural right to look to heaven for healing. (1) We have the right because of who and what God is. His very name is *Jehovah Ropheka,* "I am the Lord that healeth thee." (2) We have the right because of the example and the ministry of our Savior (Matt. 8:16–17). (3) We have this right because of the Spirit's indwelling (Rom. 8:11). All three Persons of the Godhead are pledged to this remembrance of our infirmities in saving, healing grace.

God has healed in days past in answer to prayer. God healed Abimelech when Abraham prayed for him (Gen. 20:17). God healed Miriam when Moses prayed for her (Num. 12:13–14). God healed Hezekiah when the king turned his face to the wall and with bitter weeping asked God for length of days (Isa. 38:4–5). Jesus healed the leper who in faith prayed to Him (Matt. 8:2).

At a church dinner for men and boys, I heard the testimony of one who had won the Olympic title of "the strongest man in the world." To my amazement he began his talk by telling about a divine healing experience. When he was a little boy, four years of age, the doctors said he could not live. But a godly grandfather brought his sorrow to a pastor who, in turn, prayed to God for the life of the child. The lad was miraculously delivered. The God of healing is available to hear our petitions.

January 8

Leviticus 13:1–39

THE FIRST BRIGHT SPOT

When a man shall have in the skin of his flesh a rising, a scab, or bright spot, and it be in the skin of his flesh like the plague of leprosy; then he shall be brought unto Aaron the priest, or unto one of his sons the priests (13:2).

Who would have thought the little bright spot, appearing on the person of some member of the congregation, to be a matter of such grave concern? Almost every disease begins with a small infection, but its terror lies in its strength to grow. It is so with sin. Hardly anyone becomes a colossal sinner suddenly. It is growth and confirmation in sin that are terribly disastrous, but that does not take away from the jeopardizing alarm of its first appearance.

Were it not for the first drink, there would be no drunkards. Were there no first game, there would be no gamblers. Were there no first playing with temptation, there would be no infidelity. It is that little bright spot beginning the story that leads to death.

That bright spot appears in every life, and, contrary to what many may think, it appears early in life. If our children were miniature divinities, we might hope to train them in goodness and see them live the remainder of their days in perfection.

However, children don't need to be taught to become sinners. In the so-called "age of innocence," yes, even in babyhood, an infant will know anger and impatience. It is difficult to deny the biblical observation that we are born in sin and shapen in iniquity (Ps. 51:5).

January 9

Leviticus 19:1–37

EQUALITY FOR ALL

Ye shall do no unrighteousness in judgment: thou shalt not respect the person of the poor, nor honor the person of the mighty: but in righteousness shalt thou judge thy neighbor (19:15).

On my morning walk down Swiss Avenue, I see a black man with a patch over one eye. He greets me by name. It does my heart good just to listen to his cheery voice. On one occasion, my friend got in step with me and walked back up the street by my side.

He said, "Did you know that every Sunday morning I hear you preach?"

"Oh," I said, "I didn't know that."

"Yes," he said, "I belong to the Church of God over here. I go to Sunday school and then come home and listen to my radio. I listen to you preach."

As we walked along, he began to open up to me. "You know, I go to the office of the Chief of Police and sit out there, and there's a receptionist in front of his office and she won't let me in. Along will come a rich man, and he doesn't sit out there in that office. He just walks right on in, pays no attention to that receptionist and just sits down."

Then he said, "Do you know, some day we're all gonna be up there before God, and, you know, there ain't gonna be no poor and there ain't gonna be no rich up there in heaven. There ain't nobody goin' by that receptionist, whether he's rich or poor. He ain't gonna get by that receptionist to God."

He said to me, "You know who that receptionist is? That receptionist is the Lord Jesus Christ. There ain't nobody that's gonna see God unless he goes through that receptionist. That receptionist is gonna have to take him in, and that receptionist is gonna have to introduce him. Nobody gets to God who doesn't go in with that receptionist."

What a blessed thought—and what great theology!

Leviticus 20:1–8

A BENT TO SINNING

Sanctify yourselves therefore, and be ye holy: for I am the Lord *your God (20:7).*

The Roman thought only in terms of the state. His highest goal was to bring the life of the citizen into conformity with the welfare of the empire.

The Greek made human conduct an object for philosophical speculation. He compared man as he was with man as he might be, and hence never developed a clear sense of sin. To the Greek, what we call "sin" was only a passing weakness. It was a hesitation, a turning aside from normal development.

But the Hebrew had seen the glory of Jehovah. He had seen the moral grandeur of the Almighty, and he compared man as he was with man as he ought to be.

Human nature against the background of pure holiness was dark and dismal. Its inherent lawlessness needed to be restrained. Life, therefore, became a civil war between evil tendencies and godly standards, a war in which defeat was all too frequent. It was a battle which was unceasingly fought throughout the generations, from babyhood to the grave.

Every soul was called to the conflict against the iniquitous bent of the natural self.

It was thus that the Hebrew, in the presence of the holy God, had a sense of failure, guilt, shortcoming. The ceremonial system taught him the same lesson when he came before the Lord Jehovah. Condemned in his sin and lost in his transgression, the Hebrew sought relief and forgiveness in sacrifice, such as the sin offering, the guilt offering, the trespass offering. And this finally led to Jesus, "the Lamb of God, which taketh away the sin of the world."

Where there is no sense of sin, there is no desire for a Savior. But if God is holy and pure, exalted higher than the heavens, and if He expects of us holiness and purity even as He is pure, then how greatly do we need a Savior to deliver us from our sins!

January 11

Deuteronomy 6:1–25

THE WEEDS IN YOUR GARDEN

And thou shalt teach them diligently unto thy children, and shalt talk of them when thou sittest in thine house, and when thou walkest by the way, and when thou liest down, and when thou risest up (6:7).

A friend of Coleridge, while looking at the poet's weed-filled garden, said to him, "Why don't you dig up those weeds and plant flowers?" Coleridge replied, "I don't want to prejudice the garden in favor of flowers. We just let it grow up as it is."

If you do not guide your children heavenward, Godward, Christward, churchward, you will be the only one who is not influencing them. The world will have its influence. The infidel will have his influence. The criminal element, the pimp, the procurer, the bookie, the chiseler, and the dope pusher will all have their influence. The streets of the city offer no diplomas and confer no degrees, but they educate with terrible precision. The nation's hope lies in the godly nurture and admonition of the children under the loving, endearing hands of their parents.

You ask me why I go to church;
I give my mind a careful search.
Because I need to breathe the air
Where there is an atmosphere of prayer.
I need the hymns that churches sing;
They set my faith and hope on wing.
They keep old truths and memory green,
Reveal the work of things unseen.
Because my boy is watching me
To know whatever he can see
That tells him what his father thinks.
And with his eager soul he drinks
The things I do in daily walks,
The things I say in daily talks.
If I with him the church will share,
My son will make his friendships there.

January 12

1 Samuel 1:1–28

LENT TO THE LORD

Therefore also I have lent him to the LORD; as long as he liveth he shall be lent to the LORD. And he worshiped the LORD there (1:28).

A devout, godly, and affluent couple were faithful in the church, faithful in their devotion, and faithful in their gifts. They prayed, gave to missions, and supported the work of the Lord. They had one daughter, who, one day, came home from school and announced that she had felt God's call to be a missionary. She planned to begin immediately preparing to go to a foreign field to represent her Lord as a missionary.

The parents at first accepted the news with sorrow of heart. They said, "We have given our money, our prayers, our time, our love, and our devotion, but you are the only child we have. To see you leave and go to a foreign field is almost too much." They resolved that they would take the matter to God in prayer and tell Him all about it. When they finished their praying, they had found an infinite peace and rest in Him. "Lord, not only the money we have, not only the prayers of our hearts, not only the devotion of our lives, but Lord, we also give to Thee this only child."

What a marvelous attitude!

January 13

1 Samuel 3:1–21

A MANDATE FROM GOD

Therefore Eli said unto Samuel, Go, lie down: and it shall be, if he call thee, that thou shalt say, Speak, LORD; for thy servant heareth. So Samuel went and lay down in his place (3:9).

A story that moves me every time I hear it is about my famous predecessor in the First Baptist Church of Dallas. When he was on a hunting trip with the Chief of Police of the city of Dallas, his gun accidentally fired, killing the Chief of Police.

The great pastor was plunged into an indescribable and abysmal sorrow. He felt that because he had killed a man he could never preach again. But the Lord appeared to him in the night. He appeared and spoke a second time. The Lord spoke a third time, calling the pastor again to the incomparable ministry with which the Holy Spirit had endowed him.

The man ministered forty-seven years in that pulpit. This is the same Lord Jesus.

January 14

1 Samuel 16:1–13

THROUGH THE EYES OF GOD

But the LORD said unto Samuel, Look not on his countenance, or on the height of his stature; because I have refused him: for the LORD seeth not as man seeth; for man looketh on the outward appearance, but the LORD looketh on the heart (16:7).

As a youth, in the days of the depression, I was in Chicago. I happened to be with a young fellow from Seattle, whose rich father sent him away because his stepmother did not want him around. He was a most knowledgeable, worldly young fellow. He knew all about Al Capone. I had wondered as a youngster how Al Capone could hold the city of Chicago in the palm of his hand. Well, this young fellow soon showed me. He took me to one of Al Capone's speakeasies in the middle of town, right under the nose of forty policemen who patrolled up and down there every day. It was an astonishment to me to observe the illegal gambling and drinking.

But there was another side to Al Capone. Only the Lord knows how many thousands, and perhaps millions, of dollars Al Capone poured into feeding the poor and taking care of widows and orphans. He had every precinct bound up in the hollow of his hand. When the time came to vote for aldermen or mayor, all of those people followed the slate of Al Capone to the tee, and the law could not touch him. The people who were starving to death were overwhelmed by his goodness and generosity.

Was Capone actually a worthy man? He was a gangster and a murderer of the vilest sort. The law-abiding citizens of the United States called Capone a leech, a curse. Yet they were unable to touch him because of his good works. They finally sent him to the penitentiary because of income tax evasion. This is an illustration of how differently from God people look at their deeds.

We seek to commend ourselves to God, but God says our good works are like filthy rags in His sight. If we are ever accepted in the eyes of God, it must be through Christ our Lord. There is no other way.

January 15

2 Samuel 12:1–31

GAINING THROUGH LOSS

But now he is dead, wherefore should I fast? can I bring him back again? I shall go to him, but he shall not return to me (12:23).

One time I read of a mother who was deeply devoted to the Lord. But her big, strong husband was not a Christian. They had a child who became sick and died. The father went to his wife's pastor and said, "My wife is so frail. She has spent long vigils during the illness of our little girl, and now that the child has died, I am afraid she cannot bear it. Please, would you come, pray, and lend strength?"

So the pastor went to the home to pray with the mother. As they came into the house, they heard someone speaking. They paused as they saw the frail mother kneeling before the casket of the little girl. She was praying, "Dear God, You gave and You have taken away; blessed be Your name. Our little child is safe with You, and You will care for her until You give her back to us again. But, dear God, my husband does not know that promise and strength. He is not saved; he is not a Christian; he does not know You. I pray, Lord, that You will help and strengthen him, and in this may he find You as Savior and Lord."

The man turned to the pastor and said, "I do not know the promise of which she speaks. What is the strength, and who is the personal Savior who could give such victory and triumph to one who has lost so much?"

Through that experience, the pastor easily led the husband to the Lord. There is always a secret strength in the people of God. The Lord is standing by. He is always near.

January 16

2 Samuel 24:1–25

THE MEASURE OF DEVOTION

And the king said unto Araunah, Nay; but I will surely buy it of thee at a price: neither will I offer burnt offerings unto the LORD my God of that which doth cost me nothing. So David bought the threshingfloor and the oxen for fifty shekels of silver (24:24).

When I attended the famous Passion Play in Oberammergau, I was told that an American man and his wife were once in attendance at the play. Between acts, the wife said to her husband, "Now you pick up that cross, and I will take a picture of you carrying the cross." He thought it was a good idea; so he walked over to pick up the cross. He could not even lift it. About that time Anthony Lang, the great man who for thirty years played the part of the Christus in the play, came by. The American asked him, "Why so heavy? This is just a play. This is just an act. Why is the cross so heavy?" Anthony Lang humbly and simply answered, "Sir, when I carry it, if I do not feel it, I cannot play my part."

It is thus with our devotion to Christ. If it does not cost us anything, if we do not feel it, it becomes meaningless. And that is exactly the measure of our devotion before God. If it costs us nothing, then it turns to dust and ashes in our hands.

January 17

1 Kings 17:1–16

THE GIFT OF FAITH

And she went and did according to the saying of Elijah: and she, and he, and her house, did eat many days (17:15).

Witness the faith of Elijah, who believed that God would take care of both him and the widow's household through the years of the terrible drought.

The barrel of meal shall not waste,
Neither shall the cruse of oil fail,
Until the day that the Lord
Sendeth rain upon the earth.

George Muller, by prayer and faith alone, sustained his orphanage in Bristol, England, for a generation. He once said, "It pleased the Lord to give me something like a gift of faith so that unconditionally I could ask and look for an answer." This man of prayer never asked another human being for any of his needs for food, clothing, or provisions. He asked only God, and God faithfully answered abundantly and triumphantly.

From paradise in Eden, to Patmos in Revelation, this gift of faith marks the trail of the company of the blessed, the heaven-bound saints of God. No wonder the faith chapter, Hebrews 11, sounds like a roll call of God's heroes! The gift of faith was and is their sublimest endowment. That gift is still available even in this generation.

January 18

1 Kings 19:1–18

A PROPHET'S GREAT NEED

And as he lay and slept under a juniper tree, behold, then an angel touched him, and said unto him, Arise and eat (19:5).

How grateful we are that God does not answer all our prayers! We are thus thankful concerning Elijah's prayer that he might die. If God had answered that prayer, Elijah would have died in despair. There would have been no still small voice, no commission to Elisha, no translation to heaven in a whirlwind and a chariot of fire. The Lord's plans made no provision for any tombstone for a prophet under a juniper tree.

In any case, where there is gold in a person, God sticks to that person until He brings it out. The providences of the prophet's life are like a crucible that holds the refiner's fire. Under the juniper tree, praying to die, he does not pray for fire or for rain. No one ever prays positively in discouragement. Under that juniper tree is the worst place in the world to pray for a revival. Revival prayers are heard only on the mountaintop. The only person the Lord cannot use is the discouraged person. But God does not fail. Under this juniper tree no ravens were sent, no barrels of meal and cruses of oil were provided, but God did send an angel.

As we follow the story, we are almost overwhelmed by God's marvelous goodness to the prophet. God seemed to be doubly solicitous about him. There was no angel at Tishbi, Cherith, or Zarapheth. Elijah had drunk water at Cherith, but never water drawn by an angel. He had eaten bread made from flour multiplied miraculously in the home of the widow at Zarapheth, but he had never eaten cakes made by the hands of an ambassador from the courts of glory. Elijah's flight and his journey of fear were undertaken in his own weakness, but God helped even when the prophet was running away from his post of duty.

January 19

2 Kings 2:1–25

A CHARIOT OF FIRE

And it came to pass, as they still went on, and talked, that, behold, there appeared a chariot of fire, and horses of fire, and parted them both asunder; and Elijah went up by a whirlwind into heaven (2:11).

Our spirit of commitment is like that of the English mystic poet, William Blake, when he wrote:

Bring me my bow of burning gold,
Bring me my arrows of desire;
Bring me my spear. O clouds unfold!
Bring me my chariot of fire.
We shall not cease from battle's strife,
Nor shall the sword sleep in our hand,
'Til we have built Jerusalem
In this fair and pleasant land.

Our work will not be done until Jesus comes again. Even as Elijah, we must continue in the work of the kingdom until God sends a "chariot of fire" or calls us home.

January 20

2 Kings 5:1–19

THE GREAT ENCOURAGER

And she said unto her mistress, Would God my lord were with the prophet that is in Samaria! for he would recover him of his leprosy (5:3).

How often we hear of a man dying soon after he retires because he has so little to do! Nothing destroys the fiber of a person's life like feeling useless and unwanted, having nothing to do and no purpose in life. Though many of the elderly and invalid feel they have no purpose, God has given them a ministry of intercession and prayer. They can pray for their pastors and Christian workers. I have never heard a sweeter word than what Spurgeon once said to a humble disciple, "My friend, some day when you have the ear of the great King, will you call my name?"

The message of Jesus' care and concern is addressed to the lost who also lose hope. God alone knows the number of young men and women who find themselves enmeshed in sin and compromise and nearly give up. The Lord takes a broken life and mends it. He forgives and lifts the person up. He strengthens and encourages. The Lord's great assignment in the earth is not to destroy people's lives but to save their lives that they might have strength and ability in Him. There is no person whom the Lord cannot lift up and set his feet upon a rock. He puts a song in the heart. The redeemed person can go forward forgiven and strengthened in the name of the Lord.

January 21

2 Kings 6:1–17

FIGHTING THE BATTLE

And Elisha prayed, and said, Lord, I pray thee, open his eyes, that he may see. And the Lord opened the eyes of the young man; and he saw: and, behold, the mountain was full of horses and chariots of fire round about Elisha (6:17).

Somewhere I read a story about the Supreme Commander and General of the Army, Dwight D. Eisenhower, who decided to observe his forces make the historic crossing of the Rhine River. Accompanied by another general, he fell into step with a group of Thirtieth Division infantrymen, all apparently in high spirits, en route to their boats.

Then Eisenhower noticed that one young soldier looked depressed. "How are you feeling?" he asked.

"General, I'm awful nervous. I was wounded two months ago and just got back from the hospital yesterday. I don't feel so good."

"Well, you and I are a good pair then, because I'm nervous, too. But we've planned this attack for a long time, and we've got all the planes, the guns, and airborne troops we can use. Maybe if we just walk along together to the river, we'll be good for each other."

"Oh," replied the young soldier, "I meant I *was* nervous. I'm not anymore. I guess it's not so bad around here."

Soldier in Christ's army, are you discouraged? Are you afraid of the enemy? Are you thinking of retreating? Then remember that Christ has promised to walk with you, to inspire and encourage you. As you walk in obedience to His commands, you will experience the promised Presence. He has guaranteed it; yours is but to obey.

We are never alone. We are never fighting the battle for Christ without His help or without the love, prayers, and support of a multitude of others. The angels in heaven and the stars in their courses battle for the person who is doing God's work in the earth.

January 22

2 Kings 7:1–20

WHO IS THE MISSIONARY?

Then they said one to another, We do not well: this day is a day of good tidings, and we hold our peace: if we tarry till the morning light, some mischief will come upon us: now therefore come, that we may go and tell the king's household (7:9).

As a young man, I knew the pastor of the First Baptist Church in Amarillo, a gifted and marvelous minister of the Word of God.

He resigned that affluent pulpit and went north to accept an assignment. He resigned because a survey had been made in the northern part of the United States, and the official report was this: "There are seven thousand churches with seven thousand pastors who [that year] preached five hundred twenty-six thousand sermons without a single convert and without a single baptism." Can you imagine a harsher indictment than that? The Amarillo pastor described a church which had a multi-million dollar plant, a large staff, and one of the most famous preachers in America. Yet, in the preceding year, they had only two people come for baptism.

Paid preachers and missionaries alone will never win the world to Christ. According to the Word of God, all Christians are to be missionaries, preachers, ministers, and witnesses to the truth of God in Christ Jesus.

January 23

Job 7:1–21

WHAT IS LIFE?

My days are swifter than a weaver's shuttle, and are spent without hope (7:6).

What is life? Some answers are given in earth's best literature. For example, Hans Christian Andersen wrote, "Life is a fairy tale, written by God's finger." Robert Browning wrote, "Life is probation and the earth is not the goal, but the starting point." Thomas Carlyle wrote, "Life is a little gleam of time between two eternities." Goethe wrote, "Life is the childhood of our immortality." William Shakespeare wrote, "Life is a tale told by an idiot, full of sound and fury, signifying nothing." Henry Thoreau wrote, "Life is like a stroll upon the beach."

To us who love the Lord and have given our hearts to Him, it is interesting to read in the Scriptures what God says about life. Job said our life is like the "sparks that fly upward," like a messenger sent swiftly on his way, like a ship crossing the bosom of the sea, like an eagle darting to its prey. In Isaiah 40, the inspired prime minister of Judah said that life is like a flower that fades and like the grass that withers. The pastor of the church in Jerusalem wrote, "What is your life? It is even a vapour, that appeareth for a little time and then vanisheth away." There is an unsubstantiality in life that is undeniable. It is like our breath on a cold, frosty morning. How quickly it dissipates. It is like a brittle thread, not one-tenth the substance of a spider's thread, so easily broken and torn apart.

There are certainties about life, and Number One is that it is ending. Its certain and inevitable conclusion is that we die—sometimes so suddenly, so tragically. We cast ourselves upon the mercies of God so that God will give us breath and length of days.

January 24

Job 13:1–28

SATAN'S BOUNDARIES

Though he slay me, yet will I trust in him: but I will maintain mine own ways before him (13:15).

Some years ago I had dinner with Dr. Black, the president of Robert Presbyterian College in Istanbul. He married a Bulgarian and was in Bulgaria when the Communists took it over. He told me that the strength and power of the Communists over their people is beyond imagination. He said that children will turn informers against their parents, even when they know it will mean the death of their fathers and mothers. He then added something I will never forget. There is a kingdom of darkness in this world presided over by a king, just as there is a kingdom of light presided over by Jesus Christ. He said that the kingdom of atheistic Communism is an expression of the kingdom of Satan.

There is a God in this world, and we see Him in His illimitable power, in His command of the elements and of disease. It was Satan who destroyed God's perfect creation. It was Satan who destroyed God's re-creation, made the animal kingdom vicious, and caused people to be full of murderous thoughts.

Job gives us a good example of this truth. After he had suffered his many and great losses, he asked the question as to who caused his heartache and agony. He came to realize that Satan did it under the permissive will of God.

Job 19:1–29

THE EMPTINESS OF INFIDELITY

For I know that my redeemer liveth, and that he shall stand at the latter day upon the earth (19:25).

Once I stood before the baptistry of the William Carey Memorial Baptist Church in Calcutta, India. Beside the baptistry was a large, white marble plaque which bore an inscription identifying this as the place where Adoniram Judson, Ann Hasseltine Judson, and Luther Rice were baptized into the Baptist communion. They had been sent out as missionaries by the Congregational Board of Missions. Having been cut off from the support of the Congregational Board, it was agreed that the Judsons would go on to Burma while Luther Rice would return to America to raise support.

As a young man, Adoniram attended Brown University, our oldest Baptist institution. During his college days, he returned home and announced to his parents, "I am an infidel. I do not believe in God and I certainly do not believe in Christ, and less do I believe in the church." The announcement shocked his father and broke the heart of his mother. He went out from his father's house, leaving the faith and the church, intending to live a prodigal and debauched life.

As he journeyed, he came to a country inn and asked the landlord for a night's lodging. The landlord said, "Yes, I have a room, but in the room next to it a man is dying. Would that bother you?" Judson replied, "Ha! I am not afraid of death. I will take the room."

Through the hours of the night he listened to the agony, the cries, and the convulsions of the man in the next room. He was unable to get that man out of his heart, thinking, "Is he ready to die? Is he ready to meet God?"

The next morning Judson sought out the landlord to ask about the dying man. The landlord replied, "Sir, he is dead." Judson asked, "Did you know who he was?" "Yes," said the landlord, "he was a young fellow from Providence College." Judson cried, "Providence College? What was his name?" The landlord answered, "His name was Elbert Winthrop."

Adoniram Judson was astonished and awestruck, for that was the very young man who had introduced him to infidelity. He fell on his face and asked God to forgive him. He returned to his mother and father. He made a confession of faith in the church and was received into membership. He enrolled in seminary and became our first missionary.

January 26

Job 23:1–17

THE ENTIRE PICTURE

But he knoweth the way that I take: when he hath tried me, I shall come forth as gold (23:10).

Some time ago in the Cookson Hills of eastern Oklahoma, I took a canoe trip with one of my deacons down the Illinois River, one of the most beautiful streams in the world. The river twisted and turned, and around each bend we saw things happen one at a time as we came to them. But you could stand on the top of one of the highest hills in the area and see that river for a long distance.

That is how God sees things. To us, things happen one at a time, a day at a time, and we do not know what is around the bend of the day. But God sees the entire picture, from beginning to end.

January 27

Job 24:1–25

WHO KNOWS THE FUTURE?

Why, seeing times are not hidden from the Almighty, do they that know him not see his days? (24:1).

The occult is sweeping America like a storm. Ask the magician about tomorrow. What of future life? Houdini was probably the greatest magician America ever knew, and he was followed by one almost as great, Blackstone.

Before Houdini died, he made a covenant with Blackstone that his ashes were to be scattered from a bridge in Chicago. Once a year, Houdini's widow and Blackstone, holding an object in his hand, would stand on that bridge. Houdini was to knock the object out of Blackstone's hand. Year after year Blackstone stood there with an object in his hand, crying, "Houdini, come and knock this object out of my hand. Let us know that you live." They finally quit. The magician doesn't know about the future.

Take the question to the secularists, the men of the world, the men who run the military, business, and political life. Ask them about the grave and the life to come. I remember a conversation between a young sailor and his commanding officer as they were steaming into combat on one of the great battleships of the U.S. Navy. The young fellow was afraid. Trembling, he went to the officer and said, "Sir, I am afraid. Do you have a word for me about death and the world to come?" The commanding officer replied to the sailor's question and said, "Young man, I have always felt that there was nothing but here and now, so I try to get as much pleasure out of life as I can. I know nothing of the life beyond the grave." This is the word of the whole world. The philosopher, the scientist, the magician, the man of the secular world—they do not know the future.

Does God have an answer? Does God speak to us? Does the Lord say words to us about the grave and about the life that is to come? Yes, He speaks on page after page of His holy Word.

January 28

Job 26:1–14

THE BIBLE AND SCIENCE

He stretcheth out the north over the empty place, and hangeth the earth upon nothing (26:7).

Look now to the Word of God to see what kind of scientific background is written upon the pages of God's holy Book.

The Egyptians said that the world is sustained by five great pillars, one at each corner and one in the middle. That was the science of the Egyptians when Job wrote, "God hangeth the earth upon nothing."

The Greeks were taught to believe that this world is held up by an immense giant named Atlas, upon whose great shoulders and back the world rested. That is what the learned, sophisticated Greeks believed.

The Hindu scientist and theologian believed that this earth is sustained on the back of a gigantic elephant, that the elephant stands on the back of an enormous sea-turtle, and that the sea-turtle swims in a cosmic ocean. Then they ran out of imagination and quit without saying what the ocean stands on.

However, from beginning to ending there is not a word or a syllable or a revelation in the Word of God that has contradicted or ever will contradict any true, substantiated scientific fact. The reason is very simple. The Lord God who inspired the Book is the Lord God who made these things from the beginning. That is why, when the Lord speaks through His servants, you can base your life and your soul and your salvation upon what God has said.

January 29

Job 34:1–30

LIFE IS FLEETING

For the work of a man shall he render unto him, and cause every man to find according to his ways (34:11).

The Vicar of an Anglican church in England was kneeling by the bedside of one of his wealthy parishioners. He was pleading with the man to give his heart to God. The minister said to him, "Sir, if you will give your life to God, your soul to God, your heart to God, take my hand." But the man refused. Then the Vicar pled with him, "Sir, the end is drawing near. Life is fleeting. Death is nigh. Give your heart to God. Take my hand." But again the man refused.

When the man died, his cold, pulseless hand relaxed, and in it the pastor saw the key to his safe, as though he could take his possessions with him.

January 30

Psalm 1:1–6

PROSPERITY FOR A PARTNER

And he shall be like a tree planted by the rivers of water, that bringeth forth his fruit in his season; his leaf also shall not wither; and whatsoever he doeth shall prosper (1:3).

Queen Elizabeth I sent for a merchant in London and asked him to go on a mission for her across the seas. Because he would have to be gone a long time, the man was concerned as to what would become of his business. He was afraid it would go bankrupt. The queen told the merchant to go and take care of *her* business; and she pledged that while he was gone, she would take care of *his*. The merchant went abroad. He did the work for his queen and returned. To his amazement, under her care and guidance, his business had flourished and quadrupled. That is what God will do for you if you will make Him a partner.

January 31

Psalm 11:1–7

THE DOWNFALL OF A NATION

If the foundations be destroyed, what can the righteous do? (11:3).

The greatest historian of the twentieth century was Arnold Toynbee, the famous British educator and writer. *Time* magazine, in reviewing Toynbee's study of history, said, "Toynbee shattered the frozen pattern of historical determinism and materialism by openly avowing that God is a moral force in history." Secularists describe what happens in time as being just something people are doing, but Toynbee said the great moral imponderable in the life of a nation lies in God.

Toynbee said that there have been twenty-one civilizations in the history of mankind. Sixteen of them have already perished, and Toynbee feels that without exception all sixteen perished because they were inwardly decadent. They fell because of unrighteousness. And America cannot continue to live in debauchery and drunkenness and moral decay. The great imponderable that lies in the history of a nation lies in the moral judgment of almighty God. What we read in the Bible is nothing other than what we see in daily experience, in human life, and in human history. Thus, if God judges us, it is, as the author of Hebrews says, a terrible thing to fall into the hands of the living God, for our God is a consuming fire. If God judges iniquity, every person must stand before Him guilty.

February 1

Psalm 13:1–6

COMFORT IN AFFLICTION

I will sing unto the L*ORD, because he hath dealt bountifully with me (13:6).*

My predecessor at the First Baptist Church of Dallas was Dr. George Truett. For a full year before he died, Dr. Truett suffered agonizingly. He was allergic to all pain-killing drugs. Any narcotic would make him deathly sick and nauseated. So he suffered excruciating pain for a full year. Many who loved him would ask me again and again why it was that Dr. Truett, the great man of God and the incomparable preacher of the Word, had to suffer so much for a full year. But Dr. Truett had a secret. His faith in the Lord and in the goodness of God was gigantic. He repeated many times that which he preached so often, "Not my will, but thine be done." In that faith and in that yielded submissiveness, the great pastor died.

That is what it is to be a Christian. Anyone can sing songs and be happy when all is well. But what happens when the dark day comes, when the valley stretches endlessly ahead, when illness racks, and when the bed is itself an affliction? That is when we glorify God, singing songs in the night, trusting in the goodness of the Lord. We take it to God in prayer, and ask the pastor and people who believe in the Lord to pray. We use every means God has given us—the doctor, the pharmacist, the hospital—then having prayed, having done all that we know how to do, yielded, submissive, we leave the final verdict in God's hands. If it is God's will that we live, may we praise the Lord in the gift of days. If it is God's will that our lives be closed like a book and the last chapter be written, then may we have the faith to believe that God will heal us over there.

February 2

Psalm 14:1–7

THE INSIGNIFICANT

The fool hath said in his heart, There is no God. They are corrupt, they have done abominable works, there is none that doeth good (14:1).

When I was a teen-ager, Sinclair Lewis, the famous novelist and agnostic, was still living. One day Lewis stood up in a pulpit in Kansas City and made fun of the idea of God. He said, "If there is a God, I challenge Him to come and strike me dead here in this pulpit." And when Lewis said that, the whole world of infidelity applauded. How smart! "Man, did you ever hear anything like that?" said the whole world. They headlined it in the newspapers and wrote of it in editorials. How well I remember that!

At the same time, many of our newspapers carried a column entitled "Today" written by Arthur Brisbain. Brisbain wrote about Lewis and his statement from that Kansas City pulpit. He said that Lewis reminded him of a little ant in the deserts of Arizona. Through the middle of Arizona ran the great Santa Fe railroad. This little ant got on top of one of those big steel rails and lifted his hand and said, "I am told that the head of this railroad is a man named Charles Storey. I do not believe it. If there is a Charles Storey who runs this railroad, I dare him to come out here to Arizona and step on my head." Then Brisbain said that Charles Storey would say, "It is just not worth my time." Right! Why should the Almighty of the universe, the sovereign God of time and eternity, come to earth to strike down Sinclair Lewis?

February 3

Psalm 18:1–32

THE INADEQUACY OF REASON

As for God, his way is perfect: the word of the LORD is tried: he is a buckler to all those that trust in him (18:30).

Logic and reason can explain in part, but logic in itself fails miserably and dismally. For a person to limit himself to reason or to logic is to blot out of his life the spectatular revelations of almighty God.

The Greeks played around with logic and metaphysics, and loved doing it. An author named Zeller wrote *Outlines of Greek Philosophy*. In that book he presents a Greek sophist by the name of Gargius. By metaphysics, Gargius proved that motion is impossible—logically, reasonably, intellectually. First, a thing cannot move from where it is because if it does, it is not there. Second, a thing cannot move from where it is not; that is obvious. And third, where it is and where it is not are the only possible places that exist. Therefore, a thing cannot move. Now one can think about that forever. That is logic.

Logic by itself takes you nowhere. There are people who want to live by logic, but they are always illogical. Other people want to live by reason, but they are always unreasonable. They reduce the world to an illogical and irrelevant fact.

What God has done for us is to give us another faculty, and that faculty is what exalts and raises a person up in the likeness of God. Reason can take one only so far. It cannot soar; it cannot rise. The eyes of the soul, the inward faculty that God has given a person, makes him go on and on.

February 4

Psalm 19:1–14

GOD'S TRACKS IN THE SKY

The heavens declare the glory of God; and the firmament sheweth his handiwork. Day unto day uttereth speech, and night unto night sheweth knowledge (19:1–2).

The physical sciences (the handmaidens of the Lord) speak to us plainly of God. Their eloquence is endless and infinitely variegated. In touching God's world through a physical science we reach only the frontier of the presence of the almighty Creator.

A learned French atheist was crossing the desert with a camel train. At the hour of prayer, his Moslem camel driver stopped, rolled out his little rug on the sand, and bowed toward Mecca. In sarcasm, the infidel asked him what he was doing. The driver replied that he was praying to God.

In scorn the unbeliever asked, "Did you ever see God? Did you ever touch Him? Did you ever taste Him? Did you ever smell Him?" To these questions the humble man was forced to reply, "No."

Early the next morning, after having camped for the night, the atheist looked across the desert wastes and saw camel tracks. He observed, "There was a camel that passed by here last night." The camel driver said to the Frenchman, "Did you see him? Did you smell him? Did you touch him? Did you taste him?" To which the atheist replied, "No."

The camel driver then asked, "How do you know that a camel passed by here last night?" The atheist replied, "Why, I can see his tracks in the sand." The humble, unlettered camel driver pointed up to the heavens and replied, "I can see God's tracks in the sky."

February 5

Psalm 23:1–6

THE WORLD'S NEED

Yea, though I walk through the valley of the shadow of death, I will fear no evil: for thou art with me; thy rod and thy staff they comfort me (23:4).

A Chinese correspondent was talking to an American correspondent, who happened to be a devout Christian. The Chinese correspondent said to the American, "I am a Buddhist, and my religion is so much better than yours. I have a happy religion, and I worship a happy god, but your religion is full of blood, suffering, crucifixion, and death, and when you come before your God, He is dying in shame on a cross." The American correspondent had never thought about it like that, and he did not know how to answer.

Some time later the American saw a Chinese man, starving by the side of a road. The correspondent went over to him, saw that he was dying, and called the Chinese people passing by to come and help. No one seemed to care. The American tried to find someone to help him with the dying man, but not a person would stop. They looked with contempt and disdain and passed on by. So the correspondent reached down and picked up the dying man in his arms. As he held the man in his arms and looked upon his silent face, he had his answer. Tell me, where would you take him, if you had in your arms a dying man, a victim of starvation and exhaustion? Would you take him and lay him before the fat, affluent, happy, smiling god called Buddha, or would you take him and tenderly, lovingly, and carefully lay him at the feet of One who knew what it was to be hungry, poor, in need, and in want? The faithfulness of the Son of God is God's answer to the need of the world.

February 6

Psalm 27:1–14

TRUST AND COMMITMENT

The LORD is my light and my salvation; whom shall I fear? The LORD is the strength of my life; of whom shall I be afraid? (27:1).

When I was a little boy living on a farm, I developed a large abscess on my body. When I was thin, emaciated, and unable to walk, my mother took me to the nearest large town, which was Trinidad, Colorado. There she placed me in the hospital. My doctor was a Dr. Friedenthal, a Jewish physician. Mother told him all about me and placed me in his hands. That doctor took me to the operating room, put me to sleep, and operated. I did not know him, nor did my mother, but seeking someone who could help me recover, she carried me in her arms to place me in the trust of that physician.

It was that same mother who, in a revival meeting, turned to me and said with tears, "Son, will you trust Jesus as your Savior today?" That day I did trust Jesus as my Savior. That is what it is to be a Christian. It is the committal of your life to Him. When I die, that same committal will bring peace and assurance to my soul. "Lord Jesus, into Thy hands I commit my soul. Take care of me, Lord, save me." And He will. The great act of conversion is this simple committal of your life to His keeping.

February 7

Psalm 31:1–24

FROM MOURNING TO REJOICING

Oh how great is thy goodness, which thou hast laid up for them that fear thee; which thou hast wrought for them that trust in thee before the sons of men! (31:19).

In my memory is a couple who had a little business. Both of them worked in it. They were a sweet, precious couple. On Christmas Day he had a sudden heart seizure and died. I made my way to the home, feeling so heavy-hearted. Of all days, the tragedy fell on Christmas Day! I had to go to that house to see if I could be of any comfort and encouragement to that poor young wife, with her husband lying dead before her. But One had been there before me, for she said to me, "When I was saved, I experienced God's saving grace. For the years of my life I have known His living grace. And now that my husband is gone, God has given me dying grace." Then she added, "It was God's Christmas present to my husband. For today, Christmas Day, God introduced him to the saints and to the angels in glory."

When I left that house, I left exalted and uplifted. Christmas Day brought death and separation to her, but in Christ it brought a Christmas present for him. "Today he was presented to the saints and the angels in glory." Oh, what God hath done for us!

February 8

Psalm 37:1–40

WE TRUST IN THEE

The steps of a good man are ordered by the LORD: and he delighteth in his way (37:23).

If the Lord delays His coming, a grave awaits us, somewhere, some day, some hour, some moment when the pounding waves of the sea will beat our little ship into pieces. Then the grace of God will reach down and lift us up, spare us, and save us to Himself.

Do you remember the beautiful poem by Henry Van Dyke?

O Maker of the mighty deep
    Whereon our vessels fare,
Above our life's adventure keep
    Thy faithful watch and care.
In Thee we trust, whate'er befall;
    Thy sea is great, our boats are small.

We know not where the secret tides
    Will help us or delay.

Nor where the lurking tempest hides,
    Nor where the fogs are gray.
We trust in Thee, whate'er befall;
    Thy sea is great, our boats are small.

Beyond the circle of the sea,
    When voyaging is past,
We seek our final part in Thee;
    O bring us home at last.
In Thee we trust, whate'er befall;
    Thy sea is great, our boats are small.

We shall not escape, for the pounding tides of surf and sea, the billows of hurricane force sweep us up, bear us away, and we are helpless before the driving storm. But our hope is in Him. Wherefore, be of good cheer; we believe God. If our boat is broken, and it will be, God has prepared some better thing for us—a better house, a better boat, a better fellowship, a better city. God's grace reaches out to us!

February 9

Psalm 42:1–11

REJOICE IN THE LORD

Why art thou disquieted in me? hope thou in God: for I shall yet praise him for the help of his countenance (42:5).

God's people are to be up, not down. We are to be encouraged, not discouraged. We are to work with the assurance of God's blessings upon us. We are not to labor as those who support a lost cause. There ought to be joy among our Christian people.

We are told in Philippians to "rejoice in the Lord." The spirit of victory should characterize us as much as that same spirit characterized the first-century Christians. We are not to work in a minor key of defeatism. We are not dead, nor are we even dying. It does not honor Christ when we give ourselves to attitudes of discouragement and defeat.

The joy of the Lord is to be our strength, even in surrounding darkness and gloom. We are to shine as lights in a day of unrest, uncertainty, discontent, tension, and materialistic unbelief. We are to be examples of what a Christian can really be.

Down the street from our church is a man who is daily at his post selling his newspapers. He is a Christian, and it shines in his face. He is never sad. He is always smiling, and he has a happy word for me every time I pass him. He is not rich. He is not beautifully clothed. He has little of this world's goods. But he is happy in the Lord! He is a living demonstration of what God can do for a human soul. We ought always to be like that.

God is never discouraged. He has the burden of the whole human race upon his heart as well as the sovereign responsibility for the course of all human history. Yet He remains the fountain of hope and the unfailing source of all spiritual blessing.

February 10

Psalm 46:1–11

CHRIST—THE ANSWER

God is our refuge and strength, a very present help in trouble (46:1).

In Africa I stood in the midst of a church jammed on every side by half-naked people. The church was as full as it could possibly get; even the yard was filled with people listening to the Word of God. While waiting to preach, I saw on the wall in back of the pulpit a big placard with a picture of our Lord in the center. Around the picture were these words: "Christ Is the Answer to Every Human Need." I looked at all those half-naked Africans and then up to the picture. Where the gospel of Christ is preached there is also a school, a hospital, an orphans' home, and the church. Christ is the answer to every human need. For the balm of Gilead, for the healing of a heart, for the restructuring of society, for the rebirth of the individual, for the remaking of all humanity—the answer is in Christ our Lord.

A father with three little boys was not a Christian. His wife died suddenly and left him alone with his sons. Knowing that the man was crushed and faced with an awesome responsibility, I spoke to him. "My friend, God is able to help if you will invite Him into your home and into your heart. He will be an answer to every problem. He will be a friend who is able to see you through. Take Jesus into your heart and home."

The days passed and I visited with the man again. He said, "That first step was the hardest I ever made, but having accepted the Lord and received Him into my heart and home, it has been a blessing every step of the way. I am rearing my three little boys in the love and nurture of the Lord."

There are no problems that God cannot solve, nor difficulties for which Christ is not equal.

February 11

Psalm 50:1–23

GIVING GOD ALL

For every beast of the forest is mine, and the cattle upon a thousand hills (50:10).

Every summer Dr. George W. Truett would go out to West Texas and preach. After a morning service, one of those ranchers said, "Dr. Truett, would you walk with me?" So the pastor and the cattleman walked until finally they came to a lonely, isolated place. The cowman stopped, turned to the pastor, and said, "Sir, I have come to realize that these hundreds of thousands of acres of ranchland and these herds of cattle are not mine. They belong to God, and I am but His steward. Dr. Truett, I want you to kneel down here with me and tell God that I am giving Him all of my land, cattle, and possessions." So the great pastor and that big cattleman knelt and dedicated to God everything that the man owned, with the promise that he would use it for the glory of the Lord.

In describing the incident, Dr. Truett said he supposed that was only a prayer of consecration and dedication of what the man possessed. But when Dr. Truett finished the prayer of dedication, the rancher said, "Now, Dr. Truett, having given God everything that I have and having promised God that I would use it for His glory, may I also give to God my boy? And may I ask God to save and bring back that wayward, prodigal child?"

Having dedicated to God everything in the flesh and having consecrated to Him all we have in the world, we have a right to ask a harvest in the spirit.

According to the immutable, inexorable laws of the Almighty, the harvest is certain. When I sow in the spirit, when I sow in prayer, when I sow in dedication, I have a right to expect in kind and degree a harvest from His gracious hands.

February 12

Psalm 51:1–19

COMING BACK TO GOD

Create in me a clean heart, O God; and renew a right spirit within me (51:10).

Once I read about an evangelist in India, a former Hindu, who was known by the name Sammy. He went around with a big Bible under one arm and, with his other arm, carried an umbrella above his head. Little Sammy was trotting down a road in India when he passed by some barracks where English soldiers were stationed. They were familiar with the preacher, so, as he trotted by with his big Bible and his umbrella, one of the British soldiers called to him. "Say, Sammy, how is Jesus Christ this morning?" The little evangelist stopped, drew himself up to his greatest height, looked reproachfully at the soldiers, and said, "I will answer you out of the Holy Book which came to us from your country." He then turned to Hebrews 13:8 and read, "Jesus Christ the same yesterday, and today, and for ever." And then he trotted on down the road.

That night two of those British soldiers found the modest home of Sammy, the evangelist, and knocked at the door. When he came to the door, one of the British soldiers said, "Sammy, we are ashamed of ourselves. This morning we asked you how Jesus Christ was, and you read to us out of the Holy Book, 'Jesus Christ the same yesterday, today, and for ever.'" The soldier went on, "When we were back home, we were Christians and we served the Lord. But we have fallen away, Little Sammy. We have come to apologize and ask forgiveness for what we said this morning. We want you to know that we are coming back. We are coming back into the love and service and ministry of our dear Lord." Always it is revival and true godly service when we keep our eyes upon Him and rejoice in Christ our Savior.

February 13

Psalm 56:1–13

SURRENDERING YOUR WILL

In God have I put my trust: I will not be afraid what man can do unto me (56:11).

The life of the Christian is always to be one of gentle humility and of bowing in yielded surrender to the will of the Lord. There is a famous poem by William Henley entitled "Invictus." *Invictus* is the Latin word for "unconquerable" or "invincible." Henley writes:

Out of the night that covers me,
Black as the Pit from pole to pole,
I thank whatever gods may be
For my unconquerable soul.

In the fell clutch of circumstance,
I have not winced nor cried aloud,
Under the bludgeonings of chance
My head is bloody, but unbowed.

Beyond this place of wrath and tears
Looms but the horror of the shade;
And yet the menace of the years
Finds, and shall find, me unafraid.

It matters not how strait the gate,
How charged with punishments the scroll,
I am the master of my fate;
I am the captain of my soul.

February 14

Psalm 63:1–11

MIXED EMOTIONS

Because thy lovingkindness is better than life, my lips shall praise thee (63:3).

A painting by Norman Rockwell appeared on the front of the *Saturday Evening Post.* It was the picture of the inside of a palatial home with beautiful wall-to-wall carpet. An elegant staircase wound up to the second floor. On the staircase stood a queenly mother who was manifestly affluent and who presided over the home.

Norman Rockwell captured a conflict of emotion when he painted her face. As she stood on the beautifully curved staircase, she looked down at her son who was standing with his dog on the plush carpet. The front door was open, and the rain was pouring down. The little boy, with the dog by his side, evidently had come home from school, walked through all the mud he could find, and tracked ugly blobs of mud on the beautiful carpet.

The little fellow had in his hand a valentine which he had made for his mother. His face was full of life and anticipation as he thought how happy his mother would be to receive the valentine. She looked down at the mud, at the dog, at the boy, and at the valentine he held in his hand. This painting effectively presented mixed emotions. The heavenly Father has no mixed emotions, however. He welcomes even the most wayward child and covers even the most widespread sin and ugliness.

February 15

Psalm 67:1–7

A HANDICAP

God be merciful unto us, and bless us; and cause his face to shine upon us; Selah (67:1).

A handicap is a compliment in any area of life. As such, a handicap would be a compliment from God.

If a person in the athletic world is superior, he will run or play under a handicap. If there is a race of runners and one of the athletes is unusually gifted, he will run with a handicap. The officials will pull him back at the starting point so that the other racers will have a better opportunity to run against him.

If some men are playing golf and one of them is superior, he will play under a handicap. A handicap is a compliment in the athletic world.

A handicap is a compliment also in the artistic world. One day Michelangelo looked at a stone that had been rejected. But he saw in it the most beautiful carving of a statue of David the world has ever known. Michelangelo sculpted David out of a stone that everyone else had rejected.

All poetry is written under a handicap. Poetry has to follow meter and often a rhyming scheme. Poetry is a fettered word, a chained word. It is a picture of how the handicaps of life are a blessing from God.

What can a paraplegic do? What can a chained person do? What can a blind person do? What can an invalid do? Without doubt, some of the greatest accomplishments in this earth were wrought by people who labored under a great handicap.

February 16

Psalm 68:1–35

HE IS STILL FATHER

A father of the fatherless, and a judge of the widows, is God in his holy habitation (68:5).

The Earl of Asquith, who was the Prime Minister of Great Britain in the early years of this century, was a noble and appreciated man, a man highly honored. He received many citations and plaudits in the course of his illustrious political career.

One day a servant was recounting to the Prime Minister's little girl the greatness of her father. The servant spoke of the citations awarded to him and the honors bestowed upon him. The little wide-eyed girl broke in and said, "But sir, is he still my father?" God is great and mighty, but He is still our Father in heaven. I can bless God through filial love.

February 17

Psalm 69:1–36

HE LIFTED ME

Deliver me out of the mire, and let me not sink: let me be delivered from them that hate me, and out of the deep waters (69:14).

An old Indian in Oklahoma was asked, "How did Christ save you? You say that you are saved. How did He do it?"

The old Indian took some dead leaves and laid them in a little circle. Then he took a worm and put it inside that circle. Next he set fire all the way around those leaves. As the fire burned, the worm crawled one direction, seeking a way out, then turned back again, this direction, that direction, and another. Finding himself encompassed by the flames, the worm drew as far away from the fire as he could and curled up to die. The old Indian then reached down his hand, picked up the worm, and placed it safely away from the fire. The Indian said, "That is what Jesus did to me. I was perishing and dying, and He lifted me up and saved me."

From sinking sand He lifted me.
With tender hands He lifted me.
From shades of night to plains of light,
Oh, praise His name, He lifted me.

February 18

Psalm 78:1–41

REARING A GODLY GENERATION

We will not hide them from their children, showing to the generation to come the praises of the LORD, and his strength, and his wonderful works that he hath done (78:4).

In my reading, I came across the autobiography of Henry C. Mabie, who was for many years the illustrious secretary of the American Board of Foreign Missions for the American Baptist Convention. In his autobiography, he said, "When I was four years old, my mother took me to a mission meeting. I could not understand what the missionary was saying. I did not know the language he used. I could not understand what he was talking about. But there was something that the missionary said that moved my mother, and I saw her take the gold ring off her finger and give it to missions. I was only four years old. That was my introduction to God's purposes for the world."

What we do in front of our children is indelible. When we teach them in the love, nurture, and admonition of the Lord, God works with us, and the repercussions of it are found in every area of human life. So in the dedication of our homes, our lives, our prayers, and our faithful response, we shape the children and the young people of today. They will be our preachers, deacons, superintendents, and teachers of the next generation. God bless and help us as we consecrate our efforts to that holy and heavenly assignment!

February 19

Psalm 84:1–12

A HUNGRY SOUL

My soul longeth, yea, even fainteth for the courts of the LORD: my heart and my flesh crieth out for the living God (84:2).

While I was attending seminary in Kentucky, I pastored a church in a village. One day a family moved to a large, spacious farm in our village, and the man and his large family joined the church immediately. I would see that man in the congregation every time the doors opened. As I preached, the tears would fall from his face. When I was his guest for dinner, I said to him, "In the congregation you are so moved, like a hungry man seated at the table of the Lord, like a thirsty man drinking from the water of life. Why?" The man replied, "Young pastor, for these past years I have lived way up in the mountains where there were few, if any, Christian people and no church at all. Up there, away and alone, my heart was hungry and my soul was thirsty. Now that we have moved here we come to church and just thank God for the people of the Lord."

That is the description of one who is "in Christ." There might be a thousand very fine organizations, but my soul would thirst to death just being in a wonderful organization. I want to be fed the Bread of Life. The hymn, "Break Thou the Bread of Life," does not refer to the Lord's Supper. It refers to the Bible. "Beyond the sacred page I see Thee, Lord." I want someone to open God's Book for me and speak to me the Word of heaven.

A man may lecture beautifully. His so-called ethical sermon may be full of finest admonitions. But Socrates could have said the same things. Buddha doubtless could have said it better, and Zoroaster could have placed it in even more beautiful language.

It is neither beauty of language nor ethical content my soul desires. What I want to know is this: Does God say something? My heart wants to hear, and my soul is thirsty to know.

February 20

Psalm 90:1–17

GOD'S CLOCK

For a thousand years in thy sight are but as yesterday when it is past, and as a watch in the night (90:4).

Some time ago a man from the Pentagon appeared before the Senate committee on armed services. He pointed out to that committee that Russia was building such nuclear weapons as to be able to annihilate the United States in one moment—in one surprise attack. Our country could go along a thousand years as a day, then suddenly a day would be as a thousand years, in which with one catastrophic nuclear attack the whole nation could be wiped out. Our lives are sometimes like that. Suddenly in our everyday lives something happens, and life is never the same for us.

God's clock is different from our clock. On God's clock, a thousand years is as a day and a day is as a thousand years. There is no time with God. Time is the creation in which we are imprisoned, but not so with God. To us, if a thing is near, it could be five minutes from now or an hour from now. That would be near. And to us if a thing is a thousand years from now, it is far off. To God, there is no near or far. It is all right here—present.

February 21

Psalm 91:1–16

SAVING FAITH

I will say of the LORD*, He is my refuge and my fortress: my God; in him will I trust (91:2).*

Did you ever get into a plane and notice that the door to the cockpit was open? Did you ever look through that door at those hundreds of instruments on the panel? What would I do if the landing of the plane were dependent upon me? I know not a single instrument on the panel. I know not a single knob to move, button to push, or lever to turn. If the safety of the plane depended upon me, I would surely die. I am forced to trust that pilot completely, implicitly. Because I trust him, I sit there in the plane in perfect confidence that the pilot will take it safely down to the runway. Saving faith is a like trust in Christ and commitment to Him.

Did you ever have an operation? How completely you must lay your life in the hands of the physician! While you are under an anesthetic and thus unconscious, you must trust the doctor completely. You must commit your life into his hands. That is saving faith when we place our lives into the hands of Christ.

February 22

Psalm 94:1–23

AN ASTONISHING ADMISSION

In the multitude of my thoughts within me thy comforts delight my soul (94:19).

Even philosophers and atheists are somehow persuaded about the reality of a future life. For example, Bob Ingersoll, the most blatant and popular of American infidels, once said, "You know, when we die, we will say 'We hope to meet again.'" What an astonishing admission on the part of an infidel!

Another American infidel, Tom Paine, in arguing for immortality, said that to him it was unthinkable that God created the soul just to destroy it.

Plato, in ancient literature, says, "All of the speculation and hope regarding immortality are the raft upon which our souls now are cast, waiting for some sure word on which we could be more securely and safely carried."

Cicero said, "There is, I know not how, in the minds of men a certain presage, as it were, of a future existence, and this takes the deepest root and is most discoverable in the greatest geniuses and most exalted souls." A prayer from Tennyson avows:

> Ah, Christ, that it were possible
> for one short hour to see
> The souls we loved that they might tell us
> what and where they be.

We cannot deny that there is in the human heart a longing for God, a better life, a better world, and a life after death. There is no people, society, or tribe, however degraded, that does not believe in some kind of an afterlife. The early American Indian put a bow and arrow and a bowl of food in the grave of the Indian warrior to use in his happy hunting ground. The ancient Egyptian wrapped up and placed in the grave all the things that the deceased person possessed, so he could use them in a life that was to come. This belief in an afterlife is universal.

February 23

Psalm 103:1–22

THE PITY OF A FATHER

Like as a father pitieth his children, so the Lord *pitieth them that fear him (103:13).*

A man had two sons. The older son was in college, a star athlete, a handsome specimen of young manhood. The father also had a younger son, and the little boy gave promise of being as fine and as strong as his older brother. One day, in some unexplainable accident, the little boy got tangled up with his bicycle and the wheels of a big truck. In the hospital the doctor turned to the father and said, "Sir, the only way I can save the life of the boy is to amputate his left arm and his right leg." The father said that, as he looked down into the face of his little boy, he knew for the first time what the Scriptures mean when they say, "As a father pitieth his children, so the Lord pitieth them that fear him." I thank the Lord for His goodness, His grace, and His mercy that comes down to those of us who greet Him with open arms and with open heart.

February 24

Psalm 104:1–35

THE WONDER OF CREATION

O Lord, how manifold are thy works! in wisdom hast thou made them all: the earth is full of thy riches (104:24).

Once a fellow had me look into a microscope at a piece of paper covered with red paint. Under the microscope, the solid red color on the paper looked like blobs. Then he took the wing of a butterfly and placed it under the microscope, and I looked at that. The beauty of the color and the smooth, even arrangement of the color in the wing of a butterfly was an astonishing thing to see. With a deep, moving response, I said, "Think of the pattern of the glory of God who would spend such infinite pain upon the smallest wing of a little creature!"

The Lord God who patiently arranged forty-two million of those brilliantly tinted scales per square inch on the wings of a butterfly is the same Lord God who would mark the atoms and the molecules in a person's ashes. Our bodies change all the time. Every seven years we have an altogether different physical frame, yet we are the same surviving person. Even so, though our bodies fall into the dust of the ground and die, God marks the little molecules and atoms and will raise us up the same person. In God's time our very bodies shall be raised from the dead. We shall live again!

February 25

Psalm 107:1–43

BEGINNING THE DAY

Then they cry unto the Lord *in their trouble, and he bringeth them out of their distresses (107:28).*

I got up early one morning and rushed right into the day.
I had so much to accomplish that I didn't have time to pray.
Problems just tumbled about me and each task seemed heavier.
Why doesn't God help me? I wondered.
And God answered, "You didn't ask."
I tried to come into God's presence and use all my keys at the lock.
God gently and lovingly chided me, "My child, you didn't knock."
I wanted to see joy and beauty but the day wore on gray and bleak.
I wondered why God didn't show me, but I didn't seek.
So I woke up early this morning and paused before entering the day.
I had so much to accomplish that I had to take time to pray.

The reason we do not have help from heaven is that we do not ask for it. We do not take it to God. We do not make it a matter of prayer. We rush into the day, making decisions for ourselves and leaving God out of it. Then we wonder why life can be so frustrating and disappointing. It is a marvelous thing how God can be moved to answer if we just ask Him.

February 26

Psalm 116:1–19

CORONATION DAY

Precious in the sight of the Lord *is the death of his saints (116:15).*

A dear sainted woman in our church died in the hospital from a terminal illness. The doctors had used chemicals, tubes, medicines, massages, and all of those apparati to bring her back to life. When she came into consciousness for just awhile, she exclaimed, "Oh, and now I must die again!"

What a strange persuasion some have, that when our life is done and our task is ended, we then are to be plunged into a terrible "yonder," a horrible "out there"! If the human arrangers can just delay by five more breaths our escape, then may all of the science of the physicians, the chemists, and the pharmacists be brought to bear that we may take these five more breaths. O, Lord, no! When the task is done and the life is ended and age has taken our faculties away, it is a comfort to the Christian that he may be translated in victory, in triumph, to an upper and more glorious world, joined to Christ in glory. Our translation is our coronation day. It is a great consummation toward which all life inevitably moves.

For those outside of the Lord, death is a blackness. It is a despair, it is a defeat, it is an awesome prospect. It is death forever. But to the child of God, joined to the body of Christ, death is a triumph. It is our ultimate victory that some day all of us shall experience and enjoy. We cannot be lost. We belong to His body. We are members of His very frame. If He lives we also shall be saved and shall live with Him. We cannot be lost. Christ does not lose part of His members. We are joined to Him.

February 27

Psalm 118:1–29

OVERCOMING DEPRESSION

It is better to trust in the Lord than to put confidence in man (118:8).

When I first came to Dallas, I had a good talk with Mrs. George W. Truett about her great husband, who pastored the First Baptist Church of Dallas for forty-seven years. She told me, to my great surprise, that at times the great preacher would become despondent. She shared with me that one time when he felt he had failed, she said to him, "George, when you have prayed and asked God to bless you, and when you have done the best you can, then you leave it to Jesus."

It is for us to dig the well; it is for God to send the rain and the water. It is for us to plant the seed; it is for God to make it sprout and grow. It is for us to cultivate the field; it is for God to give the harvest. It is for me to witness; it is for God to give the increase, to save the soul. When I have done the best I can, then God must do the rest, and He will.

February 28

Psalm 119:1–9

THE BOOK

Wherewithal shall a young man cleanse his way? by taking heed thereto according to thy word (119:9).

A familiar story in the annals of literature is the description of the death of the immortal Scottish poet and novelist, Sir Walter Scott. As he lay dying, he turned to his son-in-law, Lockhart, and said to him, "Son, bring me the Book." There was a vast library in Walter Scott's home and, bewildered, the son-in-law said, "Sir, which book?" The dying bard replied, "My son, there is just one Book. Bring me the Book." It was then that Lockhart went to the library and brought the Bible to Sir Walter Scott.

"There's just one Book," cried the dying sage,
"Read me the old, old story."
And the winged words that can never age
Wafted him home to Glory.
There's just one Book.

There's just one Book for the tender years,
One Book alone for guiding
The little feet through the joys and fears,
The unknown days are hiding.
There's just one Book.

There's just one Book for the bridal hour,
One Book of love's own coining;
Its truths alone lend beauty and power,
To vows that lives are joining.
There's just one Book.

There's just one Book for life's gladness,
One Book for the toilsome days,
One Book that can cure life's madness,
One Book that can voice life's praise.
There's just one Book.

There's just one Book for the dying,
One Book for the starting tears,
And one for the soul that is going home,
For the measureless years.
There's just one Book.

—*Anonymous*

February 29

Psalm 119:10–72

THE WONDERFUL PEARL

Thy word have I hid in mine heart, that I might not sin against thee" (119:11).

Many years ago in Lyons, France, a rich merchant named Peter Waldo was saved. He began to witness on the streets of the cities of southern Europe. He gathered around him men, later called Waldensians, who sang and preached Jesus on the streets. Being a rich merchant, Waldo took all his fortunes and paid for the printing of little Bibles which he gave to the people.

Here is a poem of one of the Waldensian merchants who is displaying his silks to a queenly lady.

Oh lady fair, I have yet a gem
 Which purer lustre flings,
Than the diamond flash from the jewelled crown
 On the lofty brow of kings.

A wonderful pearl of exceeding price
 Whose virtue will not decay,
Whose light shall be as a spell to thee
 And a blessing on thy way.

The cloud went off from the Pilgrim's brow
As a small, meager book,
Uncased with gold or gem of cost,
From his flowing robes he took.

Here, lady fair, is the pearl of price;
May it prove as much to thee.
Nay, keep thy gold, I ask it not;
For the Word of God is free.

God gave the Word to us freely, and He wrote its sacred pages in blood. He watered His holy Word in tears, He bathed it in suffering and sacrifice, and He handed it down to us by the hands of the angels.

Thus to believe and receive the Word of God is to believe and to receive the Word of Christ.

March 1

Psalm 119:73–96

THE DIVINE STANDARD

For ever, O LORD, thy word is settled in heaven (119:89).

In Washington, D.C., we find the National Bureau of Standards, the central measurement laboratory of the United States. It develops standards and methods for accurate measurement and disseminates precise data on the properties of matter. There is a perfect weight, a perfect inch, foot, gallon, pint, ounce, and yard. All of the other measurements in the United States must conform to that standard. If a butcher sells meat on a scale that does not match the pound weight in Washington, he can be fined and imprisoned. All of the weights and measurements in the United States follow the pattern found in the Bureau of Standards in Washington.

In the Naval Observatory, also in Washington, D.C., there is a clock which is set every day at high noon by the concourse of the stars in God's firmament. Thereafter, every clock in America is set by that one standard of measurement in Washington. The Lord God told Moses to see that he made everything in the tabernacle according to the pattern shown him on the mount. There is a tabernacle of God in heaven. God gave the pattern to Moses and had him make every part according to the pattern He showed him from heaven. So it is with the Word of God. His Word is fixed.

March 2

Psalm 119:97–104

THE GREATEST INVESTMENT

Oh how love I thy law! it is my meditation all the day (119:97).

Years ago, a marvelous Christian named John Wanamaker lived in Philadelphia. He had become a successful merchant prince with beautiful specialty department stores in New York and in Philadelphia.

He had the good fortune to be appointed Postmaster General of the United States. One day when speaking to a group of businessmen about investments, the great Christian churchman said, "I want to tell you about the greatest investment I ever made in my life." They expected him to refer to property on which he had built the block-long store in Philadelphia, or to a lucrative investment in stocks or bonds. Much to their surprise, John Wanamaker said, "When I was a boy, I worked hard, saved my money, and I bought a Bible for $2.75." This great merchant and famous government servant continued, "This was the greatest investment I ever made."

March 3

Psalm 119:105–112

BURIED WITH HIS BIBLE

I have inclined mine heart to perform thy statutes alway, even unto the end (119:112).

A talented producer of plays in New York married a beautiful woman in my church, came to Dallas to live, and was won to Christ. He grew in grace with us, redeeming the time.

One day, to my great sorrow, he suffered a heart attack and died. When I buried him I stood at the casket and looked down on his still, silent face. His wife had placed his Bible in his hand upon his breast. I said to her, "That is a beautiful thing." She said, "Yes, after he was saved he read the Bible day and night. He would put a little Testament in his pajama pocket when he went to bed. He would prop it up by the mirror when he shaved in the morning. In the funeral parlor when I looked at him, his hands seemed so empty. So I went home and got his Bible." The man was buried with the Word of God upon his breast.

March 4

Psalm 119:113–136

THE COMFORT IN THE BIBLE

Thou art my hiding place and my shield: I hope in thy word (119:114).

When dark days come, we face the swollen river and look over to the other side. Many tears have fallen on these words: "Let not your heart be troubled: ye believe in God, believe also in me. In my Father's house are many mansions. . . . I go to prepare a place for you. And if I go and prepare a place for you, I will come again, and receive you unto myself; that where I am, there ye may be also" (John 14:1–3). The heart is quieted and the spirit comforted. We commit ourselves to the love and the grace of God. The Bible brings comfort and assurance of salvation to our souls.

Thank God for the Bible,
Whose clear, shining ray
Has lightened our path
And turned night into day.

Its wonderful treasures
Have never been told,
More precious than riches,
Set round with pure gold.

Thank God for the Bible.
In sickness and health,
It brings richer comfort
Than honors or wealth.

Its blessings are boundless,
An infinite store.
We may drink at the fountain,
And thirst nevermore.

Thank God for the Bible.
How dark is the night,
Where no ray from its pages
Sheds forth its pure light.

No Jesus, no Bible,
No heaven of rest,
How could we live,
Were our lives so unblessed?

March 5

Psalm 121:1–8

CONFIDENT OF HIS CARE

The LORD shall preserve thy going out and thy coming in from this time forth, and even for evermore (121:8).

In Hong Kong, I was with Dr. T. M. Rankin, who was then the Executive Secretary of our Foreign Mission Board. We were in a little car on the back of the island. As we drove along, he pointed and said, "In that place, I was incarcerated in a concentration camp all through the years of World War II. When the Japanese came and seized Hong Kong, I was arrested and interned in that camp. When I was marched into the concentration camp with a Japanese soldier on each side of me, I had no idea whether I would live or die. What lay before me could be starvation, disease, and maybe even death. But I never had the sense of the presence of God with me as I did that day when I was marched into the camp with a Japanese soldier on each side of me."

March 6

Psalm 126:1–6

SHADOW MINISTRIES

They that sow in tears shall reap in joy. He that goeth forth and weepeth, bearing precious seed, shall doubtless come again with rejoicing, bringing his sheaves with him (126:5–6).

Do you know the name of the woman in the Pacific Garden Mission in Chicago who won to Jesus the famous White Sox ball player, Billy Sunday? I do not know her name. But think of the enormous influence of that humble woman who won the famous baseball player to the Lord.

Do you know the name of the layman who won a young teen-ager in his Sunday school class to the Lord in the stockroom of a downtown Boston shoe store? That was the conversion of Dwight L. Moody. Think of what God did through that man, and yet his name is unknown to us.

Do you know the name of the Moravian missionary who won John Wesley and George Whitefield to the faith? I have no idea who he was. His name has been lost to the world. But John Wesley led the great Wesleyan revival in England. George Whitefield began the Great Awakening in America.

Shadow ministries such as these are done for God by humble people, whom no one remembers, or even knows! But God knows, and He blesses that influence for good through the years.

That is the reason a person does not receive his reward when he dies. He does not receive his reward until the end of time.

March 7

Psalm 127:1–5

THE HERITAGE OF CHILDREN

Lo, children are an heritage of the LORD: and the fruit of the womb is his reward (127:3).

Many years ago an old Puritan named Increase Mather wrote a tract entitled, "The Duty of Parents to Pray for Their Children." He had a wonderful son named Cotton Mather. When Cotton himself became a famous preacher, he wrote a tract entitled, "The Duty of Children to Their Parents Who Have Prayed for Them." That is marvelous! A father and mother consecrate themselves for their children, and their children bless and obey the Lord in honor of their parents. This is the first commandment with promise: "Honor thy father and thy mother."

When I was a boy in my father's shop, I remember that he kept the money he made in a large leather pouch with a drawstring at the top. At the end of the week, my father would take all the money he had made for the week, put it in my hands, and say, "Son, take this to the bank."

As I walked out the door, I overheard one of the men in the shop say, "Mr. Criswell, do you trust that boy with all that money?"

My father replied, "Sir, I would trust my soul to that boy!"

It was only a few words, but when I overheard my father say that about me, I stood ten feet tall. I felt I would rather die than betray the trust of my father. He believed in me, he trusted me, and I, in turn, loved and respected him.

March 8

Psalm 136:1–26

THE WAY TO WISDOM

To him that by wisdom made the heavens: for his mercy endureth for ever (136:5).

The atheist scientist looks through a telescope. He looks and he looks, but all he sees is just more materialities. The same pseudo-scientist dissects an insect, a frog, or maybe a human cadaver. All he sees is protoplasm, cells, nuclei, structure, and bone. It is only we who know God who see the divine wisdom of the shaping of life and of the universe.

When we look through those telescopes up into the heavens, we see the glory of God and look upon the lace work of His hands. When we look down into the minute, infinitesimal microcosm of God's universe, we see the hand of the Lord painting the wing of a butterfly, placing a song in a mockingbird's heart, or revealing Himself in the innocence of a little child. I may be rude and harsh in what I say, but I do not think that any person comes to wisdom who does not know God. He may be learned in facts, he may be studied in scientific development and achivement, but he does not know the truth of the universe until he comes to know it in the Lord.

March 9

Psalm 139:1–24

GOD IS FOR US

Thine eyes did see my substance, yet being unperfect; and in thy book all my members were written, which in continuance were fashioned, when as yet there was none of them (139:16).

A sculptor pictures an angel in the solid rock before he begins to chisel it out. An artist sees a beautiful painting before he puts it on a canvas. An architect imagines a magnificent building before he draws up the plans.

Jesus is like that. He sees us at our best. He encourages us. He lifts us up. When we are discouraged He does not add to our burden and frustration. He has words of comfort. He believes in us. What a blessedness!

March 10

Psalm 147:1–20

THE REWARD OF WAITING

He healeth the broken in heart, and bindeth up their wounds (147:3).

John Milton was a great Puritan poet who wrote literature as no one has ever written outside the Word of God. He lost his sight in the cause of liberty and righteousness, standing by Oliver Cromwell and the Puritan commonwealth. In his blindness he wrote *Paradise Lost.* He also wrote a sonnet on his blindness. The last line says, "They also serve who only stand and wait."

God gives to us who wait on the Lord His finest gifts. Somehow God may take from us earthly things so that He might bestow upon us heavenly things. Sometimes God will take away from us human strength so that He might bestow upon us heaven's strength. John Milton's eyesight was taken away in order that he might see the celestial cities of God. John Bunyan was imprisoned in order that he might make a journey throughout life that leads to heaven. Alfred Tennyson was broken in heart that he might write, "Thou strong Son of God, immortal love."

The chosen nation and family of God were sold into slavery and lived in foreign captivity in order that they might love the Promised Land. To this day wherever you find the Jew, you will find in him an imperishable love for his promised home. God sometimes takes away the old Jerusalem that we might lift up our eyes to the New Jerusalem. God lets this house turn back to the dust of the ground in order that He might build for us another house, one made without hands, eternal in the heavens. God bestows His best gifts upon those who look up to Him.

March 11

Proverbs 3:1–35

THE SECRET TO HAPPINESS

In all thy ways acknowledge him, and he shall direct thy paths (3:6).

One day, while in Africa, I sat at the side of the Executive Secretary of the Foreign Mission Board at a meeting of missionaries. A young doctor was giving his report. As I listened, the Executive Secretary turned to me and said, "Take a good look at that young man, for I have something to tell you about him." After the meeting was over, the Executive Secretary said, "You noticed that young doctor? He belongs to a very wealthy family in America. When he graduated with his Doctor of Medicine degree, he was sought and offered a large salary by some of the finest clinics in the north and east. He is a brilliant young man, but he felt called by God to be a medical missionary. So we appointed him and you heard him this morning. His salary could be thousands of dollars in America, but instead his salary is one thousand dollars a year." What a marvelous dedication when a man gives himself to the will of God!

Money, fame, or success have nothing to do with happiness. God is sovereign, and He made us for a definite purpose. When we give ourselves to that plan, our hearts are filled with the presence of the glory of God. This is the sovereign grace of Him who presides over all time, history, and life.

The tragedy of human life is this. If I refuse and spurn the will of God, He raises up someone else, but He does His work. O, that all of us might have a yielded heart and be willing to obey God and to do what He has laid upon our souls to do. We will never be happy any other way.

March 12

Proverbs 10:1–32

GOD GIVES THE INCREASE

The blessing of the LORD, it maketh rich, and he addeth no sorrow with it (10:22).

In my first pastorate a young man was marvelously converted. His wife was already in the church. The young man, as the representative of a large company, had been very worldly and compromising.

After he had been a Christian about four or five months, he came to see me and said, "I do not know what to do. Since I have become a Christian, all of those things that I did before do not seem right to me, and I have quit them. It does not seem right to me to gamble at poker or to drink with my clients. But now I have lost my customers because they do not like me any more. Since I do not drink with them, they do not want to talk to me or buy from me any more. I am becoming destitute, and I do not know where to turn or what to do." I said to him, "My friend, if God does not do some great and marvelous thing for you, then there is no blessing in the Christian way of life."

The months passed, and one day that young fellow came back to me and said, "Pastor, God has done a miraculous thing for me. As it became known that I was a child of God, my customers said to each other, 'He is a Christian; he will tell you the truth; you can count on what he says; his word is his bond; he will not misrepresent what he sells.' They began to send for me and to call for me because they knew I would tell them the truth. Now I have more business than I know what to do with. God has wonderfully blessed me and helped me."

It is neither chance nor labor, but the blessing of the Lord, that gives the increase.

March 13

Proverbs 12:1–28

A WORD OF ENCOURAGEMENT

Heaviness in the heart of man maketh it stoop: but a good word maketh it glad (12:25).

Sir Walter Scott, as a young boy, was dull and slow in his lessons and, consequently, discouraged. One day, or so Sir Walter Scott relates, he sat down by Scotland's sweetest singer, Bobby Burns, who read to him some of the lines of poetry he had written. Burns put his hand on the head of the boy and encouraged him. Sir Walter Scott said he went back home and wept for joy. There was a marvelous change in his life because of that one word of encouragement.

One time I heard Gypsy Smith describe a most moving incident in his own young life. He had gone to hear Dwight L. Moody preach and Ira D. Sankey sing. After the service was over he went up to Ira Sankey, Moody's singer. Sankey, talking to the little waif of a gypsy boy, somehow by inspiration and a revelation from God, put his hand on the head of the forlorn boy and said to him, "Some day God will make of you a great preacher." It was just a sentence. It was just the warmth of a hand. It was just a smile—kind, tender-hearted, sympathetic. But that kindness changed Gypsy Smith's life.

March 14

Proverbs 13:1–25

THE DIVINE SPANKING

He that spareth his rod hateth his son: but he that loveth him chasteneth him betimes (13:24).

A little boy stands up, throws the comic book he is reading down on the floor, and says, "Every time I sit down, someone comes along and wants me to do some crazy thing!"

The father replies, "Son, that is not true. I am just asking you to run an errand for me."

"No," says the boy. "You pick on me all the time, and every time I want to do something, you want me to do something for you."

The father says firmly, "Son, pick up the book and place it quietly on the table."

The boy says, "I will not!"

The father removes his belt and, after spanking the boy, says, "Son, pick up that book and put it on the table."

The boy weeps, but he does not pick up the book. The problem is that the tears, the anguish, the hurt come from the incorrigibility and rebellion of the boy. Before any kind of regularity and normality can be established in that home, the boy has to pick up the book and put it on the table. If he does not, the home will disintegrate. The father will be a figurehead, and the boy will be incorrigible all of his life. He must repent.

Before God can do anything with us, we must give up our disobedience and turn toward God. When the boy picks up the book and places it quietly on the table, then he and his father can work things out. So it is with us. When I repent, when I ask God for His help, then things begin to fall in place. God speaks to me, I listen to His voice, and repentance leads to obedience.

March 15

Proverbs 15:1–17

CHRIST AND THE LOWLY

Better is little with the fear of the Lord, *than great treasure and trouble therewith (15:17).*

In a great art museum, I saw a picture entitled "Christ Among the Lowly." The artist had drawn a modest home and a poor family. In the picture, a father, a mother, and ragged children are seated at a table. They are bowing their heads, saying grace over a few crumbs. The artist drew above them the Savior with His hands extended in blessing.

Would you rather be in a palatial home without Jesus, or would you rather be in that poor man's cottage with the Lord's hand extended in blessing? Those riches are ours in Christ Jesus. They are ours forever.

March 16

Proverbs 15:18–33

THE TRAGEDY OF DEJECTION

A man hath joy by the answer of his mouth: and a word spoken in due season, how good is it (15:23).

In the autobiography of Frank Rutherford we read that he preached his heart out to his people. The intensity of truth burned in his soul when he preached. One day after he had poured out his soul, he went to the vestry. Not a person spoke to him. The janitor finally came in. His only remark was, "It is raining outside," and he went out and closed up the building. The pastor went home without an umbrella, was drenched by the rain, and entered his little room. He lost his heart and his ability to minister. He left the ministry. When I read that, I thought, could anyone have said some word of encouragement to that dejected man?

It takes so little to make us sad.
Just a slighting word, a doubtful sneer,
Just a scornful smile on some lips held dear
And our footsteps lag though the goal seem near,
And we lose the joy and hope we had.
It takes so little to make us sad.

It takes so little to make us glad.
Just a cheering clasp of some friendly hand.
Just a word from one who could understand.
And we finish the task we so long had planned.
We lose the fear and doubt we had.
It takes so little to make us glad.

March 17

Proverbs 17:1–28

COMPASSION RULES

A friend loveth at all times, and a brother is born for adversity (17:17).

As I was driving down the Dixie Highway to my little rural church in Kentucky, a big new car passed me at a high rate of speed. When I reached the little community, I turned from the highway and followed the road for a mile or so. Where the road made a right-angle turn, there was a high dirt embankment with a farmer's house on the top of it. At that corner, to my sorrow, I saw the wreckage of that big beautiful car. It had plowed into the embankment, going so fast that the driver could not negotiate the right turn.

By the time I could get there, the farmer and his wife were helping the injured man out of the car. He apparently had gone through the glass windshield and had been cut in many places, for he was covered with blood. The farmer was on one side of him and the farmer's wife on the other side, and they were helping him to their farm home to care for and minister to him. I presume it would have been legalistically possible for me to stand before the man and say, "Do not drive so fast. You cannot negotiate these turns at such terrific speed! You know better than to break the law and the speed limits!"

How much better for us to be like the compassionate farmer who took the hurt man out from behind the wheel. My assignment is to help. If I cannot help, then I can pray. My business is not condemning others in a censorious, judgmental attitude. Judgment belongs to God. My business is to love, to help, to pray, to forgive, to encourage, and to respond to others in compassion.

March 18

Proverbs 20:1–30

THE DISCIPLINE OF TEMPERANCE

Wine is a mocker, strong drink is raging: and whosoever is deceived thereby is not wise (20:1).

John L. Sullivan was the boxing heavyweight champion of the world in the late 1800s. In that day boxing was done with bare knuckles, and they sometimes fought for seventy-two rounds. They fought until there was a victor. As time went on, Sullivan turned aside from the discipline of an athlete and began to waste his life in drink and debauchery. About this time a sickly young fellow by the name of Jim Corbett began to train and discipline himself for boxing. When he felt he was ready, he challenged Sullivan. Sullivan's henchmen, making the rounds of the saloons, boasted that with one blow of his fist he would pulverize young Corbett. When that battle was fought between Sullivan and Corbett, it went on for round after round after round; and when it was over, John L. Sullivan lay flat on the mat. Jim Corbett was champion of the world.

Something great happened out of the experience, and that is the reason I use this story as an illustration. When John L. Sullivan stood up, he apologized to the world for his drunkenness and his debauchery, and from that day until he died, he gave his life speaking to young people and to civic meetings, pleading for temperance and discipline. The eighteenth amendment, the prohibition amendment, was added to the United States Constitution partially because of the crusading of John L. Sullivan. It is a Christian virtue for a person to be self-disciplined and temperate.

March 19

Proverbs 26:1–28

REGATHERING WORDS

The words of a talebearer are as wounds, and they go down into the innermost parts of the belly (26:22).

A woman repeated a tale about another woman. It brought misery and agony to that woman. Later it was found that the tale was not true, and the woman who bore it and scattered it abroad went to a sage and asked, "What shall I do?" The sage said, "Take a pillow of feathers and scatter them over the town." So she took a pillow of feathers and scattered them up and down the streets of the city. Then she came back to the sage and asked, "Now what shall I do?" The sage told her, "Gather them all up again." And she replied, "The wind has blown them all over. I could never find them again." Then he said, "Nor can you ever gather back all of those words you said."

When you say a thing, you cannot pull it back. You cannot unsay it, nor can you make atonement for the hurt that it has done.

March 20

Proverbs 28:1–28

THE FUTILITY OF COVERING SIN

He that covereth his sins shall not prosper: but whoso confesseth and forsaketh them shall have mercy (28:13).

A rich man, whom God had blessed, had a poor brother who was a construction worker. The rich brother said to his poor brother, "I want you to build me a house and I want you to make it the finest that money can buy—spacious, large, and beautiful." The poor brother was delighted, so he started to build the house that his rich brother had requested. But he said to himself, "This is a chance for me to make money." So he took out of the foundation the good material that should have gone into it and he put in a cheap foundation and put the money saved into his own pocket.

Instead of placing fine lumber in the building, he used cheaper lumber and pocketed the difference. Instead of installing superior plumbing in the house, he chose cheaper plumbing. Throughout the house he used cheaper materials to deceive his own brother.

When the house was finished, his rich brother came to him and said, "Let us go see the beautiful house." They stood and looked at it, and the rich brother said to his poor brother, "Brother, it is yours. This is a gift of my heart to you."

That is as true a parable of life as I know. The man who cheats, deceives, and lies destroys himself. God sees to that.

March 21

Proverbs 31:10–31

BEAUTY OF CHARACTER

Favor is deceitful, and beauty is vain: but a woman that feareth the LORD, *she shall be praised (31:30).*

Recently I had one of the most unusual experiences in my life. Some of the men in my church asked Mr. Yousuf Karsh to come to Dallas to make a portrait photograph of me for my thirty-fifth anniversary as pastor of First Baptist Church. Mr. Karsh is by far the most famous portrait photographer in the world. He has spent time with all of the great of the world. A large book, *Faces of Destiny,* contains his photographs of Albert Einstein, Albert Schweitzer, Winston Churchill, Ernest Hemingway, Pablo Picasso, and many presidents of the United States. He was born in Armenia, Turkey, and his studio is located in New York City.

As I visited with Mr. Karsh, I asked him who, out of all the great men and women of the earth he had photographed, would he select as the greatest of all? I thought he would have replied, "Winston Churchill." If you were a great scientist, you might think he would say, "Albert Einstein." But he said to me, "Out of all the people with whom I ever worked in photography, far and above the greatest to me was Helen Keller."

I said, "Helen Keller?"

He replied, "Yes, Helen Keller." She was blind and deaf. The only way to reach her was through the sensitivity of the fingers on her hands.

I asked, "Why Helen Keller?"

He replied, "One cannot describe the beauty of her character and the gentleness of her personality."

March 22

Ecclesiastes 9:1–18

A FELLOW'S WILL

Whatsoever thy hand findeth to do, do it with thy might; for there is no work, nor device, nor knowledge, nor wisdom, in the grave, whither thou goest (9:10).

No one is beat till he quits.
No one is through till he stops.
No matter how hard failure hits,
No matter how often he drops,
A fellow's not down till he lies
In the dust and refuses to rise.

Fate may slap him and bang him around
And batter his frame till he's sore;
But she can never say that he's downed,
While he bobs up serenely for more.
A fellow's not dead till he dies,
Nor done till he no longer tries.

If you think you're beaten, you are;
If you think you dare not, you don't.
If you'd like to win, but think you can't,
It's almost certain you won't.

If you think you'll lose, you're lost,
For out in the world you find
Success begins with a fellow's will,
When Christ has the whole man's mind.

Life's battles don't always go
To the stronger or faster man.
But sooner or later, the man who wins
Is the man who thinks he can.

Abraham Lincoln was born in absolute poverty. Failing at practically everything to which he placed his hand, Abraham Lincoln said, "I will study and prepare myself, and maybe my time will come." He struggled against a handicap. After many failures, he succeeded in becoming one of the greatest men in American history.

March 23

Ecclesiastes 11:1–10

BEFORE THEY FALL

Rejoice, O young man, in thy youth; and let thy heart cheer thee in the days of thy youth, and walk in the ways of thine heart, and in the sight of thine eyes: but know thou, that for all these things God will bring thee into judgment (11:9).

Recently I was preaching to the association of Southern Baptist churches in New York City. Between the morning and afternoon sessions I walked along the New York streets with one of the local pastors. Our meeting place was one block away from Bowery Street, where humanity dumps the refuse of the human race. As I walked down Bowery Street with the young minister, I turned my head to talk to him. Suddenly he grabbed my arm and yanked me aside. I looked to see why he had done that. On the sidewalk in front of where I would have stepped, had the minister not jerked me out of the way, was a poor, miserable, fallen wretch. Part of him was in a doorway and part of him was out on the sidewalk, unspeakably miserable, dirty, and fallen.

We have a Bowery Mission, and my heart cannot but thank God for the ministers of Christ who work in that mission, doing what they can to help those fallen and miserable men. But there is something better, far better. It is even better to keep the person from falling than it is to minister to him after he has squandered his life away.

It is strange how things come to your mind. Almost stepping on the man on Bowery Street, I thought about the committee's recommendation to build up our Sunday school. Rather than minister to people when their lives are ruined, why not try to get them for God before they fall?

> Better guide well the young than reclaim them when old;
> For the voice of true wisdom is calling.
> To rescue the fallen is good, but 'tis best
> To prevent them when young from falling.

March 24

Ecclesiastes 12:1–14

IT IS TOO LATE

Remember now thy Creator in the days of thy youth, while the evil days come not, nor the years draw nigh, when thou shalt say, I have no pleasure in them (12:1).

One of the devout Sunday school teachers in the church where I was once pastor said, "My husband is getting old and is very ill. I have witnessed to him for the years of our marriage, and he has always said, 'Not now.' Would you plead with him to accept the Lord as his Savior?"

I went to the home and to the upstairs bedroom. I talked to that husband and pleaded with him about the Lord. As I pressed the invitation to accept Christ as his Savior, he answered, "Oh, it is too late; it is too late."

I do not know how demons rule the human spirit, but something happened in that man's soul, and he could not stop repeating the words, "Oh, it is too late; it is too late." The crescendo of the rising sound of his voice went higher and higher, "Oh, it is too late; it is too late!" I left the room. I could still hear him say those words as I left the house. He was taken to a mental institution and he died, saying, "Oh, it is too late; it is too late!"

What does that mean? What enters the spirit of a person that shuts him out from the kingdom of God? It is the vastness of judgment into which I cannot enter.

Noah could not open the door of the ark when the people crowded around and the waters began to rise. Why? Because God shut the door.

March 25

Isaiah 1:1–31

SOME WILL BE SAVED

Except the L*ORD* *of hosts had left unto us a very small remnant, we should have been as Sodom, and we should have been like unto Gomorrah (1:9).*

Someone once said to Charles Spurgeon, "So you believe that some will not believe, accept, and be saved no matter what you do, no matter how much you preach, no matter how much you work. What a despairing doctrine!" Spurgeon replied. "Nay, not so. I know they will not all believe, repent, turn, and be saved. But I know that some will listen, some will open their hearts, some will repent, and some will be saved."

This is the comfort God gives His children in the doctrine of the remnant. Darkness, unbelief, and rejection will be in the world, but some people will be saved. God's remnant will always be called out. This is the doctrine of the Holy Spirit. In 1 Peter 1, the Holy Spirit calls and we feel His moving voice in our hearts. In Ephesians 1, the Holy Spirit seals our names, written in heaven before we were born, even before we were conceived. His grace touched us, spoke to us, and led us to turn from our sins and look in faith to the blessed Jesus.

The truth of this doctrine can be observed in any city, in any nation. The gospel will be presented to millions of people. Many of them will not listen, will not turn, or will not believe, but some will. The Holy Spirit in His elective grace will bring some people to a saving knowledge of Christ.

March 26

Isaiah 5:1–16

MORE STUPID THAN AN OX

Therefore my people are gone into captivity, because they have no knowledge: and their honorable men are famished, and their multitude dried up with thirst (5:13).

People do not think. When a person puts God out of his life, dismisses Him from his business, and forgets Him in his dreams and visions, God says that the person is more stupid than an ox and not as bright as an ass. You see, God confronts a person whether he likes it or not, and He intrudes into a person's life whether he wants it or not. It is as impossible for the mind to keep out the idea of God as it is for the tides of the sea to keep from washing up onto the shore. As God upheaves the oceans, He upheaves a person's soul.

In Seattle there was a successful atheistic lawyer. He had built a palatial home overlooking beautiful Lake Washington and the Cascades beyond. One night he awakened from sleep and sensed that his little girl was standing by his bed looking quietly into his face in the early dawn. She was so tiny standing there in her little white nightgown with her curly, black hair falling over her shoulders. The father pretended to remain asleep. After the little girl looked at her father intently for awhile, she quietly turned around and stood before the large picture window facing the Cascades and the dawn of the eastern sun.

As the girl watched the sunrise over the beautiful mountains, she began to bow back and forth and to say sweetly in childlike innocence and humility, "Good morning, God. Good morning, God." The lawyer buried his face in his pillow and cried, "O God, that I could see You, that I could know You, that I could find You." Through the quiet, humble innocence and simplicity of his little girl, he found the Lord. God intrudes into a person's life so that he cannot escape.

March 27

Isaiah 9:1–21

THE MATCHLESS CHRIST

For unto us a child is born, unto us a son is given: and the government shall be upon his shoulder: and his name shall be called Wonderful, Counsellor, The mighty God, The everlasting Father, The Prince of Peace (9:6).

For many years Korea was a part of the Japanese empire. The Japanese accepted the Shinto religion and worshiped Emperor Hirohito as a god. When the Japanese subjugated Korea, it came to the attention of the military commanders that the Baptist missionaries were presenting another Lord—Jesus. The head of the Baptist Convention in Korea was brought before the commanding officer and questioned concerning Christ.

The Korean pastor told the story of Christ's life, including His death and resurrection. And the pastor boldly and unashamedly proclaimed, "He is coming again." The commanding officer asked, "Then what?" Bravely, the Korean pastor continued to explain that every knee shall bow to Him and every tongue confess that He is Lord. The commanding officer asked the pastor if that included his emperor, and the pastor said, "Yes." The commanding officer asked if all the Baptist pastors believed that. And the president of the convention replied that all of them believed that. Therefore, the Japanese military took every Baptist pastor in the nation of Korea and put them all in prison throughout the years of that occupation. Almost all of them died, and the man who was president of the convention outlived the occupation by just a few months. These pastors literally laid down their lives for the hope we have in Christ Jesus.

I make no apology when I preach the coming again of our blessed Lord. I do not think there is any hope in the Middle East or anywhere else save in that One whose name is called Wonderful, Counselor, the Mighty God, the Everlasting Father, the Prince of Peace. Ah, to lift Him up, to preach His name, and to invite souls to love Him and follow Him is the highest heavenly privilege of human life.

March 28

Isaiah 14:1–28

EVANGELISM IN THE NEW WORLD

The LORD of hosts hath sworn, saying, Surely as I have thought, so shall it come to pass; and as I have purposed, so shall it stand (14:24).

In God's providence, He chose the English nation to evangelize the world, and thousands of missionaries have gone out. The English-speaking world still sustains in every corner of this earth men and women who mediate the mind of God that was in Christ Jesus.

When the Pilgrim fathers came to this country, they not only came to have their own church, their school, and their Christian homes, but they also came for the evangelization of the new world. William Bradford, the governor of Plymouth Colony, in his story of Plymouth Plantation, gave the reason why the Pilgrim fathers left England and finally left Holland to come to the new world:

> Lastly and which was not least, a great hope and inward zeal we had of laying some good foundation or at least to make some way thereunto for the propagating and advancing the Gospel of the Kingdom of Christ in those remote parts of the world.

One of their purposes when they came to the new world was to evangelize the people who lived in the new land. This has been God's hand in the history of the English-speaking nations—England, America, Canada, Australia, and New Zealand. As a sign of this evangelization, English has become a universal language in the multi-faceted life of the nations of the world today.

March 29

Isaiah 21:1–17

WHEN GOD TURNS HIS FACE

The burden of Du-mah. He calleth to me out of Se-ir, Watchman, what of the night? Watchman, what of the night? (21:11).

In 1914 the Foreign Minister of the British Empire was a godly man named Lord Gray. In a session of the cabinet that lasted through the night, it was decided to go to war against Germany. In the early hours of the morning, just as it began to dawn, Lord Gray walked out of the foreign office with one of his cabinet officers. When he stood on the steps he saw down the street the lamplighter putting out the gas lights. Lord Gray, seeing that, turned to his companion and said, "See, the lights are going out over all of Europe."

The Allied Powers were triumphant in the war against Germany between 1914 and 1918. "The morning cometh, and also the night." For a period after the war there was infinite optimism and rejoicing in the earth. I grew up in that wonderful era of golden optimism. I also lived to see the rise of Hitler and to see the great armies of the Allied powers drawn against the bastions of continental Europe. I lived in the days when Hitler was destroyed, but we really only traded Hitler for Stalin. We traded Facism for Communism. We traded the freedom of that golden vision of the latter 1920s for the despair that grips millions of people today. More than two billion people are under the iron hand of Communism.

The notorious French scientist, Blaise Pascal, cried, "The silence of the universe frightens me." How much more when God turns His face and refuses to answer, and a nation and a people die!

March 30

Isaiah 25:1–12

SETTING FREE THE PRISONER

He will swallow up death in victory; and the Lord God will wipe away tears from off all faces; and the rebuke of his people shall he take away from off all the earth: for the Lord hath spoken it (25:8).

He who walks with us in the morning and in the noontide of life is the same Lord God who will walk with us into the night, and into the eternity that is beyond. God has provided something better for us. I remember that as a young pastor just beginning to preach, I knelt one day by the side of an aged man who lay in his last illness. As would be expected, I prayed for the Lord to lay His hands of healing on this saint, to raise him up, and to make him well. In the middle of my prayer, the old man put his hand on my head, and shook it. He said, "Young pastor, do not pray that. I do not want to live. My wife is gone, all of my children are gone, all of my friends are gone, and I am here by myself, old and sick. My Savior is on the other side, and I want to go to be with Him and with them. Son, pray that God will release me and let me go."

So I started my prayer over again. This time I prayed, "Lord Jesus, Thy saint is imprisoned in this body of death and is longing to be set free and to be with Thee. Lord, let him go. Open the door, receive him to Thyself." The Lord answered the prayer soon after that.

The preacher, Charles Tindley, wrote the song:

> Nothing between my soul and the Savior,
> So that His blessed face may be seen;
> Nothing preventing the least of His favor;
> Keep the way clear—let nothing between.

March 31

Isaiah 28:1–13

LINE UPON LINE

For precept must be upon precept, precept upon precept; line upon line, line upon line; here a little, and there a little (28:10).

When I was in Baylor University as a young preacher, I took a course in trigonometry, all because of Professor Harrell, who was a born philosopher. Here is one of the things he said. "I saw a great building being erected. A tremendous stone was to be split in half and placed above the enormous door through which the people would enter. When I saw that big stone to be split, I imagined how the workman would split it. He would cut a slit in the middle of the stone, and then insert a wedge made of heavy steel. Using a forty-pound sledge hammer, he would beat on the wedge until the stone split right down the middle. That's how I imagined it. But instead he drilled tiny holes in the stone and placed tiny steel pegs in those holes. This he did along the entire length of the stone. Then he took a little hammer and went back and forth—tap, tap, tap, until one day the stone split right down the middle! It was beautifully done—according to the grain and the strength of the stone. I watched them elevate it above the door. Thousands of people go through that doorway into the building even to this day."

When I heard Professor Harrell tell the story, I thought of this text: "Precept must be upon precept, precept upon precept; line upon line, line upon line; here a little, and there a little."

Let us listen to the word of the almighty God and let us ask Him to bless us as we grow in the knowledge of the Lord and in the doctrine of the faith.

April 1

Isaiah 40:1–11

THE ORIGINAL EVOLUTIONISTS

The grass withereth, the flower fadeth: but the word of our God shall stand for ever (40:8).

The Bible has not changed. Every syllable is just as it was when God, through the Holy Spirit, wrote it down. The Bible was written by forty authors over a period of fifteen hundred years. They did not know each other. There was no collaboration, no collusion. Each one of them wrote as he was inspired by the Holy Spirit of God. Yet with all of the unbelievable, tragic background of the days in which the writers lived, there is no repercussion of any of that darkness and superstition in the Word of God.

The Egyptians of Moses' day had a science of anthropology. They were naive evolutionists. They believed that mankind sprang from little white worms that they found in the slime, ooze, and mud of the alluvial deposit after the Nile's annual overflow. Perhaps they supposed so because they had observed the metamorphosis of a caterpillar into a butterfly. These scientists were not far behind those today who would have you believe that your remote ancestors were flea-bitten apes hanging by their tails in a primeval jungle.

The Bible says that Moses was learned in all the science of the Egyptians. But he says nothing about those little white worms and how we were descended from them. Instead, he writes in the most majestic language in human speech: "And God said, Let us make man in our image, after our likeness. . . . So God created man in His own image."

The Bible does not reflect the scientific background of the day in which it was written. It has been kept free of error by the Holy Spirit of God.

April 2

Isaiah 40:12–31

THE PILGRIMAGE

But they that wait upon the L*ORD* *shall renew their strength; they shall mount up with wings as eagles; they shall run, and not be weary; and they shall walk, and not faint (40:31).*

All of us in our pilgrimage to the heavenly city know troubles, sorrows, and trials. Every pilgrim finds the road rough and difficult. As John Bunyan's Pilgrim in *Pilgrim's Progress,* we find ourselves in times of despondency climbing up hills of difficulty and facing giants of doubt and discouragement. It is then that many of us fall into faintheartedness and failure. To the person who does not have God as his strength and his Savior, life is a hopeless affair. The godless person always feels hopeless, for trial and trouble drive happiness and joy out of a person's life.

This world is either a place where there is no God anywhere, or it is a place where the one true God is everywhere. There is no middle ground. This world is either without cause, without meaning, without purpose, without destiny, or else it is our Father's house, and He keeps watch above His own.

April 3

Isaiah 41:1–14

IN YOUR OWN STRENGTH

Fear thou not; for I am with thee: be not dismayed; for I am thy God: I will strengthen thee; yea, I will help thee; yea, I will uphold thee with the right hand of my righteousness (41:10).

One time at the Florida State Evangelism Conference, I shared the platform with Reuben Askew, who was then the governor of the state. What he said made the headlines of the papers the following morning.

> After my election I moved to Tallahassee, the capital city, coming early in order to choose the men who were to work with me in my commissions and to form my new government. As I began to work, the pressures and burdens of my responsibilities were so heavy upon me that I could not sleep and I could not keep down my food. I thought I was going to be the first governor in the history of the state to resign his office even before he was inaugurated.
>
> In my desperation, I bowed in my room and said to myself, "What am I doing wrong, that I cannot sleep or eat?" The answer came to me as though it were a revelation from heaven, that I should ask God to help me. I knelt down before God and asked Him to help me. When I stood up, I stood up in the power of the Lord. From that day until this, I have slept like a child every night. I am in strength and in health.

People everywhere ask me: "How is it that you are so bold to speak for Christ in the legislature and the political convocation of the state?" I was a Christian before I was elected governor. I shall be a Christian after I cease to be governor. I see no reason to change in between.

Isaiah 42:1–25

WHAT IS PROPHECY?

I am the LORD: that is my name: and my glory will I not give to another, neither my praise to graven images. Behold, the former things are come to pass, and new things do I declare: before they spring forth I tell you of them (42:8–9).

To show the difference between human surmising and a prophecy from God is very simple to do. When a poll is taken, or when a politician in Washington surveys the nation and predicts that this coming November so-and-so is going to be elected, that is political sagacity, not prophecy. But suppose the same politician were to stand up in Washington and name the man who will be elected in A.D. 2180. That would be prophecy. To stand up and call the name of the President of the United States two hundred years hence is prophecy.

In the forty-fifth chapter of Isaiah, God foretells the coming of Cyrus two hundred years before he came into history. That is prophecy as it can be known only by God, the Holy One of Israel, the One who could say to Cyrus before he was even born, "I have called thee by name; I have surnamed thee, though thou hast not known me. I am the Lord, and there is none else, there is no God beside me."

For God sees the whole consummation of the age, declaring the end from the beginning, and from ancient times the things that are not yet done. Only God can thus prophesy, and that is what He has done in His Word, the Bible.

April 5

Isaiah 43:1–28

THE FRUIT OF INFIDELITY

Even every one that is called by my name: for I have created him for my glory, I have formed him; yea, and I have made him (43:7).

One of the most gifted expository preachers of our twentieth century, Dr. Harry Ironside, was pastor of the Moody Memorial Church in Chicago. One day he was in San Francisco, standing out in the street with a band of Salvation Army people, singing the praises of the Lord and preaching the message of Christ. When he made an appeal for the Lord Jesus, a blatant infidel came up to him, and addressing all the throng who were there, said, "I challenge this preacher to a debate. I will show you how the gospel that he preaches is dust and ashes!" Dr. Ironside replied, "Sir, I accept your challenge. We will set the date and the place. The place will be the Salvation Army Hall. The date will be tonight. I will bring with me one hundred men who were in the depths of despair and darkness and who were lifted into marvelous life by the Son of God. You bring one hundred men who have been saved by the gospel of infidelity, and we will have our debate tonight."

There is not even a song dedicated to infidelity! Could one scour the whole earth and find one hundred men who had been saved from darkness by the gospel of infidelity? Dr. Ironside could as easily and as quickly have said, "I will bring tonight one thousand men in San Francisco who have been lifted up by the saving message of the Son of God." The living proof of a saved person is always the best argument.

April 6

Isaiah 44:1–28

WHEN THE SPIRITUAL MERCURY IS LOW

Thus saith the LORD, thy redeemer, and he that formed thee from the womb, I am the LORD that maketh all things; that stretcheth forth the heavens alone; that spreadeth abroad the earth by myself (44:24).

One of the saddest experiences I have ever read about is the following report of a man concerning his church. "I go to God's house and find no God. I do not hear His voice in song or sermon. His grip is not in the hand of fellowship. I hear no yearnings for the lost in the message of the preacher, nor do I see it in the faces of the people. There is no God in the temple where my people worship."

What a tragedy! O, that the church might open its heart and soul heavenward and that God might come down and fill us with His moving Spirit so that when a stranger comes in the door he will immediately feel the presence of God among us!

If the spiritual mercury is low, then God's engineer is icebound, and there is no traffic in the kingdom of God. A refrigerator may preserve things that are already dead, but it never generates life. Even an egg has to be warmed under a mother hen or in an incubator if the baby chick is to burst into life. When the wires are heavy and down, the electricity is cut off from the city and it dies. No baby is ever born that is not first bathed in the warm blood of a mother's womb. Even so, the matrix in which children are born into the kingdom of God is in the warmth and prayers and in the love and tears of His people. When Zion travails, sons and daughters are born into the kingdom. O, that God could be with us as He was in the midst of that little Pentecostal group, that we might be filled with the Spirit! When we bring the Spirit with us into the house of worship, something is felt and seen and done in the congregation of God's saints. Lord, make our churches resplendent with the filling of Thy Holy Spirit.

April 7

Isaiah 45:1–19

RIGHT IS FOREVER RIGHT

I have not spoken in secret, in a dark place of the earth: I said not unto the seed of Jacob, Seek ye me in vain: I the LORD speak righteousness, I declare things that are right" (45:19).

I knew a bank president who one time refused to employ a young man at the bank because he was an atheist. The employer explained his action by maintaining that without belief in the judgment of God, all values become relative. He did not want an employee who had a relative, changing morality to handle the money entrusted to the bank. "Today," he said, "the young man may be honest. Tomorrow he may change his mind, for honesty without God is a personal whim."

Right is forever right because God made it so. What was right yesterday is right today and will be forever. What was wrong yesterday is wrong today and will be forever. God does not change, and right and wrong are rooted, grounded, founded in an unchanging God.

April 8

Isaiah 45:20–25

LOOK AND LIVE

Look unto me, and be ye saved, all the ends of the earth: for I am God, and there is none else (45:22).

Notice how plain and simple the plan of deliverance and salvation is: "Look unto me." Anyone can look. A person need not have prestige, status, or political power to look. It does not require an education to look. It does not even demand moral excellence or righteousness. The vilest and most wretched of sinners can look. How can it be that in so simple a thing as a look I could be forgiven my sins and regenerated and saved? We feel there must be something else. Surely there are deep mysterious ceremonies, rites, and rituals that are required. To look is so simple a thing, yet it is all that God requires.

I've a message from the Lord, hallelujah!
The message unto you I'll give;
'Tis recorded in His Word, hallelujah!
It is only that you "look and live."
Look and live, my brother, live!
Look to Jesus now and live;
'Tis recorded in His Word, hallelujah!
It is only that you "look and live."

April 9

Isaiah 46:1–11

GOD HAS A PLAN

Remember the former things of old: for I am God, and there is none else; I am God and there is none like me (46:9).

We see the predestinarian sovereignty of God in our individual lives. It was according to the foreknowledge and the elective purpose of God that we were begotten. No infant has any part in its own beginning. We had no choice. We had no part at all in our birth. It came in a sovereign choice of almighty God. This is true in the lives of all of us. God has a purpose and a plan for every life. His plan fits into His beautiful mosaic as He writes the human story.

How do I know that God has a plan? Because in all the years that I have been a pastor, I have observed God's plan for every life. When a person is in the will of God, he is happy, at peace; he has an infinite sense of fulfillment. He may be in the middle of the mission field. He may be half starved to death. He may be surrounded by bitter and vicious enemies. But if the person is in the will of God, he has perfect peace and rest. However, if a person is outside the will of God for his life, no matter how he may succeed, no matter how famous or rich he may become, that person is fundamentally miserable, restless, and unhappy. A great Sovereign above us directs in all of our affairs. That same mighty Sovereign has a will for you. When you are in that plan and purpose, you have joy unspeakable. When you are outside of that plan and purpose, every day of your life you are miserable enough to die.

April 10

Isaiah 49:1–26

THE MERCY OF GOD

Thus saith the LORD, In an acceptable time have I heard thee, and in a day of salvation have I helped thee: and I will preserve thee, and give thee for a covenant of the people, to establish the earth, to cause to inherit the desolate heritages (49:8).

I once heard of a man who was desperately ill in a big ward in a charity hospital. There was a custom in that ward that when a man was going to die, they put a screen around him.

One day the nurse came into that ward and, with helpers, put a screen around that man. When he looked at it he said, "O, my God, I'm going to die. I am a vile, lost sinner. O, God, have mercy on my soul. Please, God, for Jesus' sake, save me. God, save me." And the Lord Jesus in His mercy reached down and touched that man's heart and brought him comfort and forgiveness and peace in Jesus.

The nurse came and took the screen away. She said to him, "Sir, I am so sorry. I apologize. I put the screen around the wrong man. I ask you to forgive me." The man then exclaimed, "O, nurse, it was the right one. Do not ask me to forgive you. It was the best thing that ever happened to me. Nurse, I found the Lord; I have been saved." The man began to shout and glorify God.

April 11

Isaiah 52:1–15

THE TRAGEDY OF DISFIGUREMENT

As many were astonished at thee; his visage was so marred more than any man, and his form more than the sons of men (52:14).

One time I heard of an American soldier who was critically injured by the bursting of a bomb that fell in front of him during World War I in France. He lost the use of one of his limbs and was greatly disfigured. The saddest part of his loss was the destruction of his memory. His boyhood, his family name, who he was, and where he was from, were blotted out of his broken mind. For days and years thereafter he would go wherever people gathered, and lifting up his sightless eyes and disfigured face, he would cry, "Does anyone know who I am?"

It is thus with our Lord. His visage and form were more disfigured than any of the sons of men.

Isaiah 53:1–5

THE HEARTBREAK OF REJECTION

He is despised and rejected of men; a man of sorrows, and acquainted with grief: and we hid as it were our faces from him; he was despised, and we esteemed him not (53:3).

A few years ago I heard a story that I feel is one of the saddest stories I have ever heard. An American soldier from the Midwest was seriously wounded in the conflict in Vietnam, and having been nursed back to health, he returned to the States.

When he reached San Francisco, he telephoned his father and mother and said, "Mom and Dad, I have come home." And you can imagine how happy those parents were!

The boy said, "Mom and Dad, I have a friend. He has been with me in the war and I am bringing him along. Is that all right?"

They replied, "Yes, son. We would love to have him."

The boy said, "But he has been wounded. You do not realize how badly he has been hurt. He has to be cared for. He has one eye that is gone, an arm that is gone, and a leg that is gone."

"Well," said the father and mother, "we do not know about that. Son, we could not take care of a boy like that. There are government hospitals to take care of boys with such extensive injuries. We will help you take the lad to a hospital and there they can take care of him."

The boy replied, "All right, I will be seeing you soon."

The next day the father and mother received a call from a morgue in San Francisco. "We think we might have your son. Do you have a son from the Vietnam war by this name and is this your address?"

"Yes," they said. So they went and identified the lad. The boy had taken his life the previous night in a cheap hotel in San Francisco. When the couple saw his face, they immediately recognized him as being their son. But as they looked more closely, they saw that he had one eye gone, one arm gone, and one leg gone. Their rejection was more than he could bear.

April 13

Isaiah 53:6

THE PARADOX OF PROPHECY

All we like sheep have gone astray; we have turned every one to his own way; and the Lord *hath laid on him the iniquity of us all (53:6).*

Pascal, one of the greatest and most influential scientific minds of all time, wrote these meaningful words: "The greatest of the proofs of Jesus Christ are the prophecies. They are also what God has most provided for, for the event which has fulfilled them is a miracle of God." The observation of Pascal is eminently true. It is astonishing that men, under the Holy Spirit of God, should outline and foretell the life of our Lord in minutest detail. Isaiah 53, for example, written over seven hundred and fifty years before Christ, reads as if written by a man who had himself stood beside the cross of the Son of God.

No less a miraculous part of those prophecies, delivered under the inspiration of God, is the fact that they seemingly contradict one another. For that reason, until they were fulfilled in our Lord, no one could untangle them. At one time the prophet would picture the coming One as a great conqueror. In the next breath, the same prophet would describe His lowliness, sorrow, and grief. How could that be?

In one breath the prophets would present Him as the King of Heaven, the King of Glory, the King of the nations. In the next they would describe His stripes, His blood, and His atoning death. How could those things be?

Even John the Baptist did not understand. He sent his disciples to our Lord to inquire whether or not there were two Christs, one to be the Lamb of God, the suffering Savior, and the other to be the Judge of all the earth, burning the chaff with unquenchable fire.

The diverse and apparently contradictory prophecies and their fulfillment constitute the greatest attestation of the Christian faith that mind could imagine.

April 14

Isaiah 53:7–12

DEATH OF THE LAMB

He was oppressed, and he was afflicted, yet he opened not his mouth: he is brought as a lamb to the slaughter, and as a sheep before her shearers is dumb, so he openeth not his mouth (53:7).

An experience I can never forget was my visit to the largest meat packing plant in the world, the Armour Company in Chicago, Illinois. The plant was an enormous facility. First I visited the slaughterhouse for the cattle. Oh, the sound of the moaning and the lowing of the cattle as they were led to the slaughterhouse! Then I visited the slaughterhouse for the swine, and what a loud squealing of the hogs as they were led to slaughter!

Next I visited the slaughterhouse for the sheep and lambs. The room was as silent as death. The man with the long knife plunged it into the jugular vein, and the sheep or lamb would watch the last crimson blood pour out. There was not a sound, not a cry. The only sound that I heard was the sound of the machinery as it pulled the carcass around.

April 15

Isaiah 55:1–7

THE ABUNDANCE OF DIVINE WARES

Ho, every one that thirsteth, come ye to the waters, and he that hath no money; come ye, buy, and eat; yea, come, buy wine and milk without money and without price (55:1).

When we think of God in the temple, in the sanctuary, or in the center of our worship hour, we see Him where people usually think of Him. But to put God in the marketplace selling His wares is an amazing depiction of our Lord.

I remember visiting a large city in the Middle East where those who were selling water walked up and down the streets. Their call in Arabic was translated, "O, thirsting one, water!"

What God offers is different, however. First, what God offers satisfies. There is no emptiness in what He gives. It is full, abundant, and overflowing. Second, God says that if the buyer has no money, then there is no cost or price—it is absolutely free.

April 16

Isaiah 55:8–13

CHANGE WROUGHT BY THE WORD

So shall my word be that goeth forth out of my mouth: it shall not return unto me void, but it shall accomplish that which I please, and it shall prosper in the thing whereto I sent it (55:11).

The showers that fall from heaven turn into flowers, into wheat fields, into beautiful meadows and pastures, and into orchards that are fruitful as only God can make them. So the Word of God waters our souls and brings blessing and fruit to us. The change that the Holy Scriptures bring to human life and human destiny is glorious beyond compare.

God's Word can change human life. In the Fiji Islands an islander was reading God's Book. A Frenchman, watching him, finally came over and said, "So you are reading the Bible!" The Frenchman ridiculed the islander.

The islander turned to the Frenchman and said, "Do you see that boiling pot over there? Were it not for this Book, you would be in that pot!" What a glorious change the Word of God makes in human life!

April 17

Isaiah 57:1–21

THE ETERNALITY OF GOD

For thus saith the high and lofty One that inhabiteth eternity, whose name is Holy; I dwell in the high and holy place, with him also that is of a contrite and humble spirit, to revive the spirit of the humble, and to revive the heart of the contrite ones (57:15).

The text speaks of the great and mighty God in time. He inhabits eternity. Language staggers under the weight of the magnitude of the burden laid upon it. God dwelt in eternity in the aeons and ages before creation and will dwell in the great consummation of the aeons that are yet to come. He is ageless and unchanging.

The tall, graceful Sears Building is located in Chicago. It is the highest man-made structure in the world, towering a quarter of a mile high above the streets of the city. The thickness of a nickel placed on top of that vast building would be relative to the age of humanity compared to the age of creation itself. Yet creation is but a small part of the eternity before and the eternity that shall follow after. In all of the ageless aeons, God dwells.

April 18

Isaiah 59:1–21

SHARING THE WORD

As for me, this is my covenant with them, saith the LORD; My spirit that is upon thee, and my words which I have put in thy mouth, shall not depart out of thy mouth, nor out of the mouth of thy seed, nor out of the mouth of thy seed's seed, saith the LORD, from henceforth and for ever (59:21).

Once Mr. Pat Zondervan of the Zondervan Corporation made his annual pilgrimage to our church in behalf of the Gideons. He made his appeal for the distribution of the Holy Scriptures. In that appeal he held up a little white New Testament which the Gideons distribute to the nurses in America.

Mr. Zondervan told how a Christian nurse happened to have that New Testament in the pocket of her uniform so that its outline was seen by one of her patients. He thought it was a package of cigarettes and asked what brand she used. She took it out and held it up for him to see, explaining that it was the Word of God. She asked if she could read to him from it. He gave permission, and, as time passed, she read to him again and again. Under the influence of the Holy Spirit, the man confessed his sins, asked God to forgive him, and received the Lord Jesus into his heart.

As the days passed, this Christian nurse had a strange impulse to go to see that man. She went to his room. He sat up in bed and seemed to be looking at someone standing at the foot of the bed. Then he raised his arms and cried, "My Lord and my God." He fell back, and his spirit was translated to heaven.

Hearing that story, I could not help but bless the name of God for the little book and for the Holy Spirit who carried its convicting message to the heart of that lost man. Praise God that the man accepted Jesus.

April 19

Isaiah 60:1–22

RISE AND SHINE

Arise, shine; for thy light is come, and the glory of the Lord *is risen upon thee (60:1).*

It is amazing how the spirit of people made in the image of God can rise in a need or an emergency. Not long after World War II, I was on my way from Folkestone, England, to Boulogne, France. I had to stand in a long line before an immigration desk.

As the line slowly moved, I noticed the British woman in front of me with the name Emma Jenson on her passsport. She had a little girl with her, and I began to visit with them. The little girl had lived most of her life in an air-raid shelter. The mother said, "My husband, my daughter, and I were managing quite well during the war. But just a few days before the awful conflict closed, a rocket bomb burst over our home. My husband was killed and everything we had was destroyed." She pulled back the girl's heavy hair to reveal a dark, deep scar which went across her forehead and back over her head. The mother said, "I nursed our little girl to life and health."

When I expressed my sorrow, she said, "No, do not sympathize with me. There are thousands who have been hurt and injured worse than I. I am doing well. In the goodness of God only one thing was spared in our home, a typewriter. I got a job at Cambridge University typing for a professor of law. After I put my daughter to bed at night I type through the early hours of the morning and make a living supporting myself and our little child." That is the human spirit—in the face of a need to rise and shine.

April 20

Isaiah 61:1–11

THE NOBLEST CALLING

To proclaim the acceptable year of the L*ORD, and the day of vengeance of our God; to comfort all that mourn (61:2).*

One time I came across a letter that Spurgeon had written to his son. He wrote, "I should not like for you, if meant by God to be a missionary, to die a millionaire. I should not like it, were you fitted to be a missionary, if you should stoop to be a king. What are kings and nobles and diadems compared with the dignity of winning souls to Christ?" That is a great and true conviction and persuasion. A king, a millionaire, a kingdom with all kinds of emoluments and successes—these things are nothing compared to the marvelous assignment of winning people to Christ.

What Spurgeon wrote to his son is my persuasion after many years of looking at the stream of life. The noblest and finest of all dedications is that of witnessing for the Lord and seeing people come to know Christ in obedience to the Great Commission of our blessed Savior. O Lord, that we might share in a like commitment!

April 21

Isaiah 64:1–12

THE LIGHTING OF A FIRE

For since the beginning of the world men have not heard, nor perceived by the ear, neither hath the eye seen, O God, beside thee, what he hath prepared for him that waiteth for him (64:4).

At the entrance to Oxford University in England is located the Martyrs' Monument. It is dedicated to Archbishop Cranmer, to Bishop Latimer, and to Master Ridley. They were mighty preachers of the gospel, and because of their loyalty to the Lord they were burned at the stake in October, 1555. When the flames were rising, Master Ridley began to cry before the leaping fire. Bishop Latimer, tied to the stake on the other side, turned and said,

"Be of good cheer, Master Ridley. By God's grace we shall light a fire this day in England that shall never go out." In my reading I stumbled across the bill of expense that was sent to the crown for the burning of Latimer and Ridley. It was twenty-five shillings and eight pence. What a cheap fire! It did not even cost five dollars. But the martyrs trusted in God, and that day they did light a fire in England and throughout the world that burns to this hour. Christians are still preaching the gospel of the grace of the Son of God. We never fail when we are trusting God.

The sun may go out in the sky, the light of the world may turn to darkness, the tides of the sea may cease to ebb and flow, the stars may grow old and dim, and nature may rack itself on the shifts of time and fortune, but that Christ should remain dead is impossible and unthinkable, for He trusted in God. All through life and even to death He will carry us, holding us next to His heart, that we might have strength to finish our pilgrimage in this life.

April 22

Isaiah 66:1–24

THE HUMAN AND THE DIVINE

For all those things hath mine hand made, and all those things have been, saith the LORD: but to this man will I look, even to him that is poor and of a contrite spirit, and trembleth at my word (66:2).

When I was a pastor in a little country church, one of the godly deacons, a farmer, fell heir some way to a Spanish Bible. He could not read a word of it and wondered what to do with it. Then he remembered that in the community was a Mexican family. He made his way up to the house and knocked at the door. He was greeted by the father of the large family. The deacon said, "I have a gift for you, a Bible. It is written in Spanish, in your language. I am giving it to you." The Mexican took it with gratitude, saying, "Gracias, gracias."

One day after the farmer had forgotten the incident, he heard a knock at his door. There stood that Mexican tenant farmer. He said, "You know the Book you gave us? We have been reading the Book, and we have all accepted Jesus as our Savior. And it says in the Book that we ought to be baptized, and I have come to ask if I and all of my family could be baptized." They brought the matter to me. I said, "We rejoice; we thank God." So I baptized the Mexican and his large family.

Then one day a fire broke out in the tenant farmer's house. As the house was going up in flames, the farmers who had gathered around saw that Mexican dash into those burning embers and come back out with the Bible. He had rescued from the flames the Word of God and held it in his hands, a treasure forever. Scripture is supernatural in its effect upon the human soul.

Such is the Book of God. "The grass withereth, the flower fadeth but the word of our Lord," inspired plenarily, verbally, dynamically, supernaturally, "abides in glory and in power forever."

April 23

Jeremiah 8:1–20

THE TRAGEDY OF DELAY

The harvest is past, the summer is ended, and we are not saved (8:20).

One of our deacons said to me, "A family has moved next door to my house. None of them are Christians. Help me win them to the Lord."

Upon visiting the home, I found a father, mother, two boys, and a girl. They readily agreed that they should become Christians and attend Sunday school and church, but they never did. No amount of persuasion could bring them to a decision for Christ.

About two o'clock one morning, a Christian nurse from the hospital telephoned. "Pastor, a boy has been critically hurt in a traffic accident. His father is by his side. When the boy dies, it will be a terrible blow for this man. I thought possibly you could come and be with him and help him. He says he knows you." When she told me his name, I recognized the name of the man who lived next door to the deacon.

At the hospital I stood by the side of the father as we watched the life of the boy slowly ebb away. Soon the nurse turned to the father and said, "Sir, your boy is gone." She drew the sheet over the face of the silent form. The father stood over the bed, too stunned to move. Then he burst into tears and sobbed piteously, "O my God! My God! My boy is gone, and I have not lived right before him!"

The next Lord's Day the entire family was present and answered the invitation to come to the Savior. What should have been a beautiful sight was one of the saddest sights. In a lonely grave in a Texas cemetery lay the silent form of their boy who went out to meet God without hope, without salvation, without the forgiveness of sins. That boy's life was sacrificed on the altar of the sin and indifference of his parents.

April 24

Jeremiah 17:1–27

THE DECEITFULNESS OF THE HUMAN HEART

The heart is deceitful above all things, and desperately wicked: who can know it? (17:9).

A learned psychologist once stated that in years past we used to think that if we could change the environment, we could change the people. If we would take people living in poverty, squalor, and filth out of the environment in which they live and build them beautiful boulevards, sidewalks, and homes, they would be a different kind of people. That is what we used to think and teach.

In his own city there was a rat-infested, poverty-stricken, dirty part of town. With much money, the citizens of the community cleared out the filth, built beautiful streets, planted trees, and gave the people beautiful places in which to live. After the city had spent that vast amount of money and time, the people were still as decadent, degraded, and as sorry as they ever were. How a person is situated has nothing to do with the character of the person himself.

One of the most famous trials in all legal history was the trial of Loeb and Leopold. Clarence Darrow won his case (though he admitted that the boys were murderers) on the basis that they had grown up in affluent homes. They were the sons of rich families. Being satiated with all of the gifts and affluence of life, they were pampered and petted and thus sought a thrill in the murder of a little friend. That is hard to believe, but that was the verdict of the law.

However beautifully positioned we may be, even if all of the accouterments of art or affluence surround us, the human heart is still impotent and beggarly in the presence of the most glorious gift of life.

April 25

Ezekiel 18:1–20

THE CLOTHING OF THE SOUL

Behold, all souls are mine; as the soul of the father, so also the soul of the son is mine: the soul that sinneth, it shall die (18:4).

A sinful woman came off the street when Jesus was a guest at dinner with Simon the Pharisee. She bathed Jesus' feet with her tears, anointed Him with spikenard of ointment, and dried His feet with the hairs of her head. The law said that she was to be stoned (Luke 7:36–50). The law said that she was to be taken outside of the city and stoned until she died, but mercy and grace are something else. Not only is that law applicable to a malefactor, to a felon, to a murderer, or to a vile sinner, but it is applicable to all of us. There is no exception.

The trail of the serpent is everywhere in the earth. There is poison that has entered the fountain of our hearts. There is a black drop that courses through all our veins. Without rank, without station, without anything to commend us to God, we are naked, fallen, sinful, and lost before Him. For us to try to cover ourselves by our self-righteousness is to clothe ourselves in garments of filth and dirt. For one to protect himself and to shield himself from the judgment of God is as though one were to seek to hide himself behind a web of spider material—thin, fragile, frail. It is cut through with the sword of the law.

April 26

Ezekiel 18:21–32

WHO DOES THE CHANGING?

Cast away from you all your transgressions, whereby ye have transgressed; and make you a new heart and a new spirit: for why will ye die, O house of Israel? (18:31).

Surely there never lived a man who went through as many horrors as did the infamous John Dillinger. He even had the tips of his fingers cut off in order to destroy the identifying marks of his fingerprints. He lived a life of horror, and yet he became more criminal every day that he lived. He did not change. Why?

Why does the devil not change? Somehow it just does not work that way. A person does not have the power to change himself, and God will not force him to change. However, God will change the heart of any and everyone who comes to Him in confession of sin and with a plea for forgiveness.

April 27

Ezekiel 33:1–33

PREREQUISITE FOR PARDON

Say unto them, As I live, saith the Lord God, I have no pleasure in the death of the wicked; but that the wicked turn from his way and live: turn ye, turn ye from your evil ways; for why will ye die, O house of Israel? (33:11).

One of the most unusual court decisions in American jurisprudence happened in the days of President Andrew Jackson. A railway mail clerk named George Wilson killed his fellow clerk. He then stole the mail and tied himself in some way with a rope. When the train arrived at its destination they found Wilson tied up, and the dead clerk lying in his own blood. Wilson said that he had been assailed by bandits. But as the officers of the law began to question him, they found some discrepancies in his story. Wilson finally confessed that he killed his partner and perpetrated the hoax. He was tried and sentenced to be hanged in the federal penitentiary. But as time passed, people seemed to forget the dastardly act and the sorrow of the dead man's family. Political pressure was brought upon President Jackson to pardon him.

The warden of the penitentiary told Wilson that the President of the United States had pardoned him. But, to the astonishment of the warden, Wilson refused to accept the pardon. He wanted to be hanged. The warden did not know what to do. He called in the greatest legal minds, and it was finally sent to the Supreme Court of the United States. The decision written by Chief Justice Marshall was handed down:

> A pardon is a paper, the value of which depends upon its acceptance by the person implicated. It is hardly to be supposed that one under sentence of death would refuse to accept a pardon, but if it is refused, it is no pardon. George Wilson must hang.

And in the federal penitentiary at Leavenworth, Kansas, George Wilson was hanged.

Christ died for our sins. He was buried for our justification. He suffered that we might be forgiven. We have free and absolute pardon in Him, but if a person refuses that pardon, it is no longer a pardon.

April 28

Daniel 3:8–20

FIRE THAT LIBERATES

If it be so, our God whom we serve is able to deliver us from the burning fiery furnace, and he will deliver us out of thine hand, O king (3:17).

The three Hebrew young men were walking freely in the furnace. The fire did nothing but bring them the presence of the living Lord and burn up their bonds. They were free. So it is that the trials, fires, and floods that overwhelm us in our life free us from the visible world so that we might live in the invisible. Our bodies carry our souls; it is not our souls that carry our bodies. The flame and fire burn our bonds and liberate us to walk in the presence of the great and living God. This is God's way of preparing us for the victories of the kingdom. "Every one that is called by my name . . . I have created him for my glory" (Isa. 43:7). This is God's purpose for us that we might reign with Christ.

If we suffer with Him, we also shall reign with Him. No one could know victory who has not first been in a battle or a conflict. If we are to wear the crown in heaven, we first must bear the cross here on earth. I shall not cower and cringe before the warfare!

April 29

Daniel 6:14–28

A NON-COMPROMISING FAITH

My God hath sent his angel, and hath shut the lions' mouths, that they have not hurt me: forasmuch as before him innocency was found in me; and also before thee, O king, have I done no hurt (6:22).

The Christian faith is of all things and first of all authoritarian. It is non-compromising. It is absolute and final. It is that or nothing at all. The Roman Empire did not demand of those early Christians whom they fed to the lions, whom they burned at the stake, whom they plunged into boiling caldrons of oil, whom they crucified—that they give up their faith in Christ, nor did the Romans demand that they cease attending churches or do anything whereby they would separate themselves from their Lord.

The Roman Empire was of all things broad-minded in its religious policies. When the Romans conquered a nation, they accepted that nation's god, brought the god to Rome, and put him in the Pantheon with the rest of the gods they had previously collected. One of the secrets of the Roman Empire was the tolerant attitude toward all the religions of the provinces. The Romans allowed all of the gods to be worshiped.

As time went on, the leaders of Rome began to see that they needed some kind of faith or religion to hold the empire together. They found their hope for a common religion in the worship of the emperor. As a matter of patriotism, the Christian was asked to take a little pinch of incense and put it on the altar fire that burned before the image of the emperor. But the first-century Christians refused to do it! When the judge asked Polycarp, the pastor of the church at Smyrna, to place a pinch of incense on the flame that burned before the altar of the image of the emperor, Polycarp refused. He was burned at the stake because of that refusal.

Daniel 12:1–13

A GETHSEMANE EXPERIENCE

And they that be wise shall shine as the brightness of the firmament; and they that turn many to righteousness as the stars for ever and ever (12:3).

For two weeks I preached to a little country congregation in which there was no burden for the lost and no effort to win anyone to Christ. The whole revival was a daily Gethsemane to me. But before the benediction on Friday morning, a woman said, "Brother Criswell, my husband died several years ago. I am a widow with two boys. My boys are lost. Oh, that someone would help me win my two boys to Christ!"

Later I went to that mother's humble farm home. I asked the mother to get down on her knees and pray while I went out to the barn. The younger boy was milking the cows. I sat down on a box beside him and opened my New Testament. I read him those passages in God's Book that tell us how to be saved, and then I asked, "Son, would you kneel down here and pray with me?" He stopped his milking and knelt by my side, saying, "I will take the Lord as my Savior."

By that time the older boy had come in from the fields and was taking the harnesses off the horses. I read to him those precious passages. He knelt by my side, and I prayed that God would save him.

That night at church when I gave the invitation, those two boys came forward, arm in arm. It was a glorious sight, and that sweet mother shouted. Those two boys were the only souls that were saved in the meeting. When it was finished, I went away with a commitment and resolution in my heart that has colored my ministry ever since.

I believe that the praying, the working, and the dedication of the whole church ought to be to one holy and heavenly end, namely, that the lost may come to know God.

May 1

Joel 2:1–32

THE MONUMENT TO A SLAVE

And it shall come to pass afterward, that I will pour out my spirit upon all flesh; and your sons and your daughters shall prophesy, your old men shall dream dreams, your young men shall see visions (2:28).

There is no finer illustration of the outpouring of the Holy Spirit than that seen in John Jasper. Many learned professors of homiletics (the art of preaching) write that the greatest genius in the ministry that America has ever produced is John Jasper, a Negro slave. As he sorted out tobacco with his hands in the warehouse, the Holy Spirit of God came upon him. He became one of the greatest preachers in American history.

During a visit I made to Richmond, Virginia, the Foreign Mission Board sent a young man out to the airport to meet me and take me to the board meeting. Driving into the city down a freeway, we came to a big bend in the highway. I remarked, "This freeway should go straight!" The young man told me that when the highway department condemned all the property by eminent domain for the building of this great expressway, they went to the church of John Jasper, the Sixth Mt. Zion Baptist Church in Richmond. The people of Richmond said, "Do not touch one brick of this church. It shall stand here as a monument to the preaching of the slave, John Jasper." When one drives into the city of Richmond down the freeway, he will drive around a great bend, and there in the bend stands the Sixth Mount Zion Baptist Church, a monument to the slave John Jasper. God shall pour out His Spirit upon all—slave as well as free.

May 2

Amos 1:1–15

HOW TO EMPTY A CHURCH

The words of Amos, who was among the herdmen of Tekoa, which he saw concerning Israel in the days of Uzziah king of Judah, and in the days of Jeroboam the son of Joash king of Israel, two years before the earthquake (1:1).

Recently I read of a pioneer preacher who was successful in converting the frontiersmen. He was uneducated. He spoke in rude language. His library was a Bible and a hymn book. He pressed westward, preaching under an arbor, under trees, in log cabins, eventually reaching the waters of the Pacific.

Such men—though uneducated, crude, and unacceptable in any modern, cultured pulpit in America—turned this continent to Christ and established many of the churches and institutions that now bless our homes and hearts. The Holy Spirit worked with them, and God used them to turn America to Christ. Today many leaders in the Christian theological world are highly educated. They write learned tomes and speak in deep and recondite nomenclature. In the pulpit they snore theology and the people listen while sound asleep. They have emptied the churches of Europe and are beginning with the churches of America.

At a large convention in Nashville, Tennessee, Billy Graham was the speaker. He said that he could not understand why people would embrace a theology that had emptied the churches of continental Europe. I do not understand it either. Such nothingness does not have in it the moving, convicting Spirit of the saving power of God. I cannot help but compare these men with our coarse frontiersmen through whom the Spirit of God witnessed so that the people who listened were saved. The churches were founded and organized, but the learned, academic institutions were lost. When we have no Christ, we have no message. When we have no Spirit, we have no power.

May 3

Malachi 4:1–6

HEALING IN HIS WINGS

But unto you that fear my name shall the Sun of righteousness arise with healing in his wings; and ye shall go forth, and grow up as calves of the stall (4:2).

One evening a sweet family sat in my study. The husband was an engineer. Brilliant as he was, his mind had begun to disintegrate. He was on the verge of a nervous collapse. But he was married to a glorious Christian girl, and she brought him to the Lord.

The man said to me, "I was dreading those long, interminable sessions from psychiatrist to psychiatrist when my dear wife brought me to Jesus. I found the Lord and my mind is healed. I am sharper today than I have ever been and doing better work today than I ever have." I reminded him of Exodus 15, "For I am the LORD that healeth thee" (v. 26). God heals our hearts, our souls, our minds, and our bodies.

May 4

Matthew 4:1–11

THE GREATEST CONFLICT

Then saith Jesus unto him, Get thee hence, Satan: for it is written, Thou shalt worship the Lord thy God, and him only shalt thou serve (4:10).

What is the greatest struggle of the ages? Some people may say that the greatest conflict of all time must be the struggle unto death between the freedom of our democracy and the tyranny of ideological totalitarianism. Some could say it was the conflict in the wars which swirled around Germany. Some could say it was the terrible campaigns which oppressed Europe under Napoleon. Some could say it was the devastating wars of the Caesars.

But through the ages, the greatest conflict of all is between the evil of Satan and the mind and love of God. In glory, Lucifer looked upon the pre-existent Lord Christ and said in his heart, "I would be first; I would reign; I would rule." He hated Jehovah Jesus, the Lord Christ in heaven, and decided to supplant Him and to destroy Him.

It is against the Lord Christ that Satan in all of his subtlety wages war day and night. Satan chooses to take God's world away from Him and has avowed to rule over God's world in the place of the Lord Christ. When God made the universe, Satan said, "I will seize it." When Satan saw the man and the woman in the Garden of Eden, in the perfection and beauty of the Almighty, Satan said, "I will destroy them. I will keep them from ruling over the universe under Christ. I am going to seize the power for myself, and I am going to destroy the man; I am going to reign and to rule over this creation." Only the Lord Christ Himself can win the victory over this malignant spirit.

May 5

Matthew 4:12–25

THE GREAT PHYSICIAN

And Jesus went about all Galilee, teaching in their synagogues, and preaching the gospel of the kingdom, and healing all manner of sickness and all manner of disease among the people" (4:23).

One day when I was walking down a hospital corridor, a man stopped me and asked a question that I have been asked many times. Because of a serious illness in his family, he asked me if I believed in divine healing. I asked him if there was any other kind. Does anyone heal but God?

The doctor can prescribe, the surgeon can cut, and the physician can sew up the wound, but it is God who heals. The pharmacist cannot heal; the physician cannot heal; the surgeon cannot heal. Only God can heal. The surgeon, the doctor, and the pharmacist are as helpless before God as you and I are. They have to depend upon God, whether they admit it or not. The physician may be an infidel or an atheist, but he has to depend upon God for healing. There is no other kind of healing but divine healing. All healing comes from the gracious hands of the Lord.

May 6

Matthew 5:1–18

LET THE BIBLE SPEAK FOR ITSELF

For verily I say unto you, Till heaven and earth pass, one jot or one tittle shall in no wise pass from the law, till all be fulfilled (5:18).

An infidel challenged a brilliant minister to a debate on the inspiration of the Bible. The atheist stood up to deny the Word of God: "In this debate we shall not turn for proof to the Bible itself. You cannot test a thing by the thing itself. Thus we are not to prove the Bible by the Bible itself. Rather, our debate is to concern extraneous matters and materials."

Then said this brilliant minister, "That would be as though a man who had a ranch went to the assayer and said, 'I have found an outcropping of quartz on my ranch and in it are some yellow particles. I think that I have gold in those mountains.' The assayer would reply, 'Bring me a piece of that quartz with those gold specks in it.' And the ranchman would say, 'Oh, no, indeed not. For you cannot prove a thing by the thing itself, nor can you test a thing by the thing itself. You take one of the bricks out of the walls of your house and test them and tell me whether or not there is gold on my ranch.'"

Then the minister said, "Or it would be as though a man feared someone was poisoning him by putting potassium cyanide in his sugar. So he went to the chemist and said: 'I am fearful that someone is seeking to poison me. I am afraid there is cyanide in my sugarbowl.' So the chemist said, 'We will test the bowl of sugar.' 'Oh, no,' said the man, 'you cannot prove a thing by the thing itself. Take your salt shaker off the table and test it and tell me whether or not there is cyanide in my sugarbowl.'"

Then the minister went right ahead and looked at the Bible itself to see whether or not it is God-breathed.

May 7

Matthew 5:19–48

THE CONSEQUENCE OF WORLDLINESS

That ye may be the children of your Father which is in heaven: for he maketh his sun to rise on the evil and on the good, and sendeth rain on the just and on the unjust (5:45).

A mother is rearing her two boys in our church. Her husband viciously seeks to stop his wife and two children from coming to the house of the Lord. I went to see him and said, "If you do not want your wife and boys to attend church, then you would like to live in Russia. You would never be bothered with any Sunday school there. The official doctrine of the state is sheer unadulterated atheism. They are anti-God, anti-Christ, and anti-church. Why not move to Russia?" He answered, "Not I; I could not move to Russia!" Then I said, "Why not move your family to a godless town where there is no church and where the women in that town are the wrong kind of women? Why not move to a town like that and rear your boys there?" "Oh, no, I would not live in a town where there is no church, and I would not rear my family in a place where the people were godless."

That man receives blessings from God and from godly people, but he makes no contribution to the community whatsoever, even though he acts as though he made a contribution to the godliness and sobriety of his city. Worldliness makes liars and hypocrites out of us just as it did with Ananias and Sapphira and Achan.

May 8

Matthew 6:1–34

EMPTY-HANDED

But lay up for yourselves treasures in heaven, where neither moth nor rust doth corrupt, and where thieves do not break through nor steal (6:20).

A wealthy man had given his life to the world and not to God. In his last illness he became obsessed with his hands. His wife called his partner in business, asking him to come and talk to John. "Maybe you can help him," she said, "he is obsessed with his hands." So Jim came to see his old friend, whom he had known and loved through the years. As they visited, Jim finally said to John, "John, there is nothing wrong with your hands." But John looked at him and said, "Jim, look! My God, Jim, they are so empty! They are so empty!" He that soweth for worldly gain shall reap emptiness, corruption, decay, and loss. Death to the lost man becomes a mockery, a ghastly, ghostly apparition. He that soweth to the flesh shall of the flesh reap corruption, loss, disintegration.

May 9

Matthew 7:1–14

THE NARROW WAY

Because strait is the gate, and narrow is the way, which leadeth unto life, and few there be that find it (7:14).

A train was heading west across the vast, flat prairies of Kansas during a howling blizzard. On the train was a woman with a baby in her arms going to a little town called Prairie View. Because of the blinding snowstorm, she became anxious lest she not know the time and place to get off the train.

A kindly gentleman in the car noticed how anxious she was and said to her, "I see that you are anxious about how to know when you come to Prairie View. I ride this train back and forth all the time, and I know exactly where we are. When we come to your station, I will tell you so you won't have to be anxious anymore."

The train sped on and finally came to a stop. The kindly gentleman said to the mother with the baby in her arms, "This is Prairie View," and he helped her off the train. The minute she was off the train, it speeded up and went down the track.

After they had been traveling for miles in that blinding blizzard, the conductor came, looked around, and asked, "Where is that mother with the baby?" The gentleman said, "At the last stop I helped her off the train at Prairie View." The conductor exclaimed, "My God, then she got off the train to her death, for that stop of the train was at a switch, and we are just now coming to Prairie View!" The mother and her baby were left at a switch in the snowstorm.

Truth is narrow and demanding! If truth, mathematics, science, history, and geography are always narrow, do not persuade yourself that truth becomes any other thing when it pertains to God, eternity, heaven, hell, and our salvation.

May 10

Matthew 7:15–29

THE GNAT ON MT. EVEREST

Therefore whosoever heareth these sayings of mine, and doeth them, I will liken him unto a wise man, which built his house upon a rock (7:24).

A self-important college student said to his eldest brother, "What would you think if I told you that in ten minutes I could produce arguments that would utterly annihilate the Bible?" The brother replied, "About the same thing I would think if a gnat crawled up the side of Mount Everest and said, 'Watch me pulverize this thing with my left hind foot!'"

The answer of the atheist to the questions posited by life and personality is sterile and empty. It is like drinking water that does not quench the thirst. It is like eating food that does not satisfy the hunger. It is like building a house without a pattern. It is like reading a book that has no meaning. It is like running a train without an engine. It is like living a life without a purpose. The atheist believes like a fool.

Not to recognize the presence of God is to be blind in mind and soul as the fool is blind.

May 11

Matthew 8:1–34

THE REALITY OF SUFFERING

That it might be fulfilled which was spoken by Isaiah the prophet, saying, Himself took our infirmities, and bare our sicknesses (8:17).

What is to be the attitude of a child of God toward illness? We must accept the fact that illness, disease, germs, bacteria—these things that hurt us and cause us to be sick—they are here, along with the accidents into which we may fall. Death is here, and we cannot deny it.

One of the strangest of all of the denominations to me is the one that denies the reality of hurt, injury, disease, and illness. They say it is just in the mind. There is no such thing as hurt or illness or disease. At the same time they are saying this, they may have mouths full of crockery and eyes covered with heavy lenses.

I once was the pastor of a church in a town where there was a university. The mother of one of the professors in the university was a devout Baptist and belonged to our congregation. She was a big, heavy woman, and one day she stumbled and fell down the steps into the basement. She was bruised from head to foot.

The daughter ran down and helped her mother up. The daughter said to her mother, "You're not hurt. That's just in your mind." No doctor was called; no pharmacist was contacted for medication. I went out to see that mother. She was lying in her bed in pain, black and blue all over. She was hurt and hurting, but not to her daughter who believed any pain or suffering was only present in her mother's mind.

The Scriptures, on the other hand, offer comfort to those who are suffering and encourage us to seek healing from the Great Physician.

May 12

Matthew 9:1–13

THE APPEAL FOR PARDON

But go ye and learn what that meaneth, I will have mercy, and not sacrifice: for I am not come to call the righteous, but sinners to repentance (9:13).

The man who is sick but has no sense of being ill would never seek out a physician. A man who is not in debt would never seek help to pay his debts. The man who is not incarcerated would never seek a pardon. Rather, the man who is incarcerated, who is in the penitentiary, would seek a pardon. I once wrote a letter to the President of the United States, asking for the pardon of a man whom I knew. Had that man not been incarcerated, there would have been no need for the letter. It was because he was in the pentitentiary that an appeal was made for his pardon.

When a man is well, he does not seek a physician. It is because he is ill that he seeks the help of a doctor. If a man is not in debt, there is no need to help him financially. But if a man is overwhelmed by indebtedness, he desperately needs help. Thus it is with us before God. We are debtors before God and cannot pay. We are dying and cannot find health and life. We are without hope in the world. We face nothing but corruption and after that the judgment of God.

The purpose, therefore, of the law is to reveal to us our lostness, our sinfulness, our indebtedness, our shortcomings.

In that same law we are led to find mercy and forgiveness in Jesus our Lord. Without that consciousness of need and sense of lostness, we would never know the true and full meaning of Christ our Savior. There is no need for Christ if I can be saved by my own efforts.

May 13

Matthew 9:20–38

DELIVERING THE TRUTH

But when he saw the multitudes, he was moved with compassion on them, because they fainted, and were scattered abroad, as sheep having no shepherd (9:36).

A preacher was once talking to a famous actor. The preacher said, "I do not understand. You are on the platform, on the stage, and you deliver monologues and take part in dramas and plays. As you speak, you bring people to tears. What you are doing is just fictional. It is not fact; it is not true. You are just playing a part. But when I stand up in the pulpit and preach the truth of God, it does not move anyone! I do not understand."

The actor said to him, "The difference is this. When I am on the platform, I deliver a lie as though it were the truth. But when you are in the pulpit, you deliver the truth as though it were a lie."

How condemnatory that is to all of us—ministers and laypeople alike—who deliver the message of Christ! Instead of the message being something that is life and death, heaven or hell, saved or lost, how many times does it take a philosophical, an academic, a speculative, or a theological turn? God help us! Therefore, the first requirement of a soul-saving ministry is a deep conviction that we are lost without Christ and that we possess the word of salvation.

May 14

Matthew 10:1–33

THE FAITHFUL WITNESS

Whosoever therefore shall confess me before men, him will I confess also before my Father which is in heaven (10:32).

The apostles were witnesses to the truth as well as to the saving grace and power of the Son of God. In a military world they proclaimed the grace and forgiveness of Jesus Christ. Oh, how effective they were! They had no other robes except those of poverty. They had no other distinctiveness except shame and suffering. They had no other power but the weapon of the presence of the Holy Spirit. But how faithfully they delivered their message. They evangelized in the homes of the people, in the rural areas, in the country and the villages, and finally in the cities, even in Caesar's household. There the apostles faithfully gave the message of the truth of the cross and finally bore that message far away to the heathen of the known world.

The very word for "witness" in the Greek New Testament is *martus.* So often did the Christian witness pay for his faith with his own death that the word carried over into our English language is a transliteration of *martus*—i.e., *martyr,* signifying one who lays down his life for the faith.

How glorious is the testimony of the witnesses to the truth of God in Christ Jesus!

May 15

Matthew 11:1–19

THE GIFT OF MIRACLES

The blind receive their sight, and the lame walk, the lepers are cleansed, and the deaf hear, the dead are raised up, and the poor have the gospel preached to them (11:5).

Miracles of God are on every hand. They are recorded every day. The gift of miracles possessed by the saints may be temporary, but miracles and the miracle-working God are with us forever.

God does not change or evolve. His power and wisdom are this day what they were before the morning stars sang together. The fires that forged the strong bands of Orion are the same as those that were seen by Moses in the burning bush of Horeb. Israel looked upon those same fires in the *Shekinah* glory above the tabernacle and the temple. Again, those fires smote Abihu in the day of judgment, just as they consumed the sacrifice and the altar and the very dirt of the ground upon Mount Carmel after the appeal of Elijah.

The same fires rose in amber flames before the rapt attention of Ezekiel, and they sat in cloven tongues upon Peter and the apostles. They blinded the eyes of Saul of Tarsus on the road to Damascus, and someday those same fires shall clothe our glorious returning Lord when He descends through the clouds of heaven.

God does not change, nor does His power to work miracles cease.

May 16

Matthew 11:20–30

COME UNTO ME

Come unto me, all ye that labor and are heavy laden, and I will give you rest (11:28).

Some years ago I spoke at an interdenominational convocation for clergymen in Washington, D.C. While in Washington, I received a letter from a wife who said she was praying that her sixty-seven-year-old husband might be saved. After a service, with many tears he did give his life to Christ. The next night a young man waited for me after the service and, while on his knees, accepted the Lord as his Savior. When Sunday night came, I extended an invitation and God blessed it. Many were saved and came forward. But some of the clergymen present were highly offended by what I had done. They used some harsh and critical words. A part of the program each day was a panel, and when the panel met that Monday, I was called upon to defend what I had done. I was accused of conducting a cheap, melodramatic show of emotionalism which had no place in the service of Christ. I became discouraged and heavy-hearted. I spent that afternoon as sad and blue as I could be.

When it was time for the Monday night service, the man who presided over the convocation came to my room and had a talk with me. He said, "I know that this harsh criticism has really crushed you. But we knew that it would be this way when we invited you to come, and we wanted you to be yourself. If you had not given that invitation, we would have been disappointed in you. Tonight, you let the Holy Spirit lead you and do what God puts in your heart—and some of us will be praying." I felt moved by God that night again to extend an invitation. More responded and were saved.

Following the meeting, one of my critics drew me aside and apologized. He said that he had never seen anything like that.

The great purpose of the people of God is that God might use us to bring others to the saving faith we have found in our blessed Jesus.

May 17

Matthew 12:1–21

THE MASTER'S HAND

Behold my servant, whom I have chosen; my beloved, in whom my soul is well pleased: I will put my spirit upon him, and he shall show judgment to the Gentiles (12:18).

One of the most beautiful and meaningful poems I know is entitled "The Touch of the Master's Hand." It begins with an auctioneer selling an old violin. He holds it up and says, "What am I bid for this violin? One dollar? Two dollars? Who will make it three?"

Just before the old violin was to be sold for three dollars, from the back of the room an old, gray-haired man came forward. He took the violin and the bow, and wiped off the dust. He tightened the bow, tuned the strings, and began to play angelic music. When the auctioneer held it up again, he said, "What am I bid for it? A thousand dollars? Two thousand dollars? Who will make it three?" The concluding stanzas of the poem read:

The people cheered, but some of them cried,
"We do not quite understand
What changed its worth." Swift came the reply:
The touch of a master's hand.

And many a man with life out of tune,
And battered and scarred with sin,
Is auctioned off cheap to the thoughtless crowd,
Much like the old violin.

A "mess of pottage," a glass of wine;
A game—and he travels on.
He is "going" once, and "going" twice,
He's "going" and almost "gone."

But the Master comes and the foolish crowd
Never can quite understand
The worth of a soul and the change that's wrought
By the touch of the Master's hand.

May 18

Matthew 12:22–50

BREAKING THE BONDS

Then goeth he, and taketh with himself seven other spirits more wicked than himself, and they enter in and dwell there: and the last state of that man is worse than the first. Even so shall it be also unto this wicked generation (12:45).

In a meeting, as a little boy, I remember that an evangelist called to the platform a big, powerful man and sat him in a chair. The evangelist took a string and put it around the man seated in the chair and told him to break it. The man broke it easily. The evangelist then took the string and wrapped it around him three times, and the man broke it. But then the evangelist took that string and wrapped it around the man many times, and that big man did all in his power to break that string and failed. He was bound. That is how Satan works on us. He begins slowly, and we do not even realize the hold he eventually has over us. He leads us as an animal to the slaughtering house.

I must war against Satan! I must resist him! But how, Lord? A person can never find strength in himself to oppose Satan. He is no match for Satan. Satan is too deceptive, too shrewd, and too strong for flesh and blood. We lose the battle before we begin. How does a person stand to face Satan? He does it by faith in God. It is not enough just to turn over a new leaf. We must thrust the spirit of uncleanness out of us, but that, too, is not enough. Our hearts then are empty and make easy places for Satan's demons to fill. So what do we need? We need the power of God to resist Satan's darts. We must let Jesus come into our hearts. We will then have the Spirit of Jesus, and when a person has the Spirit of Jesus in his heart, the evil spirit has no place to dwell.

May 19

Matthew 13:1–30

THE SEED OF LIFE

But he that received seed into the good ground is he that heareth the word, and understandeth it; which also beareth fruit, and bringeth forth, some a hundredfold, some sixty, some thirty (13:23).

A theologian recently wrote that his nature needed to be cultivated and developed as one would weed and hoe a garden. He was saying that we are already saved, already in the kingdom, and all that we need do is to cultivate our nature. Then he gave the illustration of weeding and hoeing a garden. I would like to tell that theologian that he can weed and hoe that piece of ground forever, but he will never have a garden. To grow a garden, you must have seed, it must germinate, and it must grow and flower and bear fruit—and that is a work of God.

To begin with, no person can make a seed. He can analyze it, he can reproduce its chemical formula, he can make it look exactly like a seed, but it is without life. God must give it life.

May 20

Matthew 13:31–58

THE SIZE OF FAITH

Which indeed is the least of all seeds: but when it is grown, it is the greatest among herbs, and becometh a tree, so that the birds of the air come and lodge in the branches thereof (13:32).

A hunter in Canada came to a river that was frozen. He did not know whether the ice could bear his weight, so he got down on all fours and began to creep over that river, barely moving, thinking that any time the ice might break and he would drown in the cold waters below. While he was crawling, careful and afraid, he heard a great roar behind him. He turned his head and saw roaring out of the forest a wagon drawn by four big horses, loaded with heavy logs. The driver roared out of the forest and crossed the river. Beside him was that fearful man crawling on all fours.

That is exactly how people are. Some are fearfully crawling, wondering if they will ever make it. They wonder if God will let them get five feet from the golden gate and then let them stumble so they will not make it. Their faith is so little. Then there are others who roar out of the mountains, across the river of life, and right up to the other side into the gates of glory. Actually, one is just as safe as the other. We are not saved according to the size and proportion of our faith.

Your faith may not be as robust as that of Peter; it may not be as deeply understanding and theological as that of Paul; it may not be as sweet and trusting as that of the sainted John; but if you come to Jesus by faith, you are just as saved as the apostles who leaned on His breast. What a marvelous hope and what a precious promise!

May 21

Matthew 16:1–20

PETER'S GREAT AFFIRMATION

And Simon Peter answered and said, Thou art the Christ, the Son of the living God (16:16).

When Sir Christopher Wren, the incomparable architect of St. Paul's Cathedral in London, was buried in the vast structure that he had erected, they placed over his tomb these Latin words—*Lector, si monumentum requiris, circumspice*—"Reader, if you seek a monument, look around you." It is thus that the Holy Spirit of God would invite you to do today. Look around you! Miracles of regeneration, miracles of grace are everywhere. Men and women, boys and girls, by the thousands and the millions, have met Jesus in the way, and have never been the same again.

"Whom say ye that I am?" "Thou art the Christ of my conversion, of my experience, of my prayers, of my hopes, of my life, of my youth, of my manhood, of my old age, and of my death. Thou art the Christ, the Son of the living God." Upon this great affirmation of the Bible God will build His church, found His faith, and save the soul.

May 22

Matthew 16:21–28

WHAT CAN MONEY BUY?

For what is a man profited, if he shall gain the whole world, and lose his own soul? or what shall a man give in exchange for his soul? (16:26).

When a person gives himself to the world and sows for worldly gain, his harvest can be money, affluence, success, pleasure, and freedom from hunger, from cold, and from heat. In many ways he can find a harvest that is seemingly grand. But the apostle says that there is also another harvest in it, and that harvest is corruption, decay, loss. The apostle says that there are no spiritual rewards or harvests when a person sows just for the world.

For example, money can buy a bed but not sleep. Money can buy food but not appetite. Money can buy a house but not a home. Money can buy medicine but not health. Money can buy amusement and pleasure but not happiness. Money can buy gifts but not love. Money can buy a crucifix but not a Savior. When we sow for worldly gain, then the harvest is corruption, loss, and decay.

One time two men were driving through a beautiful estate crowned by a lovely mansion, with fertile fields all around it. The man asked his companion, "What is the value of this great estate?" His friend replied, "I cannot tell you the value of it, but I can tell you what it cost the owner." The other fellow said, "What?" And he replied, "It cost him everything he had. It cost him his soul."

May 23

Matthew 18:1–10

SAFE IN THE ARMS OF JESUS

Verily I say unto you, Except ye be converted, and become as little children, ye shall not enter into the kingdom of heaven" (18:3).

One time after Dr. Huber Drumwright had delivered the morning sermon in our church, he said to me, "Let me tell you something that you do not know. There is a professor who loves you with all his heart. He and his wife had a son who was born sickly and weak. As the years passed, he became quite frail. In his last months he was kept at home and watched over by his loving mother.

"One day as the boy neared his eighth birthday, he and his mother were listening to you preach on television. When the service was over the boy turned to his mother and said, 'I want to be saved just like that. I want Jesus to come into my heart.' The mother picked up the frail child in her arms and told him how God had spoken to his heart. She carefully went over the plan of salvation and the boy gave his heart in repentance and trust to Jesus. The boy died in his mother's arms and in the arms of Jesus."

> Safe in the arms of Jesus,
> Safe on His gentle breast,
> There by His love o'ershadowed
> Sweetly my soul shall rest.

Dr. Drumwright added, "You see now why the professor and his wife so deeply love you."

If you love a child, you show love for Jesus. If you minister to a child, you minister to the Lord. If you are kind to a little child, you are kind to the Savior. Somehow our hearts are bound up in the life of a child.

May 24

Matthew 18:11–35

THE VALUE OF A SOUL

Even so it is not the will of your Father which is in heaven, that one of these little ones should perish (18:14).

The deacons of a church were having a meeting, and they happened to be talking about the large offering that had been given to the evangelist.

One expressed the sentiment of all the men when he said, "This is ridiculous. Look at the large offering we have given to the evangelist, and just one little boy was saved. What a waste!"

When the observation was voiced, one of the deacons stood up and said, "Gentlemen, if you think it is too much, I personally will return every man's gift, for that one little boy who was saved is my son."

How does one write down in dollars and cents what God does with our gifts when He turns them into souls, into the preaching of the gospel, into the distribution of the Word of the Lord, into the ministry of the saints, and into the winning of the lost?

May God sanctify and hallow the dedication of our lives, our homes, and our children to the blessed Jesus. May God receive the gift not only of what we possess but also of what we are. May He write in His book in heaven the gift that we make to Him of our hearts and our lives!

May 25

Matthew 19:1–30

THE CROSSABLE RIVERS

But Jesus beheld them, and said unto them, With men this is impossible; but with God all things are possible (19:26).

When I stood at the Panama Canal, I thought, "What a miracle this great canal is!" The mechanism of the running of the canal and its gates after two generations is identical to what the American engineers first erected.

One reason it is such a notable miracle is that one government after another attempted to build the canal and failed ignominiously. One can see a futile attempt in the ground about eight hundred yards away—the big scar is still there. But the American engineers went to Panama, and they completed the construction of the canal. Even today it is one of the outstanding feats in all of the history of mankind. Looking upon it, I thought of the song the American engineers sang after they had achieved the marvelous result:

Don't send us back to a life that's tame again,
We who have shattered a continent's spine.
Easy work, oh, we couldn't do that again,
Haven't you something that's more in our line?

Now the stanza that everyone knows:

Got any rivers you say are not crossable?
Got any mountains you can't tunnel through?
We specialize in the wholly impossible,
Doing what nobody ever could do.

What a spirit in those American engineers! It is the exact spirit commanded by the apostle Paul.

May 26

Matthew 21:1–22

DYING ON HIS KNEES

And all things, whatsoever ye shall ask in prayer, believing, ye shall receive (21:22).

It pleases God that we bow, that we pray, that we ask, that we talk to Him as our father. We go further on our knees than in any other way, retreating to advance, falling to rise, stooping to conquer. Oh, the fellowship we have with God in intercession!

When the body of the missionary David Livingstone was discovered, he was by his bed on his knees. His faithful African friends had not entered his little hut all night long because the master was on his knees. When they finally went to him and touched him, he was dead. While he was praying at night his spirit had fled away. What a wonderful way to die!

May 27

Matthew 22:1–22

THIS I KNOW

And they sent out unto him their disciples with the Herodians, saying, Master, we know that thou art true, and teachest the way of God in truth, neither carest thou for any man: for thou regardest not the person of men (22:16).

In my Ph.D. oral examination before the group of professors seated around a table, one of them said to me, "I am sure that in your study you have come across the scoffers, the critics, and the skeptics who say that Paul, in his conversion, in his trances, and in his visions, suffered from sunstroke, seizures, and epileptic fits."

I replied, "Yes, sir. I have read that from the pen of critics and scoffers several times."

The professor asked, "What do you think about that?"

I replied, "Sir, I hold in my hands the Holy Bible, and in that Bible are thirteen books written by the apostle Paul. Read them for yourself. They are inspired letters, literature of the highest order, whether you look at them as poetry, language, imagination and fancy, or truth. If they are the result of epilepsy, seizures, and sunstroke, then may God make all of us victims of sunstroke or seizures." The defense of the faith is the man himself, his life, his character, his influence, his work. "This I know. This is my experience."

May 28

Matthew 23:1–12

HE DIED TO HIMSELF

And whosoever shall exalt himself shall be abased; and he that shall humble himself shall be exalted (23:12).

William Carey founded the eighteenth-century missionary movement that changed the whole culture and life of India. One time he was being honored by the Governor General of India. Present at the occasion was a petty government official who looked upon the Baptist missionary with contempt. At the dinner table the petty official openly said to a friend, "This William Carey, I understand, was a shoemaker." It was said for the ears of the missionary, so William Carey humbly replied, "Sir, I was not a shoemaker; I was a cobbler."

You cannot touch a man like that! Nor can you cut a man like that because he is already dead. He has died to himself. He has died to every ambition. Yet he lives gloriously.

May 29

Matthew 24:1–44

SUNRISE INSTEAD OF SUNSET

Heaven and earth shall pass away, but my words shall not pass away (24:35).

So deadly and so merciless has been the poison of rationalism in the schools, in the universities, in the seminaries, in the pulpits, that it has seemed that the prophecy of Voltaire, the atheist who died in 1788, would come to pass. Voltaire said, "One hundred years from my day there will not be a Bible in the earth except one that is looked upon by an antiquarian curiosity-seeker." It has sometimes looked as though there might come to pass what Hume, the infidel, envisioned. "I see the twilight of Christianity," he said.

Yet one hundred years from the time of Voltaire's prediction, a first edition of Voltaire's work sold in the market in Paris for eleven cents. And on that identical day, the British government paid to the Czar of Russia five hundred thousand dollars for the Codex Sinaiticus, a copy of the Word of God discovered by Count Tischendorf in the monastery of St. Catherine at the foot of Mount Sinai. When Hume said, "I see the twilight of Christianity," he was much confused. He could not tell sunrise from sunset.

Last eve I paused beside the blacksmith's door
And heard the anvil ring the vesper chimes;
Then looking in, I saw upon the floor
Old hammers worn out with beating years of time.

"How many anvils have you had," said I,
"To wear and batter all these hammers so?"
"Just one," said he and then with twinkling eye,
"The anvil wears the hammers out, you know."

And so I thought, the anvil of God's Word
For ages skeptics' blows have beat upon.
Yet, though the noise of falling blows was heard,
The anvil is unharmed, the hammers are gone.

—*John Clifford*

May 30

Matthew 25:1–30

WHO IS RESPONSIBLE?

For unto every one that hath shall be given, and he shall have abundance: but from him that hath not shall be taken away even that which he hath (25:29).

Do I have a responsibility before God for other people? Am I my brother's keeper?

Somehow God has made our lives so that we are accountable for other people's lives, and we cannot escape it. For example, suppose I know that a man is fast asleep in a certain house and I see his house begin to burn down. Am I responsible to awaken the man and tell him to flee for his life? Or am I free to stand and watch the house burn to the ground, knowing that the man will lose his life? What is it that God has done that makes me responsible for that man, whom I may not even know, whose name I could not even call?

Or, suppose I am standing on the shore of the ocean and I see a man drowning and hear him calling for help. On the shore is a large coil of rope. All I have to do is to pick up the rope and throw it to the drowning man in the sea. Am I accountable if I do not try to rescue that man? I may not know him or know his name, but am I accountable to God to try to save him? Has God made this world and framed it in such a fashion that I am responsible for the life of another?

That is an inescapable doctrine in the Bible and an inescapable truth by which God has framed us in the human family. I am accountable for the welfare of others, and I am spiritually responsible for their salvation.

May 31

Matthew 25:31–46

IT WAS TOO LATE

And the King shall answer and say unto them, Verily I say unto you, Inasmuch as ye have done it unto one of the least of these my brethren, ye have done it unto me (25:40).

Once I heard a mountain preacher in Kentucky make an appeal that we be kind and generous to those around us now because tomorrow may be too late. He described a farmer who had a loyal wife. They both worked long and hard, with the result that within a few years they prospered greatly. The husband took all the money they made and bought more land and more stock, year after year going through the ceaseless rounds of acquiring more fields to raise more corn to feed more hogs to make more money to do the same thing again. Each year the faithful wife would ask for a new silk dress, only to be refused by the miserly husband, who spent nothing on her, but everything on the stock and the farms. Finally, overworked and heartbroken, the faithful wife died prematurely and was laid to rest in the cemetery on the side of the hill.

The tragedy of what he had done came with such crushing force to the soul of the husband that something snapped in his reason. One day he was found wrapping yards and yards of the finest silks and satins around the headstone and footstone of his poor wife's grave. "But," said the mountain preacher, "it was too late."

It is not tomorrow that the recording angel begins to write in God's book of remembrance. He is writing now. It is not tomorrow that we should begin the gracious, sweet, humble ministries that so richly bless the lives of others. Let us do them now.

June 1

Matthew 28:1–20

ARISE AND GO

Teaching them to observe all things whatsoever I have commanded you: and, lo, I am with you alway, even unto the end of the world. Amen (28:20).

David Livingstone practiced an unusual course of action which some others also practice. When he had to make a decision, he would take his Bible, pray, and then let the pages open where they would. The first verse that he read he believed to be God's answer to his prayer.

David Livingstone had strong and unwavering faith. He was the first white man to explore the Zambezi River. When he was going down the river, discovering its length and breadth, the friendly Africans said, "You must proceed no further, for there are cannibals down the river. You cannot escape with your life if you go on."

Livingstone took it to the Lord in prayer. After he laid it before God, he placed his Bible on edge, then let it fall open. The verse he saw was Matthew 28:20. "And, lo, I am with you alway, even unto the end of the world." Livingstone said, "Arise, let us go."

That is the promise of the Father. That is the Spirit of Jesus with us to comfort us, to strengthen us, to help us, to stand by us, as God's advocate and intercessor.

June 2

Mark 1:1–15

GENUINE REPENTANCE

And saying, The time is fulfilled, and the kingdom of God is at hand: repent ye, and believe the gospel (1:15).

Before World War II, there were pacifists in many pulpits. When I was a young man going to school, I heard much about pacifism. Then on December 7, 1941, Pearl Harbor was attacked. After that we heard from one end of the country to the other, "I have been a pacifist, but I have changed. I am now ready to defend my country." That is a form of repentance. I have repented of my former attitude, I have changed.

There was a man in Kentucky who defended the distilleries. One day he helped pry a man out of the snow and ice in a ditch outside a bar on the edge of Louisville. The man had gotten drunk, and the barkeeper had pushed him out in the cold winter night. Staggering, the drunk had fallen into a ditch and frozen to death. The next morning when they found him, this man had to help pry him out of the snow. He said, "When we pried him up, I looked at the frozen man with mud all over his face and body, and I changed. I am now against the liquor industry. I have repented of my attitude."

Consider the testimony of a gambler. All the years of his life he made his living gambling. In his testimony he said, "One day I met a little boy. Talking to the boy, I learned that he was the son of the man with whom I had gambled the night before. I had won all of that man's paycheck. Instead of being able to take his money home to clothe and feed the boy and the family, he had lost it all to me at the gambling table. When I looked at that ragged, half-starved boy, I changed. I do not gamble anymore. I have repented of my ways."

June 3

Mark 4:1–12

THE DIVINE SELF-DISCLOSURE

And he said unto them, Unto you it is given to know the mystery of the kingdom of God: but unto them that are without, all these things are done in parables (4:11).

To know the God of revelation is necessary. If we are to know God, it must come from a divine self-disclosure. No one by searching the Scriptures can find God. Mankind in his genius and with his telescope and all his mathematical formulas can do many things, but he cannot find God.

In the *National Geographic* magazine there was a magnificent article on what our giant telescopes have discovered. We can now see the infinitude of the universe, the Milky Way, the multitude of galaxies out in space.

We can see all of this, and we can make a deduction that whoever created it was omnipotent, but we could never find out who He is or what His name is. Or we can look at the beautiful sunset—the glorious kaleidoscope of colors—when God makes the heavens show His glory. Or we can look at a graceful rainbow or at the perfectly formed flowers. From this we can deduct that whoever made them loved beautiful things. But we could never know Him or His name.

We can look at ourselves and see that we are intelligent and morally sensitive. So we could deduce that whoever created us was someone of intelligence and personality and moral sensitivity. But who is He? We can never know except by a divine disclosure.

June 4

Mark 9:1–41

A STORY OF HUMILITY

And he sat down, and called the twelve, and saith unto them, If any man desire to be first, the same shall be last of all, and servant of all (9:35).

James A. Garfield was the twentieth President of the United States. Because he was President of the United States, the people were very conscious of his presence when he came to church. Especially was the pastor proud of him. He would refer to him from the pulpit as "President James A. Garfield."

One day the President came to see his pastor and said, "Pastor, I know on the outside and before the world I am the President of the United States. But in the church I am just plain James A. Garfield." This is a beautiful story of humility! It illustrates the New Testament definition of greatness in a simple way. The humility of this famous and powerful man is a tribute not only to him but also to his Savior.

June 5

Mark 11:1–19

A HOUSE OF PRAYER

And he taught, saying unto them, Is it not written, My house shall be called of all nations the house of prayer? but ye have made it a den of thieves (11:17).

Religion in its manifestations may, in so many instances, be beautiful, expressive, and inspirational, but it leaves a life desolate, empty, and powerless. The whole world is filled with religion.

One time I was the guest of a wealthy family in Mexico City. They belonged to the state church, but they found it so empty that they were seeking some other avenue to serve God. They attended church only for funerals and weddings.

On another occasion I stood in front of Notre Dame in Paris, trying to think through the long history of that marvelous cathedral. I could think no thoughts at all because I was pressed on every side by a throng of people who were selling pornographic pictures and literature. However I tried to escape, the sellers followed me around.

On still another occasion I stood before one of the most magnificent architectural structures in the world, the Kali Temple in Calcutta, India. Above the main entrance into the temple was a large sign. Did it say, "This Is the House of God"? No. Did it read, "This Is the Gate to Heaven"? No. Did it proclaim, "Enter His Courts With Holiness"? No. Did it say, "Come Unto Me, All Ye That Labor and Are Heavy Laden"? No. Rather, the sign said, "Beware of Pickpockets." The temple was a den of thieves.

The world today, even with all of its manifestations of religions, does not provide an answer for a soul thirsty for God.

June 6

Mark 12:1–44

A FAITHFUL STEWARD

For all they did cast in of their abundance; but she of her want did cast in all that she had, even all her living (12:44).

Recently in our church an Internal Revenue agent stood up to give a testimony. He described how a great change had come into his life. He told about coming across the tax returns of a man who had an income of less than five thousand dollars a year but listed a contribution to his church of $684.

This agent went to the young man's humble cottage and knocked on the door. When the man came to the door, the agent said he had come to talk about his tax return. He said he expected the man to squirm and tremble. Instead, the man welcomed the agent. The agent then questioned the man about his salary of less than five thousand dollars and the contribution of $684 to his church. There was no flustering nor hesitant excuse; he just looked the agent in the eye and said that it was his tithe and a small offering that he gave to the Lord. The agent asked for receipts as proof. The young man was able to produce them from the drawer where he kept his church envelopes.

The agent admitted that everything was correct, apologized, and was about to leave when the man invited him to attend his church. The agent thanked him and said, "I belong to a church already." Then the young man said, "Excuse me, sir, but somehow that possibility had not occurred to me."

As he drove away, he said the last sentence of that young man stayed in his mind: "Excuse me, sir, but somehow that possibility had not occurred to me." What did he mean? He did not understand it until the following Sunday morning when the offering plate passed before him and he dropped in his usual quarter. He couldn't help but think of that young man. He worked with his hands—he was a day laborer—and he made less than five thousand dollars a year. But he had dedicated to God a tenth and had added a love offering besides.

June 7

Mark 13:1–37

THE BLESSED HOPE

Take ye heed, watch and pray: for ye know not when the time is (13:33).

George W. Truett, who was pastor of the First Baptist Church of Dallas for forty-seven years, was one of the greatest preachers of our time. He had a brother named Jim, and Jim was the son Mother Truett particularly loved. When anyone would speak to her about her great preacher son, George W. Truett, she would acquiesce kindly and say, "But have you heard my son, Jim?"

Jim Truett lived at Whitewright. Every morning Jim Truett would get up and raise the window on the east side of his house, and, seeing the dawn, he would say, "Perhaps today He will come." That is a beautiful and marvelous expression of the Christian faith and assurance, living in the expectancy of the intervention of God in human history. Never discouraged, never losing hope, for tomorrow will be a better day because God is in it.

June 8

Mark 14:1–36

A CALL TO COMPASSION

And wheresoever he shall go in, say ye to the goodman of the house, The Master saith, Where is the guestchamber, where I shall eat the passover with my disciples? (14:14).

One time I read a book about a first-century philosopher, Marius the Epicurean. He was described as sitting high up in the Roman Colosseum watching gladiatorial combat in the arena. History records that the arena of the Colosseum was covered with sand so that when the gladiators slew each other and the blood poured out, they could rake over the sand or bring in fresh sand without interrupting the bloody combat. As Marius watched those bloody combats, he turned to his companion and said, "What is needed is the heart that would make it impossible to look upon such bloodthirsty combat. The future would belong to the power that could create such a heart."

It was the preaching of the gospel that closed forever the Colosseum. It was the preaching of the gospel that forever did away with bloody gladiatorial confrontations. It was the preaching of the gospel that forever did away with the execution by crucifixion of a malefactor, with human slavery, with the custom of abandoning unwanted children to die. It was the preaching of the gospel that elevated and raised womanhood and family life. It was the preaching of the gospel that brought ministries to the poor and the suffering. There was not a hospital or orphans' home in the entire Roman empire. It was the compassionate love and caring heart of the Christian witness that elevated the world into another sphere, life, and devotion. It is that same compassionate concern on the part of God's people that is so desperately needed today. Conversion is a call to that compassionate concern.

June 9

Mark 15:1–47

THE SUFFERING SAVIOR

And Jesus cried with a loud voice, and gave up the ghost (15:37).

The very message of God, a call to repentance and dedication, is found in the Cross of our Savior. Long ago young Count Zinzendorf was a playboy who revelled in the use of his riches and nobility for worldly and selfish purposes. One day in the art gallery of Dusseldorf, he looked long and steadfastly upon an *Ecce Homo,* a picture of the suffering Savior. Underneath the moving portrait were these words:

Hoc feci pro te,
Quid facis pro me?
(This I have done for thee,
What hast thou done for me?)

The young nobleman turned from that sight of our suffering Lord to devote his life and his fortune to the propagation of the Gospel. His dedication, through the founding of modern missionary movements, has reached in loving and saving power to the farthest, darkest corners of the earth. It is thus with us all. The picture of Christ, crucified before our very eyes, compels us in God's moving and loving power to kneel at His feet, to look up into His face, to turn from our sins, and to ask the mercy and forgiveness of Heaven in His blessed and saving name. This is the power of the Cross and of the Son of God who "died for our sins according to the scriptures."

June 10

Luke 1:1–38

A TESTIMONY TO OUR FAITH

The Holy Ghost shall come upon thee, and the power of the Highest shall overshadow thee: therefore also that holy thing which shall be born of thee shall be called the Son of God (1:35).

An unbeliever could come to me and say, "Sir, if an unwed mother were to avow to you that her child was born of the Spirit without earthly father, would you believe it?" My reply would be, "Yes—if the birth of that child was foretold thousands of years before. Yes—if when the child was born the angels sang and the star of promise stood over the place where the infant lay. Yes—if when the child were grown He had power over the wind and the waves, over disease and death. Yes—if when He was slain, the third day He was raised from the dead. Yes—if when He ascended to heaven His disciples, through the centuries, were numbered by the millions and the increasing millions." Yes, a child like that could surely, truly be virgin-born according to the Word of God.

One of the greatest testimonies to our faith is found in the Virgin Birth of our Lord Jesus Christ. The Virgin Birth is prerequisite to our Lord's atonement.

June 11

Luke 3:1–18

OUR FALLEN NATURE

And he came into all the country about Jordan, preaching the baptism of repentance for the remission of sins (3:3).

A man had a pet leopard. One day the leopard was licking the hand of the master, and as he licked, his razor-like teeth scratched the master's hand. The leopard tasted blood for the first time, and immediately the ferocious nature of the animal went wild and cut its master to pieces. Underneath is always that primeval and fallen nature.

Joseph Stalin once attended a seminary of the Greek Orthodox Church. His mother had dedicated him to God as a priest. Out of the righteous home of Noah came carnal Ham. Out of the home of the man after God's own heart came the traitor Absalom. God also said that because of the sins of Manasseh He would destroy Judah from the face of the earth. And Manasseh was the only son of the good king, Hezekiah. You may know homes today where the parents are godly and righteous but the children reject Jesus Christ. It is hard to understand.

June 12

Luke 4:1–30

SOMEONE OUGHT TO PREACH

To preach the acceptable year of the Lord (4:19).

My first pastorate out of seminary was First Baptist Church, Chickasha, Oklahoma. When they built a new church some years ago, they invited me to return and preach the dedicatory sermon. As I walked through the streets of Chickasha for the first time in thirty-nine years, many memories came to my heart.

For example, I remembered one time when the Ministerial Alliance set aside a Saturday on which the city fathers allowed them to rope off a whole street. They were going to have a tremendous religious service. The people were there from all over. The president of the Ministerial Alliance opened the service. They sang a song and had a prayer. Then each pastor was called forward to invite the people to come to the service at his church.

After each pastor had done his part, the man who was presiding over the meeting said, "We will now have the benediction." I stood up and walked to the pulpit and said, "Sir, are you dismissing these people now?" He said, "Yes." I said, "Someone ought to preach to these people." He turned around and said, "Anyone want to preach?" No one said he wanted to preach, so I, being the closest to him, said, "If no one will preach to them, I will." He said, "Go ahead and preach."

That was second nature to me. I had been preaching on the curb of the courthouse every Saturday for three years. I stood up there with an open Bible, and I preached to those people on how to be saved. One can read his Bible forever and not be saved. One can preach and not be saved. One can sing about the Lord and not be saved. One can say prayers and not be saved. One can do penance and not be saved. One can write books about the Christian faith and not be saved. We must call people to salvation through faith in Jesus Christ.

June 13

Luke 6:1–26

THE DEFENSE OF PRAYER

And it came to pass in those days, that he went out into a mountain to pray, and continued all night in prayer to God (6:12).

In my reading, I came across an incident in history which did not identify the contestants but merely told the events that happened. In the Middle East, a tyrant proposed to vanquish and lead into subjection a free people. The people whom he was attempting to subdue were godly and praying people. The tyrant gathered his army together to invade the land of this free people. When they saw the tyrant coming, they gathered their forces together to confront the tyrannical invader.

Before the battle began, those who were defending themselves all bowed down in prayer. The tyrant said to his generals, "Look, they are already cowering. They are already surrendering." One of his counselors who knew the people said, "Sir, they are not cowering and surrendering. Before the battle begins, they are praying to their God." When the battle was over, the tyrant and his armies were destroyed.

It pleases God when we pray. Even though in God's sovereign, elective grace He has His hands on this world until the ultimate end of the age, He wants us to be on our knees in prayer and supplication.

June 14

Luke 8:26–56

HOME EVANGELISM

Return to thine own house, and show how great things God hath done unto thee. And he went his way, and published throughout the whole city how great things Jesus had done unto him (8:39).

Once when in Louisville, Kentucky, attending the Executive Committee Meeting of the Baptist World Alliance, I met with a small committee that has to do with world reconciliation—i.e., evangelism. In my committee were two members from Russia—a young woman named Volintina Rendena and the other the Minister of Music of the Baptist church in Moscow, Leonide Catchosfsky. It was a privilege to sit with them in that small group and listen to the report from Russia.

We talked about ministry there in a world of official atheism and religious oppression. They cannot have revival meetings; they cannot have a Sunday school; they cannot print literature; they cannot distribute tracts; they cannot have any service or convocation outside the church walls. How do they evangelize? They do it in the home.

Last year the church in Moscow baptized 128 people, of whom 80 percent had been atheists. The churches do their work under awesome oppression. If they would invite two, five would probably come. If ten were invited, twenty might come. And the people would stay all night long. They would listen to the message of Christ and to the teaching of the Bible.

June 15

Luke 9:1–27

BEARING A CROSS

And he said to them all, If any man will come after me, let him deny himself, and take up his cross daily, and follow me (9:23).

The Holy Spirit has given us two phrases to describe the same experience: "I am crucified with Christ" and "Take up your cross and follow me." But to what do cross-bearing and crucifixion with Christ refer? Some people identify these with a personal sorrow, saying, "I have a burden, a broken heart, a great frustration and disappointment, an agony, a great trial. This is my cross to bear."

Undeniably, Christians, as everyone else, have trials. We have heartaches, frustrations, and despairs. But the meaning of cross-bearing in the Bible does not even approach this matter of personal affliction. When the Lord says, "Take up thy cross," and when Paul uses the expression, "I am crucified with Christ," they are both talking about dying. Crucifixion means death. A cross is an instrument of death.

When the Lord speaks of taking up your cross, he is talking about dying. When the Lord bore His cross and made His way to a hill called Golgotha or Calvary, He came to that place to die. The cross was an instrument of execution. From the agony on that hill the sun hid its face. The Son of God cried in desolation and loneliness, "My God, why?" It was death.

Following Christ is to die to self, to vanity, to egotism, to all of the blandishments of the world. To become a Christian is literally to die to oneself. In salvation, however, that is only the beginning because death itself becomes the prelude for life in Christ.

June 16

Luke 10:1–24

READY FOR HARVEST

Therefore said he unto them, The harvest truly is great, but the laborers are few: pray ye therefore the Lord of the harvest, that he would send forth laborers into his harvest (10:2).

In the summer following my senior year in high school, I worked for J. I. Case Threshing Machine Company. In the panhandle around Amarillo, there are places where one can stand and see nothing but vast wheat fields from horizon to horizon. As I worked in the threshing machine company that summer, the men working in the wheat fields never stopped their combines. Day and night, twenty-four hours, they ran the machines, for the fields were white unto the harvest and the next day the grain would be lying lost on the ground. They were reaping, and they never stopped.

Our churches are like that. Jesus said, "The fields are white unto the harvest." People who need to be won to the Lord are legion in number. The whole world is just waiting for someone to say, "We would love to have you; we are interested in you. This is God's place and we are God's people. The Lord meets with us. Come and join us." The fields are white, the opportunities are great, and God needs someone to extend a welcoming hand to the people around us.

June 17

Luke 10:25–42

THE WARMTH OF THE HAND

But a certain Samaritan, as he journeyed, came where he was: and when he saw him, he had compassion on him (10:33).

One time I was reading the rules of a steel mill. The mill had great lathes in it where iron shafts were being made to infinitesimal diameter. The measurement was to be exactly correct. One of the rules I read was this, "Remember that the warmth of the hand will change the diameter of the shaft." The mechanic working at the big steel lathe, carving out a large engine shaft that must be perfectly measured for an airplane, is reminded that the warmth of his hand will change the diameter of the shaft.

If the warmth of your hand changes the diameter of cold steel, think how it will change a heart, perhaps a heart that is discouraged, sorrowful, or lost!

June 18

Luke 11:1–28

ANSWERED PRAYER

For every one that asketh receiveth; and he that seeketh findeth; and to him that knocketh it shall be opened (11:10).

Recently I came across the story of a sweet young boy. He was a German lad who loved the Lord and prayed often. His father and mother were very dilatory, but the son was devout. The pastor would speak of him in praise for his godliness and holiness. The headmaster of the school had told the children to be sure they were always on time. So the boy sought to be on time when he went to school.

One morning, through the fault of his parents, the boy could not get away, and when he walked out the door to go to school, the clock struck the time that he was to be there. It was a long walk from his house to the schoolhouse, and the boy bowed his head and prayed aloud, "Oh, Lord, don't let me be late for school." A man nearby overheard the boy's prayer and thought the request impossible. The clock had already struck the time for the boy to be there, yet he prayed God would not let him be late for school.

Out of curiosity the man followed the boy just to see what would happen. Do you know what happened? The headmaster of the school had put his key in the lock and somehow had turned it the wrong way. He jammed the lock and could not get the door open. So they called for a locksmith. The locksmith finished his work, the door opened, and the headmaster and the students walked in, just as that devout young boy arrived! Isn't that blessed? Even the smallest things are to be made a matter of prayer.

June 19

Luke 12:1–31

THE FIRST PRIORITY

But rather seek ye the kingdom of God; and all these things shall be added unto you (12:31).

One time I was preaching in the North Shore Baptist Church in Chicago. The superintendent of the Sunday school and a deacon in the church was James L. Kraft, founder of the great Kraft Food Corporation. After the service I was a guest in the Kraft home. Mr. Kraft related that as a young man he had a desire to be the most famous manufacturer and salesman of cheese in the world.

As a young fellow, he had a pony named Paddy and a little buggy. He would make his cheese, put it in the buggy, and drive Paddy down the streets of Chicago selling his cheese. The days and months passed, and the young man began to despair. He was working hard and long with no success. One day he pulled the pony to a stop and began to talk to him, "Paddy, something is wrong. Our priorities are not where they ought to be. Maybe we ought to serve God, give ourselves to Him, and work as hard as we can; then God will help us. But first, Paddy, let us give ourselves to God and place Him first in our lives." Mr. Kraft said that he drove the buggy home and there made a covenant that the rest of his life he would serve God first and then work as God would direct.

Many years later I was in a vast convocation in Washington, D.C., in which the speaker, James L. Kraft, said, "I had rather be a layman in the North Shore Baptist Church in Chicago than to head the greatest corporation in America. My first job is serving Jesus." If people would live like that, I believe they could change the whole course of civilization.

June 20

Luke 13:1–35

PERSISTENCE IN EVANGELISM

O Jerusalem, Jerusalem, which killest the prophets, and stonest them that are sent unto thee; how often would I have gathered thy children together, as a hen doth gather her brood under her wings, and ye would not! (13:34).

While I was standing in the airport at Nashville, Tennessee, waiting for a plane so I could return to Dallas, a man who was obviously affluent approached me. He was tall, had gray hair, and was tastefully dressed. He called me by name.

Then he introduced himself and referred to a time five years earlier when I had been in Nashville preaching at an evangelistic conference.

When I had finished my message on that occasion, I made an appeal to the laymen who were there. "In behalf of a man that you know, would you consecrate your life that he might be saved? If you would, get up, walk down the aisle to the front, and kneel while we pray together a prayer of consecration." This businessman was seated in the top balcony in the last row. He stood up and came down the stairway and down the aisle and knelt there before me.

He consecrated his life in behalf of a businessman who was not a Christian. For four years he witnessed to that man and asked him in the most prayerful way to come to Jesus. For four years the man was adamant in his refusal. Finally he went to him for the last time and said, "You know, I am afraid I have been a nuisance to you. Every time I have seen you I have talked to you about the Lord and have invited you to Christ. I have come to you about the Lord for the last time. I do not mean to be a nuisance to you. I have come to ask your forgiveness."

That man looked at him searchingly and said, "Oh, no. Pray for me; keep on asking me; do not stop. Talk to me about the Lord." That year the businessman gave his heart to the Lord. He and his family were baptized and joined the church.

June 21

Luke 14:1–24

INVITE SOMEONE TO CHURCH

For I say unto you, That none of those men which were bidden shall taste of my supper (14:24).

A young man recently said to me, "I was discharged from the Army. I descended into the gutter and was wretched, miserable, and in the depths of sin. One Sunday evening I happened to be in Dallas, walking through one of those downtown streets. A godly couple saw me, stopped me, and said, 'We are going to church. Would you go with us?' I told them, 'I have nothing else to do. I will go.' We came to the church that night and I listened to you preach. I was wondrously saved. God came into my heart. I took my GI bill and went to school and to the seminary. I am now pastor of a fine little church in northern Louisiana."

If we have never done anything in our lives but invite someone to church, it will have been worth all the toils of life. Invite someone to come and walk with you and to belong, as a member, to the family of God.

June 22

Luke 15:1–10

THE WAY OF A MOTHER

And when he cometh home, he calleth together his friends and neighbors, saying unto them, Rejoice with me; for I have found my sheep which was lost (15:6).

Our Lord is sympathetic. He is full of kindness and understanding when people err and sin. The same shoulders that carry the weight of the government of heaven bear us in deepest sympathy and understanding.

In our church, the children are given a six-weeks' course preparing them to join the church. Then the parents make an appointment to bring the children to me. I talk to them about the Lord, the church, and about being baptized.

Somehow I did not know the background of one of the children who was coming. As the child sat by the mother, I began to talk to the child. To my chagrin and exasperation, the child could not answer. I thought it was a waste of time that they should make an appointment for the child to see me when the child was unprepared. The mother moved close to the child, and in the sweetest way, the tenderest tone, and the gentlest manner, she began to talk to the child about what I was asking. Then I realized that the child was retarded. I had not known it. The mother did not say, "You stupid moron, why can't you answer these simple questions the pastor asks?" The mother instead talked kindly to the child.

I could not help but see the Spirit of God working through that sweet mother. In how many ways do we show ourselves unknowing! God does not find it in His heart to be judgmental, but He in kindness helps and encourages us. He lays it on His shoulders, lovingly and tenderly.

June 23

Luke 15:11–32

THE ATTITUDE OF THE ELDER BROTHER

It was meet that we should make merry, and be glad: for this thy brother was dead, and is alive again; and was lost, and is found (15:32).

The unsympathetic and recalcitrant spirit leads us to undo the will of God. Jonah, refusing to go to Nineveh, hating those Gentile dogs, turned the opposite way to Tarshish. When God showed mercy to the repentant city of Nineveh, Jonah sat under a gourd vine, praying that he might die. He was remonstrating with God for saving the lost!

Judas, seeing that the Lord Jesus would certainly be delivered to the Romans, sought to retrieve what little he could from a lost cause. To placate his mercenary and covetous spirit, he sold his Lord for thirty pieces of silver.

The elder brother, coming in from the fields, found that his younger brother had returned home. But instead of rejoicing, he pouted in anger and refused to enter the house. When the father came out and entreated him saying, "Son, thou art ever with me," the boy replied, "At no time did I transgress thy commandment, but when this thy son [not "this my brother"] who has wasted his life in harlotry and in riotous living, comes back home, for him you kill the fatted calf and the whole family makes merry." Heaven and earth instinctively dislike the attitude of the elder brother. The sins of the spirit are the worst sins of human life.

June 24

Luke 16:1–31

THE MANNER OF THE SAVIOR

And he said unto him, If they hear not Moses and the prophets, neither will they be persuaded, though one rose from the dead (16:31).

Thomas Carlyle was in London as the guest of a glittering socialite. She was light of mind, one of those butterflies who lives on the surface, sipping here, sipping there. In the course of the conversation she spoke of the guilt of the Jewish people in slaying the Son of God, the Savior of the world. She said that if Christ were to come today we would open our homes to Him and welcome Him. Then she said to Mr. Carlyle, "Do you agree?"

The great Scottish essayist replied (and I copied down his answer), "No, I do not agree, madame. I think that had He come very fashionably dressed with plenty of money and preaching doctrines most palatable to the higher orders, I might have had the honor of receiving a card from you on the back of which would be written 'to meet our Savior.' But if He came uttering His sublime precepts and denouncing the Pharisees and associating with publicans as He did, you would have treated Him much as the Jews did and cried out, 'Take Him to Newgate and hang Him!'"

It is quite probable that if the Lord came today, He would be no more generously received or devoutly believed in and accepted than He was in the days of the apostle Paul. For the offense of the cross—the scandal of the cross—has not yet been abolished.

June 25

Luke 18:1–17

THE NEED FOR A SAVIOR

And the publican, standing afar off, would not lift up so much as his eyes unto heaven, but smote upon his breast, saying, God be merciful to me a sinner (18:13).

In one of my pastorates a young fellow, gifted and brilliant, was accused of embezzling from the bank. He was a smart boy, and he thought that by juggling those books he could take money out of the bank undiscovered. He took thousands of dollars. But, of course, one is never that smart. The bank officials discovered his dishonesty and accused him. When he was tried before the federal judge, the mother and the father of the boy asked me to stand by him. So we went to the big city, and that boy stood before the bar. The judge seated behind the bar looked at him and asked a simple question, "Guilty or not guilty?" And the boy replied humbly and simply, "Guilty." I was standing there by his side. I had the feeling then that I represented all humanity when I stood by that lad.

If you are not guilty and can save yourself, then the grace and mercy of God is superfluous. There is no need of the Savior. But if you are a sinner and if you are dying, all of us are like that lad who looked back into the face of the judge and said, "Sir, your honor, I cast myself upon the mercy of the court." In that instance, the judge was so merciful to the young bank employee that he gave him a sentence and then probated it. I helped him live out that probation through the years that followed. It is thus with us. As sinners, we cast ourselves upon the grace and mercy of God.

June 26

Luke 18:18–30

FLESH AND BLOOD FAITH

And he said, The things which are impossible with men are possible with God (18:27).

The son of a seminary theological professor said to his father one night, "Dad, today I saw the real thing down at the mission, and it was the first time I have ever seen it." The boy had grown up in the home of a professor of theology. All the days of his life he had been conversant with and had been introduced to fine theological arguments for the person of God, for the resurrection of Christ, and for the propagation of the faith. But the boy had not seen it in action until he went down to the mission.

Any time the Christian faith is word, language, and argument, or any time it is forensic, philosophical, and speculative, it is nothing. But when the Christian faith takes flesh and blood and produces the conversion of an individual through the power of God to change human life, then it is real and factual. Some day the Christian faith will present us faultless before the Lord Himself and we will thank God forever and ever!

June 27

Luke 19:1–27

THE CONVERSION OF AN INFIDEL

And he made haste, and came down, and received him joyfully (19:6).

One of the most tremendously meaningful sermons I have read was delivered by B. H. Carroll, founder and first president of Southwestern Baptist Theological Seminary in Fort Worth. The sermon was entitled, "My Infidelity And What Became of It."

In the days of the Civil War, B. H. Carroll was an outspoken and crude infidel. He had a violent reaction against those who believed in God and in Christ. When the days of the war were over, he came home, crippled by an injury. While he was living at home, a tremendous outpouring of the Spirit of God fell on the community where he lived. One night after a revival service, he came hobbling home on his crutches. He walked through the kitchen of the house and up to his room to lie down.

A little nephew in the kitchen watched him, went to Carroll's mother, and said, "Uncle B. H. is acting so strange. He is crying and singing at the same time!" His mother, a godly, praying woman, went upstairs and into the room where her son was lying on the bed with his hands over his face. She pulled his hands away from his face, looked long and searchingly into his eyes, and exclaimed, "Son, you have found the Lord! You have been saved!" She saw the glory of God in her boy, and the little nephew heard God's glory in the gladness of B. H. Carroll's song.

There is often a strange response from a person when he is saved. He is so happy that he cries, just out of the overflowing of the saved heart. To be a Christian is to be glad in soul, to sing, to praise God. This praise creates a fellowship like the first Christian community.

June 28

Luke 20:1–18

CUTTING DOWN THE CROSS

And he beheld them, and said, What is this then that is written, The stone which the builders rejected, the same is become the head of the corner? Whosoever shall fall upon that stone shall be broken; but on whomsoever it shall fall, it will grind him to powder (20:17–18).

In the heart of Latvia's capital city stood a church with its tall, tall steeple, a lofty spire topped by a cross of wood covered with gilded metal. In 1940, the Soviet Union, in violation of its treaty with that little country, sent her Red Armies crashing into the Republic. Many thousands, including the most prominent religious leaders, were herded into boxcars like cattle and deported to Siberian labor camps. The Nazi Armies came, then again the Red Army, and Latvia became a slave state of the Soviet Union.

One morning a squad of workmen under a communist boss appeared with ladders and tools to cut down that gilded cross. None of the workmen would volunteer to destroy it. The foreman cursed and scolded, but none moved toward the unhappy assignment. Finally a young man, a leader of the Komsomol (Young Communist League) stepped from the crowd. He would cut down the cross.

It proved to be a difficult job. When his legs became numb, he climbed down to the roof to rest himself. Back up again he went and hacked away at the back of the cross until the ropes tied to it from below pulled it to the ground. Crashing to the earth, the cross fell. In the next instant, the Komsomol's safety belt broke loose and he came falling spread-eagle from the steeple to the hard pavement. With a sickening thud he fell beside the cross, dying in a widening pool of blood. The foreman, ashen and shaken, dismissed the men. Within an hour an automobile carted away the remains of the would-be hero who dared defy the Creator-Ruler of the universe.

June 29

Luke 21:1–24

PRIZED BEYOND MEASURE

For all these have of their abundance cast in unto the offerings of God: but she of her penury hath cast in all the living that she had (21:4).

A shabbily dressed man lived in a little house. He was known as being stingy, penurious, and frugal. When the pastor ate dinner, a sparse meal, with that shabbily dressed man in his humble little cottage, he was astonished to learn that this man lived on a small portion of his salary. With the rest of his salary he supported a missionary on the foreign field. Was this man a worldly success? Who would want to emulate his poverty? Look at his clothing! Look at his success! Look at the house that he lived in! Look at him! Who would follow that? Truly, there is such a difference between how God sees a thing and how the world regards it.

I remember a deacon of many years ago who had served in my church for a generation. He came to church on a bicycle. In his old age a car struck and killed him while he was riding his bicycle. I buried him. He gave every penny he possessed to the church. I am not saying that one ought to do that, nor am I implying that to be a true follower of Christ we must give all our living to the work of the Lord. The Lord never told Zacchaeus to sell everything he had. The Lord did not say that to Nicodemus or to Joseph of

Arimathaea, both of whom were wealthy men. I am merely pointing out that in our sight, in our judgment, sometimes what we think is tremendous success is a pecadillo in God's sight. It is inconsequential or insignificant. Some things that we regard as so despised and rejected may in God's sight be prized beyond measure.

June 30

Luke 23:1–49

THE FAULTLESS CHRIST

Ye have brought this man unto me, as one that perverteth the people: and, behold, I, having examined him before you, have found no fault in this man touching those things whereof ye accuse him (23:14).

One of the most moving stories I ever heard about Dr. Truett came from a man who had been with him in India. Dr. Truett had been sent on a preaching mission around the world and finally came to the vastly populated subcontinent of India. There he was invited to preach at a state university.

Before he went to the school, he was warned of the reception he would most certainly receive because of the Brahman influence in that hostile environment. The school officials warned, "When you are through preaching, people in the audience will ask you questions that are difficult to answer. They will contradict and interdict everything that you say. Do not be upset or surprised at the reception you will receive."

Dr. Truett prayed. The time came when he stood before the university to deliver God's message about Jesus. When he had delivered the sermon, he sat down. The president of the school stood behind the platform desk waiting for the vicious contradictions. He waited through a long silence. Finally a Brahman stood up and said to the president, "Sir, we have nothing against the Christ this man has preached."

We can say much against the church and the people in it. We can criticize, and much of it justly, against the way we live and do Christ's work on the earth. But it is difficult to find fault with the Son of God. The gospel message is Jesus the Christ.

July 1

Luke 24:36–48

THE SWEET REUNION

Behold my hands and my feet, that it is I myself: handle me, and see; for a spirit hath not flesh and bones, as ye see me have (24:39).

A familiar axiom in physics says, "Nature abhors a vacuum." Wherever there might be a vacuum in the earth, the forces of the universe will rush to fill it. That is why we have whirlwinds, tornadoes, and cyclones. There is a rushing in order to fill a place that has somehow become under-pressurized. Another axiom equally factual and equally true says, "The Christian faith abhors disembodiment." The Christian faith abhors a spirit without a body.

God has promised those who trust in Him that He will raise them from the dead. We cannot understand the power of God because mystery is His signature. God takes the atoms and molecules and raises them from the dead. Our bodies will be immortalized like the glorious body of our Savior when He was raised that Easter morning from among the dead.

In the First Baptist Church of Dallas there is a chapel that is dedicated to our "silent friends," those who cannot hear. Their pastor took me to see a deaf man who was dying. Gathered around him were the members of his family. The deaf man pointed to one family member after another. Then he pointed to his pastor and to me. After he had pointed to each one, he pointed to himself and then he pointed upward. The pastor said to me, "What he means to tell you is, 'You, my sweet family, and you, my pastor, I will meet you in heaven!'" The cardinal doctrine of the Christian faith is that in Christ we will see one another again.

July 2

John 1:1–34

THE INFINITUDE OF THE UNIVERSE

All things were made by him; and without him was not any thing made that was made (1:3).

Jesus created the vast infinitude of the firmament which overarches us like a chalice in the sky. How could such a thing be?

A long time ago, astrologers thought that they could count 1,022 stars. Then Ptolemy in the centuries that followed said that there were 1,066 stars. As the years passed, astronomers thought that with the naked eye they could count 1,175 stars. Then Galileo took his crude telescope, arranged the lenses, and found that there were countless stars in the sky above us. Later Herschel and Rosse with their magnificent new telescopes swept the heavens and found an infinitude of burning and blazing suns, each with its own universe and planets around it.

Now with our modern photographic equipment, astronomers have found that there are at least four hundred and fifty million suns. One cannot count the stars, the solar systems, and the planets which shine in God's glorious firmament. God made them all. They are the creation of His omnipotent hand. He made us. He created us. He wove the tissue of our physical frames. He drilled the nerve endings. He domed the brain, and He created mankind in His own likeness and image. We are both deity and dust, made like God out of the dust of the ground. We are the creation of the hands of the Lord.

July 3

John 1:35–51

EXHORTATION FROM THE PEOPLE

And he brought him to Jesus. And when Jesus beheld him, he said, Thou art Simon the son of Jona: thou shalt be called Cephas, which is by interpretation, A stone (1:42).

Recently I asked some young men from Spurgeon's College in London something about Spurgeon, the incomparable preacher of London's Metropolitan Tabernacle. Spurgeon did not give an invitation when he finished preaching. All of his sermons concluded with an appeal for people to give their hearts to Jesus, but he never gave opportunity for the people to come forward and express their faith in the Lord.

When Moody went to the British Isles and conducted great crusades in the last century, Spurgeon loved and admired him. This was surprising because when Dwight L. Moody preached, he gave an invitation and asked the people to come forward and accept the Lord publicly and openly. So I asked the two young men how Spurgeon, when making an appeal for Christ, followed it through in encouraging the people to give their lives openly to the Lord.

The young men related that when Spurgeon preached his message, the convicting power of the Spirit of God moved upon the people. One man would be weeping, one would be kneeling, one would be asking God's mercy, and one was plainly under conviction. When the sermon was done, the people of the congregation talked to those on whom the Spirit of conviction had fallen. They explained the way of salvation and personally won them to Jesus. Then they brought the newborn ones in Christ to the pastor, the pastor brought them before the deacons, and then in a church conference they were accepted into the fellowship of the church. Surely Spurgeon would be disappointed in us, for we hardly have that close, personal relationship in our churches.

July 4

John 3:1–16

PRICELESS GIFTS

For God so loved the world, that he gave his only begotten Son, that whosoever believeth in him should not perish, but have everlasting life (3:16).

God so loved the world, that He gave His only begotten Son. This is the length to which God did go in expressing His love for us. He gave His only begotten Son. What are the most meaningful and precious treasures in our lives? They are certainly not material or monetary.

For example, did you ever notice the value that we place on things that have no particular intrinsic worth at all? Did you have a little baby who died, who fell asleep in Jesus? Do you have a picture of him? Ah, how treasured is that little piece of paper! Do you have a lock of the baby's hair? It is worthless in itself.

Do you have a wedding band? On the market it wouldn't sell for much. But what value it holds for you because someone who loved you gave it to you! It represents life itself. If a man had the whole universe, and he had a boy who died in Vietnam, I can easily imagine that father standing up and saying, "I own thirty million stars and I own ten thousand universes. I own forty continents and fifty oceans. But I would give every star I own, every planet that is mine, and all the continents and oceans if I could just have that boy back again." The priceless gifts are of the soul and of the heart.

God has given us the stars and the moon to shine at night and the sun to shine by day. He has given us the earth on which to walk. But all of these things are as nothing compared to the love of God in the gift of His Son, Christ Jesus. When God gave the Lord to us, He gave Himself. When Christ died for us, the God of heaven suffered. Oh, the length to which God did go to express His love for us!

July 5

John 3:17–36

HOW MANY BLESSINGS?

For he whom God hath sent speaketh the words of God: for God giveth not the Spirit by measure unto him (3:34).

The gift of the Holy Spirit is for us when we repent of our sins, believe and trust in Jesus, and thus are saved. Jesus bestows the Holy Spirit without measure.

The Holy Spirit is a person. He is here; all of Him is available to every believer. His possession of us may be partial, but our possession of Him is total. He lives in His believer-house fully, completely, eternally.

We act as if we would evict the indwelling Spirit of God. We refuse Him access to some of the compartments of our hearts. We keep Him out of many areas of our lives. What happens when we do cleanse our hearts and make room for His filling? Some maintain that when we yield our members to Christ, we receive a second blessing.

Do I believe in a second blessing? Yes, indeed! Does the Scripture teach a second blessing? Yes, indeed! And the Holy Bible also teaches a third blessing, and a fourth, and a hundredth, and a thousandth. As we keep on yielding and surrendering, the Holy Spirit keeps on blessing, on and on, again and again and again. Oh, for the constant refilling of the Spirit!

July 6

John 4:24–42

THOSE CALLED OUT

And many of the Samaritans of that city believed on him for the saying of the woman, which testified, He told me all that ever I did (4:39).

As I was preaching in the Baptist Church downtown in Buenos Aires, Argentina, I was deeply impressed with the pastor of that church. He is tall, dark, handsome, and brilliantly educated. He has a doctor's degree in medicine, a doctor's degree in psychiatry, and a doctor's degree in theology. He presides over his church with grace and gentility. He is absolutely one of the most charming, gifted, and best-educated young ministers to be found in our entire Southern Baptist communion.

When I returned to the Southern Baptist Seminary in Buenos Aires, I mentioned to the professors in the seminary how impressed I was with that young man. The faculty members asked, "Do you know where he came from?" I said, "No." They said, "This afternoon you had tea in the home of an aged missionary. Years ago that missionary was in a marketplace in Buenos Aires. There came to the marketplace a poor, bedraggled woman who had a little baby in her arms. That missionary won the poor disheveled woman to the Lord. The brilliant young minister who impressed you so much was the child of that poor woman."

There are poor people who could be called the flotsam and jetsam of human life, but God is not done. He is still raising up Spurgeons, Moodys, and Truetts. He is still saving souls.

July 7

John 5:1–21

RESURRECT THE DEAD

For as the Father raiseth up the dead, and quickeneth them; even so the Son quickeneth whom he will (5:21).

On a journey to Alaska, I sat in the plane by the side of a Belgian atheist. He spoke to me of the freedom of being an atheist. He was unbound and free. Listening to him, you would think that he had found true glory, but actually, he described a panorama of death. He does not see, he does not hear, he does not feel, and he does not know. He is not quickened.

How does a dead person save himself? How does a dead person hear? How does a dead person feel? All the preaching in the world will not resurrect a dead person. If you would like to try it, go to the cemetery. Many dead people are out there. Preach to them. All the tearful, heartbroken cries and intercession of parents for their children will not resurrect the dead. Resurrection is a gift of God. God must unstop the ears. God must quicken the soul. It is as great a miracle as when God created you. It is as great a miracle as when God resurrected us from the dead to our spiritual life in Christ.

July 8

John 5:22–47

A TIMEPIECE FOR ETERNITY

Search the scriptures; for in them ye think ye have eternal life: and they are they which testify of me (5:39).

Peter Waldo founded the Waldensian church centuries ago. He was the scion of a wealthy, affluent family, and was living his life, as so many young, affluent men do, in a big way. During a dinner party, the young friend seated by his side suddenly dropped his head to the table and died. Peter Waldo began to search for answers to the meaning of life. He found it in God. Thereafter Peter Waldo, giving up his life of ease and fortune, stood on the streets, in the marketplace, on the highway, and preached the gospel of the grace of the Son of God.

Martin Luther was a nominal Christian and churchman. One day, as a young man, he was walking with a friend when lightning struck his friend, who died before Martin Luther's eyes. After that, the big German gave his life to a search for the meaning of God's breath in us.

One of the noblemen of England, on his way to his execution, passed by his clergyman. He stopped and placed his watch in the hands of the minister. He said, "Sir, the timepiece is yours. I am now to live in eternity."

July 9

John 9:1–41

GET OUT AND GO

I must work the works of him that sent me, while it is day: the night cometh, when no man can work (9:4).

Years ago, a preacher and his wife went to begin a work in Juneau, which is located in the panhandle of Alaska. There it sometimes rains more than one hundred inches a year. As the pastor and his wife began their work and as the days passed, the rain fell and fell and fell. The wife, oppressed in spirit, began to sit by the window and cry. Some of the people came to her and said, "Do not do that. Get up and get out in the rain; do something."

She did get out. She and her husband went berry picking in the rain. Alaska is covered with berries and all of them are edible. There is not a poisonous berry in Alaska. Some of them taste like cantaloupe, some of them taste like watermelon; some of them are on little bushes. There are blueberries, blackberries, green berries, and purple berries. I never saw so many berries in my life.

They went out in the rain and caught king salmon. They also went out in the rain and shot ducks. They went out in the rain and did whatever anybody else did out there in the rain. And they did the work of God in the rain. The time is never perfect; it is never just right. There are always handicaps and discouragements. But we must get out and go.

July 10

John 10:1–29

SECURITY IN SALVATION

And I give unto them eternal life; and they shall never perish, neither shall any man pluck them out of my hand (10:28).

Our salvation is always instantaneous. The gift is always immediate. The Gospel is, "Look and live, wash and be clean, believe and be saved." Many things may lead up to it, such as the hearing of the Word, the preaching of the Gospel, prayer, and sometimes agony of spirit, civil war in the soul. But when it comes, always that glorious gift of redemption is instantaneous.

Second, salvation is absolutely complete. It is all-sufficient and all-adequate. It needs and lacks nothing else. All of the waters of Neptune's ocean could not wash the stain of sin out of our souls. All the sweet spices and perfumes of Arabia could not cover the guilt of our sin. But the blood of Jesus Christ is all-sufficient, it is complete, it is adequate.

And last, salvation is irrevocable. When God gives us Himself, He does not take Himself back. When God bestows upon us salvation, He does not let us fall into the abyss and into hell. His merciful gift of life is irrevocable; it is a forever; it is now, and in the world that is to come.

July 11

John 11:1–27

THE EYES OF THE SOUL

Jesus said unto her, I am the resurrection, and the life: he that believeth in me, though he were dead, yet shall he live (11:25).

There are powerful truths that cannot be intellectually substantiated because the intellect, the reason, the logic cannot grasp it. Many things that we receive by faith we cannot intellectually defend. For example, Plato said a man can salute the truth by force of instinct as something akin to himself before he can give intellectual account for it. One can receive it and believe it because it is something like him. And yet, as Plato says, one cannot give an intellectual account for it.

There is no better illustration of that than something which happened in the life of a deacon in my college pastorate. The deacon taught psychology. One day he brought me a textbook in his field of science. At the end of that book the author had said something about himself. Briefly, the scientist said, "I have been an unbeliever. I have not believed in immortality, and I have denied the resurrection. But since I began writing this book, my father and my mother died; and though I can neither explain it nor intellectually defend it, I cannot believe that my father has ceased to be and that my mother is altogether gone. I believe my father is somewhere and my mother is somewhere. Though yesterday I denied both immortality and resurrection, today, after the death of my father and my mother, I believe in both of them."

God had enlightened his inward soul and he began to see with the eyes of his soul, looking at the invisible. This is the work of the Spirit of God.

July 12

John 11:28–57

SUBSTITUTIONARY SACRIFICE

Nor consider that it is expedient for us, that one man should die for the people, and that the whole nation perish not (11:50).

Sin, or the breaking of the law, does several things. Sin separates. It will separate a person from God. It did so in the Garden of Eden. When Adam, who had been in fellowship with the Lord, talking with Him face to face, transgressed God's commandment, he hid himself. When he heard the voice of the Lord God walking in the garden in the cool of the day, Adam could not be found. Thus it was that Christ our Savior, who became our sin, was separated from God on the cross. He cried, "My God, my God, why hast thou forsaken me?" Sin separated the dying Son from the Holy Father.

Sin robs. It leaves us naked, wretched, and lost. Look at Jesus in His actual substitution for us. The artists are most kind. I have never seen a picture of Jesus, dying on the cross, but that the artist somehow managed some piece of clothing to cover His nakedness. But Jesus did not die clothed. He died stripped. He died naked. Sin deprives. The soldiers took away everything He had, even His clothing.

Sin kills. Christ our actual substitute died even so for us. He was numbered among the transgressors as one of us, and for our sins He bowed His head and said, "Father, into thy hands I commend my spirit." Thus he bowed His head and died. In Christ there is an actual substitution. The teaching of the substitutionary sacrifice of Christ is not a figment of the imagination, it is not fictional. Christ died actually "in our stead."

July 13

John 12:20–50

A GLORIOUS OPEN DOOR

The same came therefore to Philip, which was of Bethsaida of Galilee, and desired him, saying, Sir, we would see Jesus (12:21).

In 1950, I was on a three-month preaching mission in Japan. It began at the northernmost island and went down to the southernmost. At one place in the islands, an officer in the Japanese government took me to a governmental compound. General Douglas MacArthur, who was a great Christian, ruled the empire of Nippon. MacArthur sought with Bibles and missionaries to bring the Christian witness to the Japanese.

Every time I preached we had at least one hundred fifty or more converts. It was the most glorious open door I have ever seen. This officer took me to a governmental compound and assembled the people to whom I would preach. The auditorium was covered with rice mats on which the people sat and listened. When I was through, each one was given a card which was perforated in the middle. The top card read like this: "I accept Jesus Christ as my Savior. I do it now." The bottom card said, "I want to know more about Jesus." After each one in the group had been given the card at the end of my appeal, a man stood up, and pointing to the top card he asked me a question, "If I sign this card, then what?" That question burned like fire in my soul. There was no church; there were no Bibles. That question covers the gamut of the kingdom of God. The strategy of the work and patience of our Lord requires a discipling, a baptizing, and a teaching. When that strategy given of God is not carried through, faith becomes anemic.

July 14

John 13:1–17

AN ACCOUNTING

For I have given you an example, that ye should do as I have done to you (13:15).

On a pastor's desk I saw a little motto, "Occupy Till I Come." I occupy God's pulpit, and we rejoice in fellowship with one another, waiting until He comes. We are blessed by the sacred privilege and wonderful opportunity to be a part of God's church. This is God's world. He sits above the circle of the earth, and all things ultimately are in His order and elective choice. He has placed our possessions in our hands to use for His glory until He comes.

One time I was talking to a member of my church who has an accounting firm. I was amazed to find out how much he gave to the church. When I exclaimed about it, he opened his billfold and showed me a card in large letters which read, "He is no fool who gives away what he cannot keep in order to gain what he cannot lose." If I could just remember that! God has given me the body in which I live, and it belongs to Him. I am to use it until He comes. All of the things that we share in our lives belong to Him. When our hearts are filled with that persuasion, belief, and assurance, there is a hallowedness about everything in our lives—what we are, what we possess, the church of which we are members, the fellowship we have with each other, our opportunities and open doors to serve Jesus—all is affected when we remember that we belong to Him. Someday in His grace we will give account of our stewardship and how we have used what God has given to us.

O Lord, may our lives be filled with rejoicing and may every step of the way be one of victory and joy over what You have purposed for us!

July 15

John 14:5–14

THROUGH CHRIST ALONE

Jesus saith unto him, I am the way, the truth, and the life: no man cometh unto the Father, but by me (14:6).

Let me make three avowals concerning the divine truth that we are saved by Christ alone. First, our salvation is always personal and not legalistic, ceremonial, or ritualistic. It is always and ever personal. We are saved not by a code, not by a law, not by a set of rituals or ceremonies, not by observing days or times, but we are saved by our personal relationship to Jesus Christ. It is He who saves us and He alone. Such a personal relationship is beautifully illustrated in human life and experience. When a man falls in love, the whole tenor of his life becomes something else. He seeks to please that someone whom he loves, to do things for the love of his life, to be cognizant of her wishes and desires. Becoming a Christian is exactly like that—one has fallen in love with Christ.

Second, our salvation is always inward and not outward. It is of God and not of ourselves. One can be a Sunday school teacher and be lost. One can be a deacon and be lost. One could have been a member of the church since birth and still be lost. Before we join the church, we must be saved. Salvation is something only God can do for us. There is not anything a person can do for me that saves me.

Third, it is spiritual and not material. It is of faith and of promise. It is looking to God.

July 16

John 16:1–33

THE COMFORT OF THE BLESSED LORD

These things I have spoken unto you, that in me ye might have peace. In the world ye shall have tribulation: but be of good cheer; I have overcome the world (16:33).

When I went to the funeral of my father I sat in the little chapel, my mother by my side, leaning against me, and the preacher said, "Late, late one night I went by the hospital to see Mr. Criswell. I stood by his bed and said, 'Mr. Criswell, how are you?'"

And my father replied, "Sir, the nights are long and lonely, but Jesus is with me. He comforts me and helps me."

What a wonderful thing to say! The comfort of the blessed Lord Jesus is always available to His children. Sometimes when people bury their dead, they will be hesitant about coming to church. If church is just another liquor party or just another social gathering, I say burn it up, tear it apart, dismiss it, be done with it. But if church is a place where Jesus is preached and the Lord is lifted up and God is named, then in the midst of my sorrow and grief, make a place for me to be present, for I need God's comfort and God's help. That is Christ to us.

July 17

John 17:1–26

THE RESPONSIBILITY OF EXAMPLE

And for their sakes I sanctify myself, that they also might be sanctified through the truth (17:19).

The testimony of Otto Graham, the world-famous football quarterback of the Cleveland Browns, appeared in the newspaper. Graham was asked, "When did a personal faith become vital to you?" He was a Christian and the entire newspaper world knew it. The quarterback replied, "Soon after our first child, Duane, was born six years ago, I began to think seriously about the important things of life. I wanted my son to have a sense of God in his soul. I saw clearly that my life has some definite reason and purpose back of it which human reason could not explain. My wife Beverly and I then decided that our children would be given the best opportunities in religious training and that we would be conscious at all times of our obligations to God and our need of Him."

The reporter continued, "Have you ever had any unusual answer to prayer?"

Graham then described a marvelous incident in his life and closed with these words, "This much I know for certain. I give God complete credit for the wonderful life I have had. I believe prayer is the key to successful living, and I want my children to grow up in that knowledge."

How wonderful to consecrate your life for someone else! Parents must dedicate themselves to God in behalf of their children. Then the parents can live before the children so as to lead them into the fullness of the knowledge of the glory of God.

July 18

John 19:1–30

THE PROSTITUTED TREE

Where they crucified him, and two other with him, on either side one, and Jesus in the midst (19:18).

Among the trees that grew around Jerusalem in the days of Caiaphas the high priest was one that was tall and towering, a beautiful and magnificent specimen of God's handiwork. Woodcutters chopped down that beautiful tree. They defoliated it of its beautiful leaves; they tore off its branches; they ripped off its bark; they cut its body in two and made a harsh, rude, cruel cross. They prepared it for crucifixion, that is, the execution of a traitor, a malefactor, an enemy of the people.

In the days of Pontius Pilate, there was one man who towered above all others. He was the Son of God, holy, pure, heavenly, perfect in His life, merciful, compassionate, unselfish, giving Himself for those who needed the healing touch and the saving presence of God. Debased, degraded, bloodthirsty men took Him and stripped Him of His glory. They divided among themselves His garments, even casting lots for His seamless robe. They took His naked body, nailed Him to that cross, and lifted it up above the earth and beneath the sky. One end of that tree was placed down in the dirt; the other end reached up toward God in heaven. The outstretched crossbeams turned toward the east and the west, as far as the east and the west do go. Held against the tree was the agonizing, suffering, naked, dying Son of God.

After the agony was over, men separated the dead man from the dead wood, but inseparable forever in memory and in mind, in thought and in history, are that man and that tree, that Christ and that cross. The hole in the ground where they placed the tree became the pivot around which swings the destiny of the civilized world. In the power and in the glory of God, that dead man lives again, raised from among those who have fallen into the arms of corruption and decay.

July 19

John 20:19–23

A WORTHY GIFT FOR AN UNWORTHY SOUL

He breathed on them, and saith unto them, Receive ye the Holy Ghost (20:22).

Jesus breathed on His disciples and said, "Take ye the Holy Spirit." Sometimes we tremble before the proffered gift. We shrink from taking the priceless possession offered by the hand that was pierced to purchase it. And sometimes, just as we by faith reach forth our hands to grasp it, we shrink back saying, "I am not worthy; it is too much for me."

On a visit to the Soviet Union, I looked upon the dazzling riches of the Russian Czars as they were displayed in the armory in the Moscow Kremlin. I thought of a story of the great Emperor Alexander. On an occasion, in the presence of his bodyguard, he turned and presented to one of his humblest, most menial servants a magnificent golden cup. The poor vassal drew back and said, "Your Majesty, it is too much for me to take." The Czar hesitated and then, thrusting the chalice into the hand of his servant, replied, "But it is not too much for me to give!"

We also shrink from taking the precious gift of the Holy Presence, saying, "I am not worthy; it is too much for me." But Jesus, with His nail-pierced hands stained with the blood that purchased this gift for us, presses the gift into our hands saying, "Take it! Take it! It is not too much for Me to give." Let us look up into the face of our Savior and say, "O blessed Lord Jesus, unworthy as I am, I take it."

The gift of the Holy Spirit is ours forever for the receiving.

July 20

John 21:1–25

WAS SHE SAVED?

He saith unto him the third time, Simon, son of Jonas, lovest thou me? Peter was grieved because he said unto him the third time, Lovest thou me? And he said unto him, Lord, thou knowest all things; thou knowest that I love thee. Jesus saith unto him, Feed my sheep (21:17).

An evangelist was asked to hold the funeral service of a little girl. Being an itinerant minister and not a member of the community, the evangelist asked the parents, "Was the little girl a Christian? Was she saved?"

The father and mother replied, "We do not know. We intended to talk to our little girl about the Lord, but we put it off, and the days passed by. We are not able to say, but her Sunday school teacher will know."

The evangelist went to the Sunday school teacher and asked, "Was the little girl a Christian? Did she know the Lord?"

The teacher said, "I do not know. I meant to talk to her about the Lord Jesus, but I put it off. The Sunday school superintendent will know."

The evangelist went to the Sunday school superintendent and asked, "Was the little girl a Christian?"

The Sunday school superintendent said, "I do not know. I intended to talk to the child about her soul, but I kept putting it off."

Can you imagine anything more sorrowful and tragic than to be given the responsibility of the souls of people, and instead of answering that responsibility with a dynamic, consecrated effort, to reply to the mandate of heaven, "I have too many other things to do; I am too busy. Some other time when I am not so burdened down, I will; but not now."

July 21

Acts 1:1–26

THE REWARD OF PERSONAL TESTIMONY

But ye shall receive power, after that the Holy Ghost is come upon you: and ye shall be witnesses unto me both in Jerusalem, and in all Judaea, and in Samaria, and unto the uttermost part of the earth (1:8).

When a country boy visits the city, he has a world of revelation before him. I grew up in the country and in a little town. When I was a youth I went to New York City for the first time. You cannot imagine the effect that big city had upon a young country boy. It was overwhelming. I walked from street to street and place to place just looking.

As I walked, I saw an enormous building which looked like a vast Greek temple. Standing on the other side of the street from that building, I noticed an enormous chiseling of words in the frieze that decorated the entire building. This is what I read: "Neither Snow Nor Rain Nor Heat Nor Gloom of Night Stays These Couriers From the Swift Completion of Their Appointed Rounds." I tried to stop a New Yorker to ask him what it meant, but he walked rapidly by. I tried to stop another one to ask him what it was all about, but he also kept on walking. Finally I was successful, and I asked the man as he paused, "What is that building there and of whom are they talking?" He said, "Son, that is the United States Post Office for New York City, and that is the biggest building in this town and the biggest post office in the world." I remember that noble tribute when I see a mailman coming to the door.

Oh, what a magnificent phenomenon if that could be said about God's people delivering the message of the Lord personally! God blesses personal testimony in a powerful way.

Acts 2:1–24

THE DIVINE SIGNATURE

Ye men of Israel, hear these words; Jesus of Nazareth, a man approved of God among you by miracles and wonders and signs, which God did by him in the midst of you, as ye yourselves also know (2:22).

In God's library of books, the signature is "Miracle." Ours is a world of miracle and wonder because God created it. A universal law of physics proclaims that heat expands. Cold has the opposite effect; the object contracts. That universal law continues until God intervenes. Water will contract as it gets colder, but when the temperature falls to 32° F., it expands. Why? Because had water continued to contract when it got colder, freezing ice would have, by its weight, fallen to the floor of the ocean. The ocean would have been solid ice at both poles from the bottom to the top. The great currents that ameliorate the temperatures of the world would have been impossible. A person could not live near the center of the earth because the torrid heat would burn him up. Such is a miracle of God.

In the field of biology a law states that in human life all the cells have a certain number of chromosomes. There are forty-eight chromosomes in every cell of the human body. In the miraculous process of mitosis, every cell will split down the middle and there will be forty-eight in one and forty-eight in the other. This happens, except, in the miracle of God, in the female ovum where there are twenty-four and in the male spermatozoon where there are twenty-four. When the male spermatozoon fertilizes the female ovum, the twenty-four chromosomes from the man and the twenty-four chromosomes from the woman combine, and the child, therefore, has forty-eight chromosomes in all the cells of his body. The child will inherit characteristics from both the mother and the father. One cannot explain the miracle of birth except through almighty God.

July 23

Acts 2:1–47

THE FAVOR OF GOD

And they, continuing daily with one accord in the temple, and breaking bread from house to house, did eat their meat with gladness and singleness of heart, Praising God, and having favor with all the people. And the Lord added to the church daily such as should be saved (2:46–47).

Somewhere in the earth there is always revival and a marvelous visitation of God from heaven. When the church at Jerusalem lost its power in Judaizing compromise, the churches at Ephesus and at Antioch became the glory of the Lord. When the church at Antioch compromised its witness, the church at Milan came forward to shine like a lighthouse before the world. When the churches of Alexandria, Carthage, and North Africa became mere shells of formalism, the churches in Gaul were battling barbarism and turning the heathen to Christ. When the church at Rome became formal, wealthy, and lacking in spiritual impact, the people of Ireland were turning with one accord to the glorious gospel of Christ.

When the Unitarian defection emptied the churches of New England and brought disaster to our Christian institutions, the pioneer preacher was pressing beyond the Alleghenies, calling the frontiersmen to repentance and faith in Christ, establishing churches throughout the Midwest and the far West, and laying the foundations for our Christian schools that bless us and ennoble our work today.

In an hour when mass evangelism is decried and belittled, Billy Graham is preaching to more people than any other emissary of heaven since the days of the launching of the Christian movement. In a day when downtown churches are supposed to die, the First Baptist Church in Dallas is growing as it has never grown before. Always there is God's rich outpouring of heavenly grace somewhere in the earth, and it can be ours for the asking.

July 24

Acts 3:1–26

THE JUST ONE

But ye denied the Holy One and the Just, and desired a murderer to be granted unto you; And killed the Prince of life, whom God hath raised from the dead; whereof we are witnesses (3:14–15).

The far-famed English preacher, Charles Haddon Spurgeon, became seriously ill at the age of fifty-eight and was taken to Menton, a city on the French Riviera. It was hoped that the soft breezes and the sunshine might bring health to the great pastor. Instead, he grew steadily worse and died. A friend of the great preacher, sitting by his side as he lay dying, said to him, "Mr. Spurgeon, what is your gospel now?" And the London preacher replied in four simple words: "Christ died for me." That is the gospel that will save us from our sins and bring us to salvation. Christ suffered for our sins, the just in behalf of the unjust, that He might bring us to God.

July 25

Acts 4:1–31

YOU AIN'T GOT NO RELIGION

And when they had prayed, the place was shaken where they were assembled together; and they were all filled with the Holy Ghost, and they spake the word of God with boldness (4:31).

In my first little country pastorate I said to one of my men, "You know, I cannot talk to anyone about the Lord. I am just so timid and afraid." He said to me, "Young pastor, do you know what the matter is?" I said, "No. I don't." Polished, cultured, educated people will always observe the amenities of life. They will always be nice and often will not be honest and forthright. An uneducated, uncultured, unlettered rural man sometimes will tell you frankly and openly what he thinks. My humble parishioner said, "The trouble with you is you ain't got no religion." I was his pastor! I stood in the pulpit of that little church on Sunday and opened the Bible and preached to him. The nerve of that fellow telling me I "ain't got no religion!" But he made an impression on me I have never forgotten.

Certainly, if I do not have any religion, I have nothing to share with anyone. I have nothing to say. No wonder I fear and tremble and am hesitant and timid. I have no Good News to tell. If a person were starving and I had bread, would I be timid? If I met a person who was thirsting to death and I had water to give him, would I be too shy to offer it? The sweetest thing I could ever share, the noblest gift I could ever bestow, the grandest news this side of heaven itself is the Good News—Jesus. That is the gift of the spirit of God. We are to be bold in the faith.

July 26

Acts 5:1–42

AN INEVITABLE SACRIFICE

And they departed from the presence of the council, rejoicing that they were counted worthy to suffer shame for his name (5:41).

It is almost an unfailing rule that when you stand before a decision that demands a sacrifice, it is likely God's will. Devotion to our Lord is often at great sacrifice.

My ministry was just beginning when World War II broke out. In the city where I was pastor, an enormous army camp was built to train soldiers to go overseas and fight in the war. Some of the experiences that happened during that war burn in my mind vividly and dramatically.

In a French railroad station where numerous soldiers were gathered, there stood a mother with her youngest son. When the train came, the mother gently kissed her son, watched him get on the train, and observed as it pulled out of the station. The boy took out his handkerchief and waved it toward his mother. The mother had a little French flag in her hand as she waved back to her son. After the train pulled out of sight, the mother collapsed in the station like a crumpled flower. Some of the other soldiers ran to her. One of them bathed her face with water and brought her again to consciousness. As she revived, she began to sob, almost half-consciously. "My husband was sent into the war and he will not come back. My eldest son will not return, for he, too, has been killed. My second son has been called into service, and he has been gone for years. Now my youngest son, the widow's staff, has been called and he has left me." As the mother sadly, almost unconsciously, repeated those sorrowful words, she happened to see the little French flag that had fallen out of her hand. When she saw it, her eyes flashed. She picked it up, held it high, and began to cry, "But vive la France!"

July 27

Acts 6:1–15

CHANGING LIVES

And the word of God increased; and the number of the disciples multiplied in Jerusalem greatly; and a great company of the priests were obedient to the faith (6:7).

A humble preacher was once seated in a hotel lobby along with a loud and blasphemous infidel. The infidel said to the preacher, "You and your prayers! Let us see you pray for me and convert me." The preacher in that hotel lobby knelt down by the side of the blatant infidel and prayed for his soul that he might be saved. When the infidel stood up he laughed and said, "Ha, I'm just the same. Nothing has been changed in me." The preacher humbly replied, "But wait. God is not done yet." Sometime later that humble preacher was looking at a newspaper from another town in which there was an article about a layman who was holding a heaven-sent, Spirit-filled revival meeting. The preacher saw the name of the layman who was leading the revival, and it was the infidel for whom he had prayed in the hotel lobby.

If you want to look at the power of God unto salvation to change people's lives, look around you. It is everywhere. The effect the filling of the Holy Spirit has upon sinners outside the fold of grace is miraculous.

July 28

Acts 7:1–60

A SLEEPING PLACE

And he kneeled down, and cried with a loud voice, Lord, lay not this sin to their charge. And when he had said this, he fell asleep (7:60).

The early Christians took the Greek word *koimeterion,* "a sleeping place," and applied it to the place where they laid aside their beloved dead. Transliterated into English, *koimeterion* becomes "cemetery." The world never used the word until Christians applied it to the laying away of their dead.

In India, I have watched people bury their dead by the scores. They place the bodies on platforms, surround the bodies with wood, and then set them on fire.

We are told that the catacombs in Rome are miles of subterranean passages where the Christians hid when they were persecuted by the Roman Caesar. Actually, the catacombs were dug out of the rock on which the eternal city of Rome is built so that the Christians could have a place to lay away their beloved dead. At that time, burning the body was the heathen custom. So the Christians felt they should not follow that custom. Because the Christians refused to burn their dead, they dug subterranean caverns and lovingly laid their dead away.

William Cullen Bryant, when he was but eighteen years of age, wrote his first great poem on American soil, called *Thanatopsis.* Here is how it closes.

> So live, that when thy summons comes to join
> The innumerable caravan which moves
> To that mysterious realm, where each shall take
> His chamber in the silent halls of death
> Thou go not, like the quarry-slave at night,
> Scourged to his dungeon, but, sustained and soothed
> By an unfaltering trust, approach thy grave
> Like one that wraps the drapery of his couch
> About him, and lies down to pleasant dreams.

July 29

Acts 8:1–25

THE SCATTERING OF THE WORD

Therefore they that were scattered abroad went every where preaching the word (8:4).

One of the bitterest antagonists of the Bible was the dogmatism of the church itself seeking to substitute for the Bible human doctrines, creed, and edicts. The Bible was taken from the hands of the people and was denied them for hundreds of years. Martin Luther was a grown man when he said, "I have never seen a Bible," and he was an ecclesiastic.

John Wycliffe translated the Bible into the language of the people. He wanted to make it possible for all to know the Word of God. Before the Inquisition could slay John Wycliffe, he died and was buried. But the inquisitors exhumed and publicly burned his body and cast the ashes upon the River Swift. If any man in England was found with a Bible, the Bible was hung around his neck and he was publicly hanged and burned. What the English inquisitors did not realize was that when they burned the body of John Wycliffe and scattered his ashes on the River Swift, the river flowed into the Avon and the Avon flowed into the Severn. The Severn flowed into the sea, and the sea lathed the shores of the world including the new land of America. Wherever the sea carried the ashes of John Wycliffe, there God scattered the truth of the Word of the living Lord.

We have learned of the people of Russia who are hearing the Word of God for the first time. In the Philippines there are fifty tribes who have the Word of God. More than one hundred tribes in Old Mexico already have the Word of God in their own language.

July 30

Acts 9:1–18

A LIVING STONE

But the Lord said unto him, Go thy way: for he is a chosen vessel unto me, to bear my name before the Gentiles, and kings, and the children of Israel (9:15).

A young man was told by his doctors that he could not go to the mission field. He was warned that if he were to go to the mission field, he would immediately die. The young fellow replied, "But I am going." The doctors asked, "Why? You are not physically able to face the hardships of those assignments. You will certainly die. Why do you insist on going?" The young fellow answered, "Doctor, did you ever see a great bridge over a broad river? The bridge stands because large stones are buried in the earth below. These foundation stones upon which the bridge rests are unseen but essential. I am going to be one of those hidden, buried foundation stones."

The boy went to the mission field, and he died as the doctors had warned. But God saw him, and He used that boy even in his fleeting days.

July 31

Acts 13:1–43

A MANDATE FROM HEAVEN

As they ministered to the Lord, and fasted, the Holy Ghost said, Separate me Barnabas and Saul for the work whereunto I have called them (13:2).

Standard Oil Company once said to a young man who was the son of a missionary, "We will give you thus-and-thus salary if you will be our representative in the Orient." The young man refused. The company came back and doubled the salary. It was an astronomical amount, thousands and thousands of dollars a year. The young man refused. The executive from the oil company finally asked, "What is the matter? How much money do you want? How much salary would it take for you to work for and be the representative of the Standard Oil Company?" The young man replied, "There is nothing wrong with the salary. I am overwhelmed by it. The trouble is this. The job is too little. God has called me to be a witness and a representative for Him, and I cannot turn aside from the mandate from heaven to accept salary and prestige from Standard Oil Company."

August 1

Acts 15:1–35

SERVING EVEN IN DEATH

It seemed good unto us, being assembled with one accord, to send chosen men unto you with our beloved Barnabas and Paul, Men that have hazarded their lives for the name of our Lord Jesus Christ (15:25–26).

A colleague with whom I attended seminary was later president of our Southern Baptist Convention. He recounted a story about a college friend of his who gave his life to be a missionary. The young man, though trained in another country, was later appointed to what was then the Belgian Congo. All during the time that his friend was training, the two corresponded regularly. Then, when the friend went to the Congo, his letters stopped. My colleague wondered what had happened to the young missionary. He learned that as his friend was going up to his mission station in the Congo, he contracted a jungle fever and died before he ever reached his destination. The Congolese buried him under a large spreading tree on the banks of the Congo River. My friend said to me, "When word of what had happened to him came back to our school, more than sixty men and women volunteered to take his place." Then he added, "When word came back to his home church that the man had died on the way to his mission station, thirteen boys and girls volunteered to prepare themselves to take his place."

God sees to it that any witness, any sacrifice, any word that we may offer to Him never falls to the ground. God blesses and multiplies the witness forever.

August 2

Acts 16:25–40

THE COST OF STANDING FOR TRUTH

And they said, 'Believe on the Lord Jesus Christ, and thou shalt be saved, and thy house (16:31).

One time I listened to a learned New York rabbi who said, "The great difference between the Jew and the Christian is this: To us there is no need of salvation. Since we are the children of Abraham, we are saved. There is no such thing as having to be saved." But the preaching of John the Baptist and all those who followed after him was this: We are all sinners, Jew and Gentile, bond and free, male and female, and we must repent of our sins and find forgiveness in Christ Jesus. That was the preaching of Jesus Himself.

We do not seem to have the fearless courage in us today to stand before a sinful, gainsaying, and Christ-rejecting world. We mollify our witness, and we compromise with the evil in the world. It is a rare person who will stand up and say the truth at a price. It is so much easier for us to say sweet, complimentary, and compromising words rather than oppose evil, unbelief, rejection, sin, wrong, and iniquity. The Lord said, "Woe unto you when all men speak well of you," when everyone has a tendency to praise you. They do so because you are not opposing their sin. You are not standing up for what is right, and you are not presenting the truth of God as it is in Christ Jesus.

August 3

Acts 17:1–34

THE OLD-TIME POWER

Now while Paul waited for them at Athens, his spirit was stirred in him, when he saw the city wholly given to idolatry (17:16).

Many years ago I was in Spurgeon's Tabernacle, seated with that little band that remains in the greatest Baptist church that ever existed. Back of me were two old men. One of them said to the other, "Did you ever hear Spurgeon preach?" He replied, "Yes, many times. He was my pastor." The man asked him, "How was it? How did he preach? What was Spurgeon like?" The man replied, "Sir, I do not like to criticize the preachers of today, but it seems to me that they just talk and lecture. But when Spurgeon stood up to preach, sir, there was power in his preaching."

How many times do I stand in my pulpit saying words, repeating clichés, doing what has been habitual for us to do all our lives? At a certain hour we are here. At another time we do this or the other. At this time we listen to a sermon. Then at this time we look for the benediction. Then at a certain time we go home and forget it.

Lord, send the old-time power,
The Pentecostal power!
Thy floodgates of blessing
On us throw open wide!

Lord, send the old-time power,
The Pentecostal power,
That sinners be converted
And Thy name glorified!

We assemble ourselves in the presence of the Lord to worship. As we listen to Him, we should ask what He would have us do.

August 4

Acts 19:1–41

THE INFLUENCE OF SUPERSTITION

Many of them also which used curious arts brought their books together, and burned them before all men: and they counted the price of them, and found it fifty thousand pieces of silver. So mightily grew the word of God and prevailed (19:19–20).

Whenever a civilization or a people turn away from the true God, they turn to all kinds of superstitions—astrology, fortune tellers, witches, and clairvoyants. That is a strange streak in human nature. I can hardly believe the number of witches, fortune tellers, and spiritist mediums active in America today. Our country has many colleges, universities, and scientifically-oriented institutions, and yet we are being drowned by witchcraft performed by people who are charlatans of the first order.

For example, few newspapers in America today would publish an issue without including an astrologer's column. You might ask the editor, "Why do you publish such inanity and idiocy in these astrology columns?" He will reply, "We dare not publish the paper without astrological forecasts because people by the thousands read them."

What a strange thing! Whenever you take God out of human life, when you take Jesus out of the human heart, there is a vacuum. But it does not stay empty. The vacuum is immediately filled with all kinds of superstitions, astrology, necromancy, and fortune telling.

August 5

Acts 20:1–27

SHAPING A MESSAGE

For I have not shunned to declare unto you all the counsel of God (20:27).

The modern pulpit is characterized by softness and compromise. I once heard an unusual story. A deacon was with the preacher of the evening just before the service began, and he opened the door a bit to see who was seated in the congregation. He looked over the people and said to the speaker, "I see some Presbyterians here. Do not say anything about the Presbyterians." Then he saw some Methodists and said, "Do not say anything about the Methodists." Next he said, "I see a few Catholics. Do not say anything about the Catholics." Finally he scanned the audience carefully and said, "I do not see a Mormon. Preacher, give 'em fits!"

What an insult to the truth of almighty God that we shape our message according to the response of the people who might be present! God bless the person who declares the whole truth and counsel of God!

August 6

Acts 20:28–38

LOVING THE FLOCK

Take heed therefore unto yourselves, and to all the flock, over the which the Holy Ghost hath made you overseers, to feed the church of God, which he hath purchased with his own blood (20:28).

Dr. George W. Truett, my predecessor, was one of the greatest men that I have ever seen. During my youth, he was to me and others an idol, a hero, and a great messenger of God. I loved to hear him as he would come to the university, to the convention, or to a pastor's conference, always speaking, with great effect and moving spirit.

Dr. Truett was a personal friend of John D. Rockefeller, Sr., who had a profound love and admiration for the pastor. Mr. Rockefeller was superintendent of the Sunday school at Euclid Avenue Baptist Church in Cleveland, Ohio. One day when that church was without a pastor, Mr. Rockefeller and the members of the church decided under God that they would seek to persuade Rockefeller's friend, George W. Truett, to come and be pastor of the Cleveland church. They sent a committee to Dallas to visit with Dr. Truett and to persuade him to come to Cleveland, but Dr. Truett refused. They talked to him repeatedly, but he still refused.

Finally, a committee was sent to Dallas to offer Dr. Truett any salary or provision he wanted. But he replied, "I cannot come." The committee finally said in desperation, "Dr. Truett, could you be moved?" He said, "Oh, yes." The committee, immediately sensing an opportunity, said, "So you can be moved! What would it take to move you?"

The great pastor replied, "Move my people, and I will move with them." This spirit will make a church great.

August 7

Acts 22:1–30

A DEFENSE OF THE FAITH

Men, brethren, and fathers, hear ye my defense which I make now unto you (22:1).

The best defense of the Christian faith is a person's affirming testimony, "This I know."

A medical missionary in Africa can say, "I was on the way from Jerusalem to Damascus, and while I was in medical school and interning in the hospital, I met the Master. I turned from a lucrative practice in a great American clinic and gave myself to be a representative of Christ in this darkened continent." That is powerful!

Or a businessman can say, "I was on the way from Jerusalem to Damascus, and I was seizing upon opportunities to become wealthy, but my life was empty, barren, and sterile. I was unhappy and restless, and I found the Lord." That is great!

Or a professor in the school may say, "I was an agnostic with no meaning in life. I was on my way from Jerusalem to Damascus, and in the meaninglessness of my life I found the Lord. Now, all of life has wonderful purpose and marvelous meaning."

Or an alcoholic or addict can say, "I was on the way from Jerusalem to Damascus, down, down, and down. As I was falling in helplessness before my addiction, I found the Lord."

Tell me, what could a philosopher, an atheist, or an agnostic say about that kind of a defense? The Christian faith is not an argument, a hypothesis, a theory, or a theological discussion. The Christian life and faith is a great experience. "I have found the Lord." What can you do with a person as he recounts his conversion? To obviate and to deny what the person is saying, you would have to obviate the person himself—his life, his character, his work, and his ministry.

August 8

Acts 24:24–27

NO MORTGAGE ON TOMORROW

And after certain days, when Felix came with his wife Drusilla, which was a Jewess, he sent for Paul, and heard him concerning the faith in Christ (24:24).

God says that no person has any mortgage on tomorrow. We do not know what tomorrow may bring. Satan deceives us when he persuades us that we are having a good time in the world and that we will have to give up joy and happiness if we become Christians.

A man stood up to testify. "When I became a Christian," he said, "I gave up many things. I gave up the liquor bill. No longer do I fall into delirium nor am I terrified by hallucinations nor do I have a dark, heavy hangover. I gave that up when I became a Christian. I also gave up the wrecking of my home and the leading of my children down to hell. I gave up gambling my check away and leaving my family in want. I gave up my dirty and foul mouth and my evil mind. I gave up the squandering of my life and salary. Now I am free of my chains and slavery and I am free in Jesus Christ. It cost me much. I gave up much to become a Christian."

This is so true. We give up the world's tears, despair, darkness, sin, filth, chains, slavery, and death, and we walk out free into the grace of God. All who have accepted Jesus as Savior have found Him unfailingly true.

August 9

Acts 26:1–20

SPEAK A GOOD WORD FOR JESUS

Whereupon, O king Agrippa, I was not disobedient unto the heavenly vision: but showed first unto them of Damascus, and at Jerusalem, and throughout all the coasts of Judaea, and then to the Gentiles, that they should repent and turn to God, and do works meet for repentance (26:19–20).

Wherever people were, there did Paul preach: on the river bank to a group of women in a prayer meeting in Philippi; at the Agora in the heart of the great intellectual city of Athens; and upon Mars Hill before the Areopagus (the Athenian Supreme Court); in ships battered and beaten by raging winds; before Felix and Festus, Roman procurators; before Agrippa, king of the Jews; and finally, before Nero and the Praetorian Guard—wherever he could, he witnessed to the grace of God in Christ Jesus.

And that is our call, our paragon, our example. Under the shade of a tree, on a city street, in a private home, anywhere is a good place to speak of what Christ has done for us. The carpenter can lay down his saw and his hammer and talk to a worker by his side. A blacksmith can take off his apron and lay down his iron tongs and talk to a man who happens to be in the shop. A secretary can prayerfully witness to someone as she works in an office in one of those tall buildings. To someone seated by your side, you can say some good words about Jesus and what He has done for you. It is a high prerogative and a holy assignment; it is an open door and an infinite privilege for the child of God to speak a good word for Jesus.

August 10

Acts 27:1–41

THE HOLY AND HEAVENLY BLESSING

Wherefore, sirs, be of good cheer: for I believe God, that it shall be even as it was told me (27:25).

When I was a boy, the marshal of our town lived across the street from our house. He and his wife and two small children attended our little Baptist church. Since our family was always at church, I saw them every time the door was opened. We came to cherish and to love them.

One dark night a robber shot the marshal, and the next morning when our little town awakened, we found him lying in his own blood. It was an indescribable sorrow.

We always had a testimony at prayer meeting on Wednesday night, and on the Wednesday after the memorial service for the marshal, his wife stood up to witness to the grace of our Lord. She was soon to have another child, and said, "This has been a great trial for me, left alone as I am with these two little children and the one that soon will be born, but God has been with me. The Lord has strengthened me, and I bless and praise His name for the loving care with which He has remembered me."

You can imagine the effect a testimony like that would have upon a small boy. I am still encouraged by it. No trial can overtake us but that God gives us strength to bear it. Out of the tears and the disappointment will come a heavenly blessing that the Lord has prepared for us.

August 11

Romans 2:1–9

THE INFLUENCE OF EVIL

Who will render to every man according to his deeds (2:6).

In Amarillo I had a friend with whom I graduated from high school. We were in the same Sunday school class and were good personal friends. We went to Baylor University together, and to my sorrow and amazement, he young fellow turned out to be an infidel, an atheist. I went to his room ›ne night to talk to him. He was seated under a lamp reading Thomas ʾaine's *Age of Reason.* Tom Paine had been dead for one hundred fifty ears. But really dead? The influence of that evil-thinking man has exended through the decades after his body has turned back into dust.

Think of the dividend for evil that wicked people will receive at the udgment bar of almighty God. We never escape the influence of evil in ›ur lives.

August 12

Romans 2:10–29

'HE SECRETS OF MEN

In the day when God shall judge the secrets of men by Jesus ;hrist according to my gospel (2:16).

One time when I was in the British Museum, I asked directions to the :lgin Marbles. The reason I wanted to see them was this. When Lord Elgin :onquered Greece, he took to London the incomparably beautiful pieces ›f statuary from the front of the Parthenon. Phidias carved the beautiful tatues and placed them high up at the front of the Parthenon. I wanted to ee them because of a story that I had heard about Phidias, one of the reatest sculptors the world ever knew. He was working meticulously, ealously, and painstakingly on the back side of one of the statues. He was :onscientiously carving the fold in the garment and carefully chiseling the alling tresses of the hair. Someone came to Phidias and asked, "Why are ou working so carefully on the back of these figures? They are to be ›laced high above the people at the top of the temple and no one would ver know."

Phidias replied, "But God sees it."

So when I went to the British Museum and was directed to the place vhere the Elgin Marbles are exhibited, I looked at the back of the statues. 'he story was true, for the incomparable artist and sculptor had as beauifully carved the back where only God could see as he had the front where he people could see.

August 13

Romans 3:9–20

UNIVERSALITY OF MORAL DISCERNMENT

What then? are we no better than they? No, in no wise: for we have before proved both Jews and Gentiles, that they are all under sin (3:9).

There is no family, no tribe, no people, nor any nation so degraded that it does not have a moral code of what is right and what is wrong. What the people think to be right and what they think to be wrong may be strange to us, but everyone has some moral sensitivity.

When Charles Darwin went around the world, he came to the tip of South America and found a group of islands called Tierra del Fuego. He wrote that he had found in those islands a tribe so degraded that they had no moral sensitivity. He said, "I have found the missing link between the animal and the man, for these Tierra del Fuegans are without sensitivity." Some Christians in England read Darwin's statement and sent missionaries to Tierra del Fuego. Soon they reported that the Tierra del Fuegans were noble in their life and virtuous in their deportment. They had been won to Christ and were now disciples of the Lord. When Charles Darwin learned of the evangelization of the Tierra del Fuegans, he himself became a subscriber and a faithful contributor to the Church Missionary Society of London, England, which had sent out the missionaries. There are no people in the world who have ever lived or ever shall live in whom that spirit of moral discernment is not present.

August 14

Romans 3:21–31

GUILT PRECEDES FORGIVENESS

For all have sinned, and come short of the glory of God (3:23).

An illustration of the superfluity of grace and mercy in self-righteousness is found in the instance of a man who stands before the bar of a federal court. He is innocent. So he stands before the judge and says, "I am innocent: I am not guilty." But the judge replies, "I know that, and this court will show you mercy and grace."

The man rightly and indignantly replies, "Mercy? Judge, Your Honor, what do you mean by mercy? I do not want mercy! I am innocent. I am not guilty, and all that I ask of this court is justice. I want my rights, because I am not a culprit or a criminal. I am innocent! And I do not want mercy!" If a man pleads mercy from a judge, that means he is guilty, he has done wrong. And he casts himself upon the mercy of the court. He cries, "May the court be merciful, forgiving, and understanding. I cast myself upon the sympathies of the court and I ask for mercy."

It is the same thing when we stand in the presence of God. If a person can stand in the presence of God and say, "Lord, I am innocent, I have never sinned. There has never been wrong in my life. I have obeyed perfectly all that God has required of me from the day I was born, and I stand here in this court asking for justice. Give me my rights." Then the Lord God can say, "How excellent! There has never been evil in your heart and life. Walk into the presence of My kingdom. Welcome, perfect you." However, who among us would claim perfection and equality with the holy Creator God? Rather, every one of us has fallen short of God's perfect mark. We are all alienated from our Lord because of our sinfulness.

August 15

Romans 4:1–25

PILGRIMAGE TO SAINTHOOD

For what saith the scripture? Abraham believed God, and it was counted unto him for righteousness (4:3).

An extreme instance of self-persecution in order to seek praises from God appeared in an article from the United Press. "A mother of seven children burned herself at the stake in the hope of becoming a saint, the police reported. Officers said that Angelida Borsen, age forty-eight, piled up straw and soaked it and herself with gasoline. Then she tied and gagged herself and set fire to the straw. Mrs. Borsen, afflicted with cancer, got up every night in her farm home to pray. She read the Bible constantly and became convinced that her illness stemmed from her sins, her family said. Relatives said that apparently she hoped that by dying in a terrible fashion her sins would be atoned." How tragic! The doctrine of justification by self-righteousness or self-merit is of the flesh and ministers to human pride. "If I do these things, if I suffer these things, if I obey these things, then I will commend myself to God and I can be saved. I can do it."

Not only is self-justification a persistent and appealing doctrine to our fallen human nature, but it sounds plausible. You could point out that people must be taught and trained to be good and to be righteous.

This doctrine of self-merit is the common denominator of all false religions. However religions may differ in a thousand categories, they all have this one feature in common: that we save ourselves by doing good, by keeping commandments, by observing rituals, by doing things—the work that supposedly commends us to God.

August 16

Romans 5:1–11

ONE BY ONE

But God commendeth his love toward us, in that, while we were yet sinners, Christ died for us (5:8).

The text brings to mind the emphatic truth that the Christian faith is personal. It is inward; it is individual. The Christian faith is the religion of the one lost sheep, the one lost coin, and the one lost boy. God does not look at us by gobs and buckets-full and oceans-full, but God looks at us one by one. He knows our names and He knows all about us.

Sometimes looking out into the blue night sky, one will see an extensive nebula which looks like a vast conglomerate, but if he looks at it through a telescope, he will find it to be a galaxy of individual stars. When we look at the mass of mankind, we are prone to lump them all together into a vast limbo of the unknown. But God looks at mankind individually, one by one.

The Christian faith begins with a personal experience when we are born into the kingdom and into the family of God. There is no other way that we become a part of it except to be born personally, individually, into it. We cannot become Christians by the godliness of others, nor are we Christians because we are born into a Christian family or because we are being reared in a Christian nation. Someone facetiously said that one might as well say that because a fellow was born in a garage he was a car or because a rat lives in a stable he is a horse. No! To whatever family we were born or in whatever country we hold citizenship, we are Christians only because we have been individually born again into the family of God.

August 17

Romans 6:1–13

THE RESURRECTION HOPE

Knowing that Christ being raised from the dead dieth no more; death hath no more dominion over him (6:9).

Recently a member of my church placed in my hand a little book entitled, *The Jefferson Bible.* In the preface, Jefferson said that he took the Bible and reduced the volume down to the things that were actually words of the Lord Jesus. He pared off all the misconceptions from the accrued story that one finds in the four Gospels. What he found remaining was the most sublime and benevolent code of morals that has ever been offered to civilization. Then when I turned to the end of his Bible, I saw that Jefferson left the Lord Jesus dead in the sepulcher. That is no gospel.

A little boy was standing before a window in which were numerous pictures, and in the center was a picture of Jesus on the cross. The little urchin on the street was looking at that center picture. A kindly man came by and, placing his hand on the shoulder of the boy, said, "Son, what are you looking at?"

The little boy, almost unconsciously, started to describe the picture of the Lord Jesus and the sadness of the cross. "They nailed Him to the cross, they crucified Him, they killed Him, and He died."

The man walked off. The little boy suddenly became aware that the visitor had walked away. The boy said, "Say, mister, wait up." He ran and caught up with the man and said, "Say, mister, He rose from the dead!"

That is the gospel. Jesus was crucified for our sins, He was delivered for our offenses, but He was raised from the dead by the power of God. That is the gospel Paul preached.

August 18

Romans 6:14–23

THE PENALTY TEACHES

For the wages of sin is death; but the gift of God is eternal life through Jesus Christ our Lord (6:23).

We teach our children that fire burns and that pins stick. The child learns. The penalty teaches the youngster. So it is when we go down the road of life. We see a flashing red signal and hear a bell ringing, for a train is coming. The railroad company is not our enemy when it flashes the sign and rings the bell. The company does this to protect us and spare our lives. If a bridge is out, the highway department builds a barricade across it. The barricade keeps us from being destroyed.

So it is with God. Someone has said there are five hundred references in the New Testament to hell. That is, God's Word has placed five hundred signs which say, "This way leads to hell. Stop! Look!" When people disregard them, nothing is left but judgment, death, and damnation.

August 19

Romans 7:1–25

A NEW SPIRIT

But now we are delivered from the law, that being dead wherein we were held; that we should serve in newness of spirit, and not in the oldness of the letter (7:6).

We see the effect the preaching of the gospel has upon a human heart when that heart opens to the Lord. Once we were dead to sin, but now we are alive to God. Sin loses its allurement and attractiveness when we accept Christ. False prophets come with veils over their faces, supposedly to hide their glory. But something always happens to show us these people as they really are.

When we were in London, the Maharajah Guru held a convocation of all his followers, and they marched through the streets of London by the ıousands. I stood there and watched them march by. Once he was in Houston at the Astrodome, and many of his followers bowed down and issed his feet and worshiped him as the great messiah. If you are a :hristian, you cannot bow down and kiss his feet and accept him as the ue messiah. There is something inside of you that rebels. To you it is ffensive and repulsive. You are a different kind of person; you are dead to in and alive to God. That is the most remarkable thing that happens to a erson when he is saved. His language is different. His interests are different. He is alive to that to which others are dead. He is dead to that to which thers are alive. The person who opens his heart to faith in Christ has a ew love, a new vision, a new hope, a new life, a new dream, a new way, a ew goal, and a new tomorrow. He has been saved.

August 20

Romans 8:1–11

HE ESSENCE OF CHRISTIANITY

There is therefore now no condemnation to them which are in hrist Jesus, who walk not after the flesh, but after the Spirit (8:1).

What was the message that Paul delivered? It was that Christ died for ur sins, that He was buried, and that the third day He rose again, all ccording to the Scriptures. When Paul preached the Gospel, that is what e preached—Christ and Him crucified. That is the faith. That is the ubstance and the essence of Christianity. The beginning of the Christian aith, the middle, and the end of it is the Lord Jesus. When Paul preaches ıe Gospel that atones for our sins and saves us from death, he is preachıg Christ. When the apostle John writes of the revelation of the Father nd the eternal life through Him, he is writing about Christ. When James, ıe pastor of the church at Jerusalem, speaks of the great lawgiver and ıdge, he is talking about Christ. And when the author of the epistle to the Hebrews speaks of the great High Priest in heaven and the mediator etween God and man, he is talking about Christ. The Christian faith is :hrist. Take that away—take the Lord out of it—and it is nothing.

The Gospel that Paul preached was Christ and Him crucified, and the ower of it, the effect of it, upon the Galatians was glorious indeed. It was miraculous. It took the whole believing multitude of them out of idolatry and paganism and set them in the glorious liberty of the Son of God. The light of heaven was on their brow. Their lips cried, "Abba, Father," and the presence and power of Christ was in their hearts. They were a new people. They arose in Christ to liberty and life, inspired by the glorious new life in Jesus. Indeed, the transformation was miraculous.

August 21

Romans 8:12–27

WE CANNOT LOSE

And if children, then heirs; heirs of God, and joint-heirs with Christ; if so be that we suffer with him, that we may be also glorified together (8:17).

When I began to preach, my first churches were in the country. I observed that young men with whom I went to school were called to famed pulpits and high-steepled churches. I was left out in the country. I used to wonder if God had forgotten where I was, if God even remembered my name. But as I look back over it now, I realize that giving me those years in rural churches was the best thing God ever did for me as a preacher.

God moves in a mysterious way
His wonders to perform;
He plants His footstep in the sea
And rides upon the storm.

His purposes will ripen fast,
Unfolding every hour;
The bud may have a bitter taste,
But sweet will be the flower.

Blind unbelief is sure to err
And scan His work in vain.
God is His own Interpreter
And he will make it plain.

Back of your life, back of human history, and back of the whole universe in which we live is the sovereign purpose and will of God. He guides us toward the ultimate and final consummation when we as joint-heirs with our Lord shall inherit the kingdom. Comforting and triumphant, His will is victorious. We cannot lose!

August 22

Romans 8:28–34

A LOST CAUSE?

And we know that all things work together for good to them that love God, to them who are the called according to his purpose (8:28).

Many years ago, when I was a youth, I read a book by a great missionary, Mrs. Howard Taylor, entitled *Borden of Yale.* Mr. and Mrs. Howard Taylor (he, the son of Hudson Taylor, the founder of the China Inland Mission) came to Baylor University in my freshman year to speak to our volunteer band. It was through this visit that I bought the book about a young millionaire missionary who belonged to the Borden family, the family who founded Borden Milk Company. In his twenties, in the springtime of his life, and just as he was beginning his missionary work on a foreign field, the young man suddenly died.

Was it a defeat? A despair? A lost cause? A poem in that book by an unknown author has stayed with me through the years. God's cause is never defeated. Note the triumphant tone sounded in that poem.

On the far reef the breakers
    Recoil in shattered foam.
Yet still the sea behind them
    Urges its forces home;
Its chant of triumph surges
    Through all the thunderous din—
The wave may break in failure,
    But the tide is sure to win.

O mighty sea, thy message
    In changing spray is cast:
Within God's plans of progress
    It matters not at last

How wide the shores of evil,
How strong the reefs of sin—
The wave may be defeated.
But the tide is sure to win.

August 23

Romans 8:35–39

THE GENERATION GAP

Nor height, nor depth, nor any other creature, shall be able to separate us from the love of God, which is in Christ Jesus our Lord (8:39).

T. DeWitt Talmadge was one of the most unique preachers of American history. He described the conversion of his family. His grandparents went to hear Charles G. Finney preach. Wonderfully converted, they returned home to try to win their children to Jesus. The children smiled and went off to a party. We say that there is a generation gap today; actually there has always been a generation gap. As the children left the house, the mother said, "I'm going to stay on my knees, praying for your salvation until you come back." When they came back, there was that dear mother who had found the Lord down on her knees, praying for those children.

The next day the parents heard their daughter weeping in her room. They went upstairs, opened the door, and there she was under deep conviction. She said, "One of my brothers is in the barn, and one is in the wagon shed, both under deep conviction." They went out to the barn, and there was Elijah Talmadge, who later became a preacher, bowed down before God. They went to the wagon shed, and there was David, the father of T. DeWitt Talmadge, under great conviction from God. The entire family was saved. They lived in a little village, and word soon spread of the marvelous grace of God upon the Talmadge family. When Sunday came, more than two hundred people accepted Jesus as their Savior in the church service. The effects of the atonement of our Lord are incomparable. They are indescribable. They are beyond what tongue, pen, poem, or song could ever tell.

Romans 10:1–8

FROM DESPAIR TO REVIVAL

Brethren, my heart's desire and prayer to God for Israel is, that they might be saved (10:1).

A mission in Africa had fallen into despair. One day the tribal chief appeared before the mission and said, "I hereby renounce the Christian faith. I am going back to my heathen gods."

In desperation the mission quit its work and bowed before the Lord in prayer and intercession. As a result, a great, sweeping Pentecostal revival swept through the tribe. Even the tribal chief began preaching the gospel of the Son of God. The word he used to proclaim the gospel was literally translated, "Joy is killing me." We can grease all the wheels that turn in the organized life of the church, but the church will finally come to a standstill, unless it is bathed in prayer and the whole foundation is laid upon intercession and appeal to God.

A godly minister named Richard Newton, a preacher of great power in the nineteenth century, wrote:

> The principal cause of my leanness and unfruitfulness is owing to an unaccountable backwardness to pray. I can write or read or converse or hear with a ready heart; but prayer is more spiritual and inward than any of these, and the more spiritual any duty is the more my carnal heart is apt to start from it. Prayer and patience and faith are never disappointed. When I can find my heart in frame and liberty for prayer, everything else is comparatively easy.

One need not decry the organized life of our church any more than he would decry the minister's preparation in study. But God does not work only in the brilliance of the pastor nor does the Spirit necessarily move in the finely tuned organized life of the church. There has to be something over and beyond if power is to come from God.

You can build a house without prayer. You can run a business without prayer. You can live in the carnal world and enjoy it without prayer. But you cannot do God's business without the Lord.

August 25

Romans 10:9–15

A MIRACLE OF GRACE

For whosoever shall call upon the name of the Lord shall be saved (10:13).

Some years ago West Dallas became famous because Bonnie Parker, Clyde Barrow, and Raymond and Floyd Hamilton—notorious robbers and outlaws—grew up there. Hattie Rankin Moore accepted the Lord and was baptized. She became deeply interested in West Dallas. When Raymond Hamilton was electrocuted in the penitentiary at Huntsville, Texas, she stayed up all night with the mother of that prodigal boy.

Raymond Hamilton had a brother serving a life term in Alcatraz and Hattie Moore was also interested in him. When she learned that I was going to San Francisco, she asked me to visit Floyd Hamilton in Alcatraz.

After crossing the bay and going through extensive security investigation, I was locked up in an iron cubicle with Floyd Hamilton. We talked for more than an hour, and at the end of the hour we knelt together on the steel floor of the prison. He clasped my hand warmly, giving his heart to the Lord Jesus. He said, "If God ever lets me out, the first thing I will do is come to Dallas and walk down the aisle in the church, and I will be baptized in confession of my faith in the Lord Jesus."

As the years passed, Hattie Rankin Moore died. Floyd Hamilton was pardoned, and he came down the aisle of this church and was baptized. From that day until this he has gone from city to city witnessing to the love and forgiveness of God in Christ Jesus. That is a miracle of grace.

August 26

Romans 11:1–36

THE PERIL OF BONDAGE

According as it is written, God hath given them the spirit of slumber, eyes that they should not see, and ears that they should not hear; unto this day (11:8).

We do not need to do anything to be damned in this life. All we need do is to fail to respond. As the lack of response characterizes our lives, we will find ourselves unable to respond. That is a strange fact of life.

Take my arm and bind it to my side, leaving it bound for a certain period of time. Then loose the bandage, and I will not be able to raise it or to use it. The nerves would have atrophied.

If I close my eye and leave it closed for a certain period of time, I will not be able to see out of it. It will have lost its ability to react to wave lengths. I would be blind.

It gives you a strange feeling to see the fish in Mammoth Cave in Kentucky. They are just like all other fish. They have sockets where their eyes ought to be, but they have no eyes. For generations they have lived in that dark cave in Kentucky, and now they have lost the ability to see.

We are like that in our souls and in our volitional will. If we do not respond, the day may come when we cannot respond. The volitional will can cease to be able to respond; it will have atrophied.

August 27

Romans 14:1–23

KNEELING TO PRAY

For it is written, As I live, saith the Lord, every knee shall bow to me, and every tongue shall confess to God (14:11).

A stranger from Great Britain once visited the Continental Congress in America. He was eager to see George Washington, and he asked a man in the hall, "Which one of those men is George Washington?"

The stranger replied to the visitor, "When the Congress goes to prayer, the one who kneels is General George Washington." There is a beautiful and meaningful testimony in a kneeling man.

August 28

1 Corinthians 1:1–17

HE COULD NOT THROW THE ROCKS

God is faithful, by whom ye were called unto the fellowship of his Son Jesus Christ our Lord (1:9).

George Whitefield, one of the preachers from Oxford, was denied the pulpits of England. Therefore, he preached outside in the Commons or on a riverbank. One day when George Whitefield came to preach at Exeter in southwest England, a ruffian came whose pockets were filled with rocks. He was going to break up the meeting. He stood there and began listening to George Whitefield. He said, "I don't want to throw these rocks at him in the prayer so I'll wait until the prayer is over." Then Mr. Whitefield read his text. The ruffian said, "I'm not going to throw these rocks at him while he is reading the Bible. I'll wait until the text is read." And when he had read the text, George Whitefield launched into his message about the grace of God in Christ Jesus.

The ruffian never threw the rocks. After the message, he made his way to the preacher and said, "I've come here with my pockets full of rocks to break up this meeting, but instead God has broken up my heart." The man was saved, gloriously converted right there on the spot. That is the effect of the preaching of the Gospel of the grace of God in Christ Jesus.

August 29

1 Corinthians 1:18–31

THE HARVEST FROM PREACHING

For after that in the wisdom of God the world by wisdom knew not God, it pleased God by the foolishness of preaching to save them that believe (1:21).

When Paul stood before Felix and Drusilla, he did his best. He preached the gospel, though he never did win Felix or Drusilla to the Lord.

That is the way with our testimony. We enter a great soul-winning appeal, but not everyone is going to listen. A person will fail in many attempts, appeals, and invitations. The Lord Jesus did not win the rich young ruler. Nor did He succeed in winning the Sadducees, the scribes, and the elders. In fact, they crucified Him. Nevertheless, He won some. God always will do that for us when we are faithful, when we witness, and when we testify. Not all will turn, believe, and be saved, but some will.

In my own heart, I have the same spirit that Spurgeon had when he was accosted about the futility of preaching to those who were not chosen in the sovereignty and elective purpose of God. He said, "But, sir, when I preach and am faithful to the Word, there will always be some who are chosen who will be saved."

That is our strength and our comfort. Wherever we have opportunity, we should invite others to the Lord, deliver the message of Christ, say a good word about Jesus, and encourage in the faith. Many will not listen or respond, but some will. You did, I did, and I bless God for those who preached the gospel to me. I listened, and I praise His name for the grace of God that saved me!

August 30

1 Corinthians 2:1–9

LET ME REST IN THEE

But as it is written, Eye hath not seen, nor ear heard, neither have entered into the heart of man, the things which God hath prepared for them that love him (2:9).

When I was a young man, I heard of a great scientist and doctor, Alexis Carrell, who had kept a chicken heart alive for twenty-seven years. He stopped the experiment because he found he could keep it alive forever by feeding it and taking away the waste. Science can do the same with the protoplasm in our bodies. To encourage such an artificial method of extending life implies that it is terrible to die. We keep protoplasm alive as long as we can because death is so horrible.

Can you believe that God has so forgotten us, and heaven is so blotted out against us, that with our last breath we must strive to breathe yet one more time? If there is work I can do and a task that I might be able to offer to God, then may God give me health, strength, wisdom, and length of days to do it. But when my task is finished and my work is done, then, Lord, let me rest in Thee.

To the Christian, death is not a horrible thing. Thanks be to God who has given us every treasure, every assurance, and every hope in Christ Jesus our Lord!

August 31

1 Corinthians 3:1–10

THROUGH STAINED-GLASS WINDOWS

I have planted, Apollos watered; but God gave the increase (3:6).

Men in the kingdom are different! They are different in affinities and predilections. They are different in personalities and in idiosyncrasies. They are different in temperament and abilities. The grace of God is not like a steam roller that irons out all the wrinkles of our individualities. We are still ourselves, though serving God. I think of the many preachers I have heard in my lifetime. They are so different. I think of a man like the elder Gypsy Smith. I think of a man like B. B. Crim, the Texas cowboy. They are preaching the same message, and yet they are so fundamentally diverse in approach, thought, and presentation. There is just one sun, but look at it through a stained-glass window. The same light shines through red, blue, yellow, and green. God's people in His kingdom are like that.

The prophets were like that. Amos was a country preacher. When you read his book you can almost smell the fresh, open forests out in the fields. He talks like a country man. He uses the language and imagery of a farmer. But Isaiah was a court preacher, and we notice his poetic imagery, his chaste and courtly language, yet both men were prophets of God. God uses us all in our diversities.

September 1

1 Corinthians 3:11–23

THE COLD WATERS OF DEATH

And ye are Christ's; and Christ is God's (3:23).

After a long and eventful life, Alfred, Lord Tennyson, wrote the immortal lines of "Crossing the Bar." This poem expresses for us all the hope of seeing Jesus when we cross the cold waters of death.

Sunset and evening star,
    And one clear call for me!
And may there be no moaning of the bar,
    When I put out to sea,

But such a tide as moving seems asleep,
    Too full for sound and foam,
When that which drew from out the boundless deep
    Turns again home.

Twilight and evening bell,
    And after that the dark!
And may there be no sadness of farewell,
    When I embark;

For tho' from out our bourne of Time and Place
    The flood may bear me far,
I hope to see my Pilot face to face
    When I have crossed the bar.

September 2

1 Corinthians 4:1–21

A FOOL FOR CHRIST

We are fools for Christ's sake, but ye are wise in Christ; we are weak, but ye are strong; ye are honorable, but we are despised (4:10).

When I was a high school student in Amarillo, I took part in the forensic extracurricular activities. I won a silver loving cup for memorizing a famous patriotic address and delivering it. I was also a debater. Donald Honey and I represented our school all over West Texas debating other teams. We spoke before every civic club in the city of Amarillo.

The biggest law firm in Amarillo asked me to visit them. They said, "We will send you to college and pay for your education." Being poor and not knowing whence the money would come for me to attend school, I was moved by the tremendous invitation. They offered to send me through college and law school if in the summer time I could work for the firm. When I was graduated with a law degree, I could then become a partner in their law firm. When I replied that I could not accept the offer because God had called me to be a preacher and a pastor, they exclaimed, "How could a young man like you waste your life being a preacher?"

To the secular world, Christianity is a fanaticism and a madness. They do not understand our commitment.

September 3

1 Corinthians 6:1–20

THE TEMPLE OF GOD

What? know ye not that your body is the temple of the Holy Ghost which is in you, which ye have of God, and ye are not your own? (6:19).

Dr. W. F. Powell, when he was pastor of the First Baptist Church of Nashville, Tennessee, called me one day and said, "I am sending to you a young man by the name of John Clifford. He is the most promising young preacher I have ever seen in my life. He has just held a revival meeting for us and God poured out His Spirit upon the meeting."

John Clifford came to see me, and I was amazed. He was one of the most handsome young men I had ever seen. He was about six feet four inches tall and had beautiful curly hair. He was a magnificent specimen, and he was a man of God. I said to him, "We shall arrange for your coming here to lead our people in a glorious revival meeting."

He came. Some time later, unknown to me, he was seated at the back of the auditorium. After the service was over, when everyone had left, one of the most disheveled, dirty-looking, unkempt men I ever saw came and spoke to me. He said, "Pastor, do you know who I am?" I answered, "No, I never saw you before." He said, "I am John Clifford." He died a young man, diseased, and in delirium from alcohol.

September 4

1 Corinthians 9:1–16

ARE THERE FOES?

For though I preach the gospel, I have nothing to glory of: for necessity is laid upon me; yea, woe is unto me, if I preach not the gospel! (9:16).

Some years ago when I was in Oklahoma, I heard of two Southern Baptist missionaries named Hogan and Hayes. In the midst of an awesome trial, Hogan said to his friend Hayes, "I am quitting; I am going back home. This is too much."

So Hayes said to his friend and fellow missionary, "I understand, I know; but before you go, would you sit down and sing just one song with me?"

Bradford Hayes got his guitar and strummed the tune as they sang:

Am I a soldier of the cross,
A follower of the Lamb?
And shall I fear to own His cause,
Or blush to speak His name?

Must I be carried to the skies
On flow'ry beds of ease,
While others fought to win the prize,
And sailed thro' bloody seas?

Are there no foes for me to face?
Must I not stem the flood?
Is this vile world a friend to grace,
To help me on to God?

Sure I must fight, if I would reign;
Increase my courage, Lord;
I'll bear the toil, endure the pain,
Supported by Thy word.

When they got through singing the song, Hogan turned to Hayes and said, "I am staying."

God never called us to flowery beds of ease. He called us to be His workers, His servants, and His witnesses. However life may turn in His gracious hands, let us affirm "to God be the glory." The tears of Paul's discipleship and apostleship are always evident.

September 5

1 Corinthians 10:1–33

THE DIVINE SCREWS

There hath no temptation taken you but such as is common to man: but God is faithful, who will not suffer you to be tempted above that ye are able; but will with the temptation also make a way to escape, that ye may be able to bear it (10:13).

Some time ago a baby boy was born with a deformed foot. And as the lad grew, that deformed foot became a severe handicap to the little fellow. His father, loving him very much, took the boy to doctor after doctor, but none could help. They gave him up.

That father got many books on the subject and read and studied them. He learned about every bone in the foot. He studied every articulation—the tendons, the nerves, the muscles. He made a strange-looking box with screws and felt washers at various angles. Then he took his son and put that deformed foot in that strange-looking box and tightened those screws. The little boy cried, and the father tightened the screws until the boy was in agony. The father would come home from work in the evening and the little boy would cry to his father, but the father would tighten the screws. Day after day, week after week, month after month, when the father would come home from work, the boy would cry in agony, and the father would mingle his tears with the boy's as he tightened the screws.

The day came when the father unloosed the screws, opened the box, and said, "Son, stand up." And the boy stood erect for the first time. As the days passed, the boy gained strength in his foot and walked erect. There was no deformity. That boy grew to be a man and one day, over the grave of his father, he wept tears of gratitude and loving appreciation.

Maybe the father, being human, tightened a screw just one turn too much, but our heavenly Father never does. He knows exactly how much we can bear.

September 6

1 Corinthians 12:1–11

IT IS GOD!

But all these worketh that one and the selfsame Spirit, dividing to every man severally as he will (12:11).

When I was in college and seminary, I looked at some of my fellow students and thought, "I do believe God makes mistakes." I never in my life saw such unpromising students for the ministry and the work of the Lord. Some of them just could not learn. But as time has gone on and these years have passed, I review sometimes in memory those fellow students. Some of those men I thought were the most unpromising are the greatest chaplains in the United States Army, the Air Corps, and the rest of the branches of our armed services. Others of them are magnificent professors and teachers. Some of them are the finest denominational leaders and missionaries, strategists, and statesmen who walk the face of the earth. When we equate God's gift with a natural endowment, we have missed it. It is not how a person looks. It is not his stature. It is not his physical form or presence, whether majestic or menial. It is God! It is God who makes him shine and flame and burn. It is God who makes him resplendent and incandescent. It is a gift of the Lord, a grace gift.

Thomas Chalmers had a sterile and barren ministry in a little place in Scotland called Kilmeny. But then he had an experience with the Lord. When the people went to church expecting those dull, dry services, all of a sudden they had a burning flame in front of them. The people were amazed and overwhelmed by the miraculous transformation of Thomas Chalmers. It was a grace gift.

September 7

1 Corinthians 12:12–18

THE BODY OF CHRIST

But now hath God set the members every one of them in the body, as it hath pleased him (12:18).

The Holy Spirit bestows upon us different gifts. No two of us are alike, as no two leaves are alike, and as no two snowflakes are alike. But however we differ, we all bear testimony of the one saving Spirit.

The difference between the spiritually minded person and the materialistically minded person is this. The materialist sees nothing but an infinite collection of unconnected, unrelated, broken, distorted, fragmentary, disordered facts. He is the existential philosopher. For him, life, the world, existence, and creation have no meaning. All came from nowhere, and all are going nowhere.

But to the spiritually minded person, every created thing has a part in the divine purpose of God. All are parts to make up the ultimately perfect whole. As the spiritual person progresses in understanding, he sees the number of basic laws diminish until at last they all are reduced to one—namely, the one that lies beneath the innumerable phenomena of nature—the Spirit of God. All living unity is spiritual, not physical; it is inward, not outward. The works of the Spirit of God are ever characterized by diversity, complexity, and multifariousness—not sameness.

Our unity is not that we are all alike in a dull, wearisome monotony, but that we are all made in His image. Our unity is not one of outward uniformity but one of inward motivation. We are all activated by the same living principle, the same quickening Spirit, the same animating vision. We are all moving toward the same holy end.

September 8

1 Corinthians 12:19–28

THE GIFT OF THE FRAIL

Now ye are the body of Christ, and members in particular (12:27).

We all, even the feeblest members, have a worthy contribution to make to the body of Christ. Without these humblest members, the body is not complete.

For more than half a century the First Baptist Church has conducted noonday, pre-Easter services in a downtown theater. My illustrious predecessor, Dr. George W. Truett, conducted them for twenty-five years, and I have continued that tradition for more than thirty-five years.

Long ago, when I had just come to be the pastor of the church, I finished delivering the message at one of those noonday services and walked through the front lobby of the theater. There I was met by a small, elderly, stooped lady, dressed in an old-fashioned, black dress. She said to me, "I have been so eager to see my new pastor, but I am too old and sick to go to church. Since today was such a beautiful, warm day, a neighbor brought me downtown to attend this service in order that I might see you. I wish I could help you but I am too old, too sick, and too poor. All I can do is pray for you."

I put my arms around that stooped and aged lady and said, "All you can do is pray! My sweet, little mother in Christ, that means more than anything else in the world. You speak as though it were so small. No. It is the greatest help of all. God hear you as you call my name before the throne of grace and ask His power to fall upon me."

September 9

1 Corinthians 13:1–13

THE GIFT OF GIVING

And though I bestow all my goods to feed the poor, and though I give my body to be burned, and have not charity, it profiteth me nothing (13:3).

Paul does not say that philanthropy in itself, if unaccompanied by love, profits nothing. A bequest of a million dollars will profit an institution whether bequeathed in anger to rob a hated son, offered in vainglory for the praise of others, or presented in ostentation.

Philanthropy that blesses a good cause can be a selfish instrument ministering to one's hope to be known as a generous soul. It can be used to advertise one's affluence or to attempt to buy one's way into heaven or to uphold one's image in a business community. But without love, the philanthropy profits the giver nothing.

Andrew Fuller once asked an English nobleman for a donation to William Carey's mission endeavor. The nobleman in contempt flung a gold crown on the table in response to the appeal. Andrew Fuller returned it to the rich man, saying, "My Lord demands the heart. Without the heart, I cannot take it." The nobleman felt the rebuke. Realizing that he could give and lose or give and receive, the nobleman accepted the returned gold coin. Then he sat down at his desk and wrote out a generous check for the mission enterprise. "There," he said, "take this; this comes from the heart." James Russell Lowell wrote:

> Not what we give, but what we share,
> For the gift without the giver is bare.

September 10

1 Corinthians 15:1–19

THE LIVING IMAGE OF HIS MIND

Yea, and we are found false witnesses of God; because we have testified of God that he raised up Christ: whom he raised not up, if so be that the dead rise not (15:15).

One of the most unusual of all prefaces to a book is that printed in 1515 in the Textus Receptus, the first Greek New Testament. Erasmus wrote these words: "These holy pages [referring to the Greek New Testament] will summon the living image of His mind. They will give you Christ Himself, talking, healing, dying, rising, the whole Christ in a word. They will give Him to you in an intimacy so close that He would be less visible to you if He stood before your very eyes." What an amazing statement! Christ is revealed to us in the Word of God more fully, more gloriously, more intimately than if we looked at Him standing in our presence with our naked eyes. The Christian faith is Christ, and it is our response of devotion to and love for the Lord that makes us Christians. It is Christ.

Let me illustrate. You can have Confucianism without Confucius. If you just gather together all the maxims of ancient Chinese culture, you can have Confucianism. You can have Hinduism without their sages and their mahatmas. You can have Christian Science without Mary Baker Glover Patterson Eddy. You do not need any of them, but you cannot have Christianity without Christ. The Christian faith is our Lord. And it is love for our Lord that makes it ours.

September 11

1 Corinthians 15:20–34

VICTORY IN DEATH

For as in Adam all die, even so in Christ shall all be made alive (15:22).

Years ago when I began my ministry among very poor people, they did not embalm their dead. Because they had no money, the poor buried their dead in a cheap, box-like coffin. At the cemetery, the family would stay and listen to the clods of dirt being shoveled on the box below.

Death had a harsh visage and those dear, poor people to whom I ministered wept and cried. But whether I hold the funeral today in beautiful surroundings in a marble chapel or whether I conduct it in a rural cemetery, it is still the same. There are no degrees in death. But there is victory for those who die in the Lord.

September 12

1 Corinthians 15:35–58

A DEFEATED CHRISTIAN

But thanks be to God, which giveth us the victory through our Lord Jesus Christ (15:57).

A defeated Christian is a travesty on the name of God. It is easier to smile than to frown. It takes sixty-four muscles of the face to frown, only thirteen to smile. God wants His people to be a happy people, a walking exclamation mark, not a walking question mark. We are to live on Sunshine Square, facing the heavenly side of the street. Even though the theology may be wrong, the spirit is right in the little song that the child Pippa sings on her one-day-a-year vacation from her toilsome work in the silk mills.

> The year's at the spring
> The day's at the morn;
> Morning's at seven;
> The hillside's dew-pearled;
> The lark's on the wing;
> The snail's on the thorn;
> God's in his heaven—
> All's right with the world.
>
> —Robert Browning's
> *Pippa Passes*

It is easy for us to become a prey, to be bogged down with discouragement and depression. There are so many who are ready to lament that the kingdom of God is an impossible dream and that the organized church is in shambles. It is easy to be persuaded that the whole world of Christendom is moving backward. Ecclesiastical pallbearers are a dime a dozen. Some of the church's critics are like hungry buzzards who cannot wait until the last trace of life is gone to pick the flesh from the bones.

Oh, that we might look to the heavenly Father with thanksgiving for His blessings and with confidence in His providential care!

September 13

2 Corinthians 1:1–7

THE MEANING OF SUFFERING

And our hope of you is steadfast, knowing, that as ye are partakers of the sufferings, so shall ye be also of the consolation (1:7).

A missionary named James Chalmers of England was sent to the cannibals of New Guinea, that big island north of Australia. Addressing the mission group that sent him, he said:

> Recall the twenty-one years. Give me back all of its experience. Give me its shipwrecks, give me its standings in the face of death, give it me; surrounded with savages with spears and clubs. Give it me back again with the spears flying about me, with a club knocking me to the ground. Give it me back, and I will still be your missionary!

He returned to New Guinea and was slain. He laid down his life, murdered by those same vicious cannibals. Yet those were the people who helped our American airmen during World War II when they were shot down and washed upon the shores of the South Pacific islands. Instead of killing and boiling the American servicemen for food, these former cannibals won them to the Lord.

God's purposes for us are known only in the sufferings of Him who is the Lamb slain from before the foundation of the earth. It is the Christ of the cross alone who is able to interpret the meaning of our suffering.

September 14

2 Corinthians 1:8–24

THE SENTENCE OF DEATH

But we had the sentence of death in ourselves, that we should not trust in ourselves, but in God which raiseth the dead (1:9).

Recently I reread a description of the great Black Plague that swept over London in 1665 and 1666. The wagons went down the street each morning ringing a bell as the driver announced, "Bring out your dead; bring out your dead." There were so many dying that they had no time for funerals. They just gathered the bodies and buried them in vast common graves. In those awful and tragic days, an awesome fire destroyed London. London has fewer marks of medieval times than any of the great cities of Europe, simply because it was all destroyed and burned.

Then I read about the preachers during that time. Many of them fled their pulpits and churches, but those who stayed were not preaching about trivialities, inconsequentials, insignificances, and ephemoralities.

Those preachers preached to the people about life and death, about God, about the judgment, and about how to be saved.

What is the difference between the preacher who would preach in those awesome days of the Black Plague in London and the way a preacher preaches in the pulpit today? In that day death was imminent. Today it is a little further removed, but nonetheless coming. We have the same responsibility today to point people to Christ, that they might be saved, as Christians were in the days of Paul, in the days of the Black Plague, in every generation. We are a dying people, and we need God.

September 15

2 Corinthians 3:1–18

PREACHING IN THE STREETS

But we all, with open face beholding as in a glass the glory of the Lord, are changed into the same image from glory to glory, even as by the Spirit of the Lord (3:18).

The Christian faith is factual. It is never hypothetical. It is never metaphysical. It is never speculative. The state church of England pushed John Wesley out and did not allow him to preach in an Anglican church. So John Wesley, George Whitefield, and Charles Wesley conducted their services out in the streets wherever people would gather to listen. Their heavenly efforts saved the nation from the bloody French Revolution.

One day Wesley was preaching in Epworth, when the angry neighbors gathered a wagonload of his converts and took them all to the magistrate. They forgot to think through the accusation. The magistrate looked upon that wagonload of Wesleyans, turned to the angry neighbors, and asked, "What is the accusation?" There was long silence. One of them finally spoke up and said, "They think that they pray better than other people." Then another long silence followed. Another one spoke up and said "They pray all day long." A long silence followed again. Then a man spoke up and said, "They converted my wife."

This interested the magistrate who said, "How was that?" The man replied, "Well, she had a tongue that was as sharp as a razor, and now she is meek as a lamb." The magistrate said, "Take these people back, and may God grant that they can convert the whole town of Epworth!"

September 16

2 Corinthians 4:1–18

A BALL OF FIRE

While we look not at the things which are seen, but at the things which are not seen: for the things which are seen are temporal; but the things which are not seen are eternal (4:18).

When I began preaching at seventeen years of age, I listened to those marvelous experiences that people claimed to have had in the Lord. They saw balls of fire from heaven, they saw lights, they saw angels from heaven. I had no experience like that. I was saved as a ten-year-old boy. As I listened to those unusual testimonies, I concluded that I was not born again. I was not saved. I was not regenerated.

When I was a youth beginning to preach, on Sundays I would preach in my little church, then every night during the week I would get down by the side of my bed and cry unto God, saying, "O God, I am not saved. I am not really born again. I am not actually a Christian, for I have not seen a light, I have not seen an angel, and I have not seen a ball of fire from heaven." Those were the most agonizing days in the world. All that I had done as a ten-year-old boy was in faith to accept Jesus as my Savior. With many tears I had gone down to the front of the church and given my hand to the pastor; I told him that I had given my heart to God, and I asked that I might be baptized and become a member of the church.

As the years have gone by, I have become convinced without any doubt that my salvation is as certain as my Savior. I was saved just by trusting in the Lord. Never an angel. Never a light. Never a ball of fire. Never anything apart from Jesus Christ and His atonement! I am saved by accepting the Lord, by trusting in Jesus, His Word, and His promise.

September 17

2 Corinthians 5:1–14

WE CANNOT FORGET

For the love of Christ constraineth us; because we thus judge, that if one died for all, then were all dead (5:14).

A North American Indian stood up and said, "There came to our tribe a man who told us about and extolled the God of the white man. We told him to leave. And there came another man and he said, 'Do not drink any more firewater. Do not get drunk, and do not steal.' We paid no attention to him. Then there came a man and he told us about a God who came down from heaven to live among us, who so loved us that He shared our lives and died in our place for our sins, and who opened the doors whereby we might be saved and enter heaven." And the Indian said, "I could never forget it."

Somehow I have that persuasion about all of mankind, whether they accept it or not, whether they believe it or not, whether they are saved or not, somehow they cannot forget it. The world is not the same since Jesus died in it. And this planet somehow is not like other planets because here the foot of the cross was set, and Jesus was raised beneath the sky. And we who have embraced the Lord cannot forget it. This He did for you and for me. "Who loved me and gave himself for me." It is the love of Christ that constrains us. It is the goodness of God that brings us to repentance (Rom. 2:4). It is the appealing, atoning grace, the mercy, the sobs, the tears, and the blood of our Lord that brings us and binds us to God. I somehow cannot forget it.

September 18

2 Corinthians 5:15–17

A NEW MAN

Therefore if any man be in Christ, he is a new creature: old things are passed away; behold, all things are become new (5:17).

An unusual story illustrates the transforming power of the grace of God in Christ Jesus. There was a man who was a drunkard. He took his paycheck and spent it on alcohol. He lived in the dirt and vomit of the gutter. His children were ragged and hungry; his wife was neglected and starved; his home was a shambles. His furniture was repossessed and the family lived in an open, barren house. In the kind and merciful providences of God, the transforming power of the cross of Christ reached down to this runkard and he became a new man, a regenerated man. The furniture 'as returned to the home, the payments on the mortgage continued, and iere was born a new life and a new day.

Then one of his old cronies began to ridicule him about becoming a 'hristian and about believing the Bible. One of the barbs of sarcasm and dicule concerned something that Jesus did in His miraculous power— ırning water into wine. That critic said sarcastically, "Do you mean to tell ie that you believe that stuff in the Bible? Take that story of the Lord hanging water into wine, do you believe such a thing as that?"

And the man replied, "Sir, I am no theologian. I'm an unlettered and neducated man and I am not able to answer. I don't know how He did it. ll I know is this: that in my life he changed beer into furniture, whiskey ıto mortgage payments, and drunkenness into the worship of God, and ıat is good enough for me!"

All the days of my conscious life I have studied the Bible. All I know is ıis: aboundingly I see God's grace around me, and that is good enough ɔr me. I see the goodness of God working in the lives of our children, and ıat is good enough for me.

September 19

2 Corinthians 5:18–21

N AMBASSADOR FOR HEAVEN

Now then we are ambassadors for Christ, as though God did eseech you by us: we pray you in Christ's stead, be ye reconciled to od (5:20).

I remember reading of an incident in the life of the great statesman, ohn R. Mott, one of the finest Christian leaders who ever lived in America. lott, a missionary to Japan, was chosen by President Calvin Coolidge to e the United States Ambassador to Japan. Mr. Mott replied, "Mr. Presi-ent, God has called me to be an ambassador from the courts of heaven, nd since that call, I have been deaf to all other invitations."

The first priority and the great mission and goal in life is to be a worthy 'itness, ambassador, and emissary from the courts of God, representing ıe grace of God in the Lord Jesus Christ.

September 20

2 Corinthians 6:1–10

DEATHBED REPENTANCE

For he saith, I have heard thee in a time accepted, and in the day of salvation have I succored thee: behold, now is the accepted time; behold, now is the day of salvation (6:2).

In the city of Dallas a famous businessman was ill in the hospital. I went to see him. He said to me, "The doctors say I will surely die. Will you kneel down by my side and pray? Tell God that if He will spare my life, I will serve Him all the rest of my days. You will see me in every service at your church. I will be a faithful servant of God." I knelt by his side and, holding his hand, I told God for him that if the Lord would spare his life, he would serve Him the rest of his days. The man said, "Amen." God heard the prayer and blessed that man. He was given strength and length of days.

I never saw him in my congregation. He never even bothered to attend church, much less give his heart and life in service to Jesus. Finally, I buried him. He died outside the faith, without God and without hope.

We need to serve God *now.*

We need to repent *now.*

We need to be saved *now.*

Deathbed repentance is vain and futile.

September 21

2 Corinthians 9:1–15

A CHEERFUL GIVER

Every man according as he purposeth in his heart, so let him give; not grudgingly, and of necessity: for God loveth a cheerful giver (9:7).

Any young couple could woo and win and marry simply by pointing and grunting and (as I read about courtship in one country) rubbing their noses together. A missionary friend of mine described to me some years ago the marriage ceremony used by an old tribal chief. When the young brave found the maid of his choice and brought her before the chief for purposes of matrimony, the old chief looked at the boy and said, "Want 'er?" The brave then grunted affirmatively, "Unh!" The chief looked at the maiden and asked, "Want 'im?" She grunted affirmatively, "Unh!" The chief then snapped, "Got 'um!" And that was that! But where are the cake, the kisses, the orchids, the church bells, the wedding march, the preacher, and all the wonderful, wonderful things that make the day an occasion to remember forever? We have to confess the truth. We like the style of a thing.

If we, God's creatures, care so much for the manner in which a thing is done, how much more must God, in whose image we are created, care for it! He, too, loves the way a thing is done—the spirit of it, the heart of it, the manner of it. For example, I suppose God loves any kind of a giver. Some give grudgingly, with a miserly spirit, under the pressure of necessity. Does God like that? No, He only puts up with that. Then what does God like? God loves a cheerful giver. We may not give the biggest gift in the world; but what we have, let us give with all the gladness of heart and soul. And God delights in that spirit. He is pleased with the way it is done.

September 22

2 Corinthians 11:1–15

THE MASTER OF DECEIT

And no marvel; for Satan himself is transformed into an angel of light (11:14).

In the days of World War II, I remember seeing pictures of beautiful women on the front pages of the newspapers. These were pictures of alluring women in the employ of the enemy. These women were paid to seduce a high-ranking officer in order to discover military secrets and then deliver the secrets to the enemy.

That is how Satan works. He is beautiful and seductive but also treacherous. Satan can also be likened to the mind and voice of a brilliant and gifted theological professor. He speaks in learnedness and eloquence, but he denies the faith. He empties Scripture of its inspiration; he takes deity away from Christ and makes Him just another man. He robs the church of its hope of a glorious tomorrow. That is Satan. If I could picture Satan as he really is, I would picture him as a great, popular leader of government who comes forth as a champion of the people. He soothes the people into believing that he is their great benefactor and patron. He is smart, shrewd, and deceptive, but beyond his soft voice, there is destruction and ruin.

September 23

2 Corinthians 11:16–33

POURING OUT LIFE

If I must needs glory, I will glory of the things which concern mine infirmities (11:30).

On the front page of the *Dallas Morning News* there appeared the picture of a minister of the British government as he stood before a student group at the University of Glasgow. He was a strange-looking spectacle because the students, who evidently disliked the British government at that time, had come prepared for him. When he was introduced and stood on the platform, they pelted him with rotten eggs and vegetables and finally with flour. As I looked at the picture of the insults they planned and executed on that minister of the British government, my mind went back to an earlier occasion when in that same university another man had been introduced to the student group. On that day, the chancellor of the university presented to the young men of the University of Glasgow God's missionary, David Livingstone.

History records that when David Livingstone stood up and walked to the front of the dais to speak to the group, the students looked at him earnestly. They saw his hair burned crisp under the torrid, tropical sun. They saw his body wasted and emaciated with jungle fever. They saw his right arm hanging limp at his side, destroyed by the attack of a ferocious African lion. When the students looked at him, they stood up with one accord in awe and in silence before God's missionary. There is a power in consecration and devotion that grips the human heart and it is difficult to belittle or ridicule it.

The power of the church has always been in its consecration and in its devotion—in the blood of the martyrs, in the songs of those who praised God while they were being burned at the stake, in the pouring out of life unto death in behalf of the name of Christ.

September 24

2 Corinthians 12:1–9

SUFFICIENT GRACE

And he said unto me, My grace is sufficient for thee: for my strength is made perfect in weakness. Most gladly therefore will I rather glory in my infirmities, that the power of Christ may rest upon me (12:9).

Colchester, which is northeast of London, is the city where Charles Haddon Spurgeon was converted. In the city hall there is a beautiful marble room dedicated to the Colchester martyrs who were burned alive for their firm adherence to the faith. On the tablet is printed a heraldic motto, "No Cross: No Crown."

As I read of the Colchester martyrs, who were burned at the stake because they loved and read the Word of God, I could not help but think of one of the famous infidels of America, who, speaking before a popular audience about the tortures of the Inquisition, said, "There is not much of the martyr about me. I would have told those inquisitors, 'Now you write it down, anything you want me to confess, and I will sign it. You may have one God or a million; you may have one hell or a million, but stop persecuting me!'" He would have cowardly turned aside from his own cherished beliefs if thumbscrews were put on. What a difference the Word of God makes in a person! I believe God; I believe His Word.

September 25

2 Corinthians 12:10–21

THE COST OF COMMITMENT

And I will very gladly spend and be spent for you; though the more abundantly I love you, the less I be loved (12:15).

One of Hugh Latimer's sermons had greatly displeased his majesty King Henry VIII. The king demanded that the preacher publicly apologiz for his message of offense. Latimer, God's preacher, stood before Kin Henry VIII and read his text, the same one he had used the Sunday befor Then, addressing himself, he continued, "Hugh Latimer, dost thou kno before whom thou art this day to speak? To the high and mighty monarc the king's most excellent majesty, who can take away thy life if tho offendest: therefore, take heed that thou speakest not a word that ma displease. But then consider well, Hugh, dost thou not know from whenc thou comest—upon whose message thou are sent? Even by the great an mighty God, who is all-present, and who beholdeth all thy ways, and who i able to cast thy soul into hell! Therefore, take care that thou deliverest th message faithfully." Latimer proceeded with the same sermon he ha preached the preceding Sunday, but with considerably more energy!

Soft, supercilious, obsequious, sycophantic Christianity is an affront t God. Men such as Hugh Latimer spoke with great conviction and truth an were willing to seal it even with their lives.

September 26

Galatians 1:1–9

DISCERNING SPIRIT

As we said before, so say I now again, If any man preach any other gospel unto you than that ye have received, let him be accursed (1:9).

The famous French philosopher, Renan, was educated to be a ministe He was a professor in a theological school. He was the skeptic of skeptic yet he had such a romantic and dramatic attitude about Jesus that I have even quoted him in some of my own sermons. The things he would say were unusually superlative. But notice this observation. Dr. Pressence said of Renan, "Renan very skillfully undermines Christianity while profuse in its praise; he buries it in flowers. He comes to the tomb of the Savior not to weep and worship like the women of the Gospel, but to stifle with perfumes and spices any lingering spark of life in the religion of Jesus. He does not deal a blow with a sharp sword; no, he embalms. But the result is the same as though he had made a violent attack."

It is possible, literally, to destroy the Christian faith in sweetness, in perfume, and in broad-minded, convictionless liberalism. May God grant to us all a discerning spirit of wisdom to keep us true to *the* gospel.

September 27

Galatians 1:10–12

THE SHALLOWNESS OF BROAD-MINDEDNESS

For I neither received it of man, neither was I taught it, but by the revelation of Jesus Christ (1:12).

There are those who teach us not to reach any final conclusion but rather to keep our minds "open," and by that these liberal thinkers mean for us not to believe anything with finality. Let everything remain in solution, in limbo.

When one takes per se the position of broad-mindedness, he embraces with it an innate and congenital accompaniment that speaks of a cheap shallowness, like a river that is three miles broad and three inches deep. The only difference between a swamp and a river is that one has banks and runs in a channel, and the other is broad and spreads itself all over. It is possible to be so lacking in conviction that one is as spineless as though he were a jellyfish—without backbone, without strength, without "morphus," without form at all.

There was a broad-minded, liberal minister who resigned, and after his announced resignation one of his parishioners came up to him and said, "Oh, how we feel the loss in your leaving." The parishioner added, "You know, before you came, I cared not for God nor man nor the devil, but under your fine preaching I have come to love all three!"

God has not left us to our own devices. He has given a sure and certain word and timeless principles by which we are to govern our lives. There is no need to risk human frailty, but rather there is the assurance of divine wisdom in the revelation of Jesus Christ.

September 28

Galatians 2:1–21

A TOWERING VERSE

I am crucified with Christ: nevertheless I live; yet not I, but Christ liveth in me: and the life which I now live in the flesh I live by the faith of the Son of God, who loved me, and gave himself for me (2:20).

Sometimes in a great mountain range there will stand up—high, elevated, and lofty—a marvelous peak. One time while flying along the coast of Alaska, our Southern Baptist Missionary, Chron, said, "I've been flying along here for fourteen years and this is the first time I have ever seen the weather clear." It was a beautiful day and those mountain ranges were breath-taking. As we flew along, there came into view a peak towering above all the others—Mount Fairweather, rising fourteen thousand feet out of the blue ocean. Solid white, it looked like a gigantic snow cone.

There are texts in the Bible like that. In the great range there will be a towering verse that somehow has in it the very presence and breath of God. Pure, holy, piercing the blue of the sky, it also penetrates our deepest souls. This is one: "I am crucified with Christ: nevertheless I live; yet not I, but Christ liveth in me: and the life which I now live in the flesh I live by the faith of the Son of God, who loved me, and gave himself for me."

September 29

Galatians 3:1–11

ADDING TO THE GOSPEL

But that no man is justified by the law in the sight of God, it is evident: for, The just shall live by faith (3:11).

When Martin Luther was on his knees climbing up the Scala Sancta before the church of Saint John Lateran in Rome, trying to do penance, seeking to work his way into heaven, trying to find forgiveness of his sins by observing rituals, ceremonies, and the law, it was there that the verse from Galatians, as from Habakkuk, came like a thunderbolt into his soul, "And the just shall live by faith." He walked down those steps, back to Wittenberg, and he nailed the Ninety-five Theses on the door of the church and the Reformation was on! The great thundering instrument in the hands of Martin Luther was this book of Galatians with its text, "The just shall live by faith."

Today the one great heresy that constantly affects the Gospel of Christ is the Galatian heresy of trying to add something to faith in order that we might be saved, as though the grace of Christ, the cross of Christ, and the blood of Christ alone are not enough to save us. The heresy that one must believe Christ and add something else to the saving Gospel is ever with us and apparently shall be until the consummation of the age.

September 30

Galatians 3:12–24

BREAKING THE CHAIN

Wherefore the law was our schoolmaster to bring us unto Christ, that we might be justified by faith (3:24).

The keeping of the law is like a chain—one does not need to break all of the links to break the chain. Just break one link and the chain falls. It is thus with the law, Paul avows. One can try to keep all of the laws; but if he breaks only one of them, he is cursed. The Book says so. A man could be saved by keeping the law, but he would have to keep all of it; and when he broke one part of it, immediately he would fall into sin and be lost. Therefore, if we are ever saved, we are saved by faith, by trusting Christ, by casting ourselves upon the mercies of God.

The purpose of the law is to show us that we are sinners, to reveal to us our lost condition. We have faults, failures, shortcomings, and sins before God, doubly revealed to us in the Mosaic legislation. The *paidagogos* (Greek), the slave who in Roman life took the child by the hand and led the child to the teacher at the school, is the picture of the law, which Paul says, leads us to Christ, to confess to Him our shortcomings and our sins. The law shows us that we are a dying people who cannot save ourselves. If we are ever saved, we are saved in the love, mercy, and grace of the blessed Lord Jesus.

Galatians 4:1–20

THE ADOPTION OF A WAIF

To redeem them that were under the law, that we might receive the adoption of sons (4:5).

Years ago there walked down a city street a ragged little orphan newsboy. He passed by a beautiful mansion. The lawn was neatly kept, the house impressive, the driveway inviting. The lad wandered up the driveway and before he fully realized what he was doing, he rang the doorbell. Mr. Lowery, the owner of the spacious home, opened the door and looked down upon the frightened, surprised boy.

Not knowing what to say, the ragged newsboy blurted out, "Mister, do you have a little boy?"

Mr. Lowery, most amused, answered kindly. "No, son, Mrs. Lowery and I do not have any children."

The youngster replied in eagerness, "Oh, I'd give everything I own if I could be your little boy and run and play on this beautiful lawn."

Then in one of those unusual providences of life, Mr. Lowery turned and called his wife. The queenly woman walked down the expansive stairway in the hall and stood by the side of her husband as he asked, "Dear, would you like to have a little boy?"

She quickly replied, "Oh, yes!"

The big man turned to the lad and said, "Son, come in, come in."

As the boy walked into that palatial home, he kept his promise. He reached in his pocket and pulled out thirteen cents and offered the pennies to the big man, saying, "Sir, this is all that I have."

We are just like that when we offer to God what little we have to buy our salvation. But the big man took the boy's hand, closed it around his thirteen pennies, and said, "Son, you keep them, for I have more than enough for us both." And he took the lad into his house and adopted him. That is exactly what God has done for us! We were waifs, poor and outcast, but God has bestowed upon us the privilege of sonship. He adopted us into the family of heaven, and we are heirs and joint-heirs with Jesus Christ our elder brother.

October 2

Galatians 6:1–10

GOD IS NOT MOCKED

Be not deceived; God is not mocked: for whatsoever a man soweth, that shall he also reap (6:7).

We are all under the great judgmental commandments and visitations of the Almighty in heaven. All that God does is universal.

For example, gravity is a reflection of the hand of the Almighty. One finds gravity here in the earth. It affects the smallest things and the greatest things in God's creation. Gravity is in the stars, spheres, and planets, as well as on the moon. It is universal because God is universal. Fire is also universal, whether it be in the heat of the sun or in the earth or in the farthest star. All of God's character is revealed to us through His universality. Sowing and reaping are universal. Paul wrote, "Be not deceived; God is not mocked: for whatsoever a man soweth, that shall he also reap" (Gal. 6:7). There is no escape. The judgment of God pursues a person's wrongdoing. There is no hiding from it.

During the days of prohibition, I pastored in a small town that had only one store. The druggist, while selling his medicines, also sold bootleg whiskey under the counter. As the days passed, he became very affluent. He was not a Christian. I stood by his side and watched his twenty-four-year-old son die of cirrhosis of the liver caused by the liquor his father sold under the counter. Be not deceived; God's judgmental power is universal. God is not mocked.

The great Redeemer came to break that awesome judgment of the fire and fury of God against our sins that we might have hope in God.

October 3

Galatians 6:11–18

GLORYING IN THE CHRIST

But God forbid that I should glory, save in the cross of our Lord Jesus Christ, by whom the world is crucified unto me, and I unto the world (6:14).

On one occasion I went from Hong Kong to Macao, the Portuguese Colony now under the surveillance of Red China. I saw a most impressive sight. On a high hill with tremendous flights of steps leading up to it from the heart of the city is what remains of Saint Paul's Cathedral. All that is left is the facade of the church and on top of it a towering cross. In a violent earthquake, accompanied by fire, hurricane, and storm, the entire church was destroyed, but there remained that front wall with the cross rising upon the pinnacle.

John Bowring (1792–1872) visited Macao and was so impressed by the spectacular sight of the facade of that church with the cross at the zenith that he wrote the beautiful hymn, "In the Cross of Christ I Glory."

> In the cross of Christ I glory,
> Tow'ring o'er the wrecks of time;
> All the light of sacred story
> Gathers round its head sublime.
>
> Bane and blessing, pain and pleasure,
> By the cross are sanctified;
> Peace is there that knows no measure,
> Joys that thro' all time abide.

God has turned ugliness into beauty, and the curse into blessing, through the cross.

October 4

Ephesians 1:1–14

FREEDOM OF CHOICE

According as he hath chosen us in him before the foundation of the world, that we should be holy and without blame before him in love (1:4).

My whole life is bound up and enmeshed with a plan, a purpose, and a choice into which I do not enter at all. Freedom of choice belongs to moral accountability—I am morally responsible. But there is also in this world a sovereignty which is greater than my life, greater than history, and greater even than the creation of mankind. Those two things, the sovereignty of God and the free moral agency of mankind, are two lines of development that we cannot reconcile. We only observe them. Charles Haddon Spurgeon said of those two lines, "I cannot make them meet, but you cannot make them cross."

John A. Broadus said that to look at the sovereignty of God and the free moral agency of mankind is like a person looking at a house. You can never see more than half of it at a time. I can stand and see two corners, but I cannot see the other two. I can walk around the house and see two sides at a time, but two are hidden from me. I cannot see all four sides of the house at the same time. But someone above me could look down on that house and see all four sides at once. So it is with us. We cannot see but alternately one half of the house at a time. But the Creator who presides above us can see all of it at once.

October 5

Ephesians 1:15–20

EYES OF THE SOUL

The eyes of your understanding being enlightened; that ye may know what is the hope of his calling, and what the riches of the glory of his inheritance in the saints (1:18).

One of our great English poets wrote, "The seeing eyes see best by the light in the heart that lies." Seeing with the eyes of the soul—this is the intuitive insight (which is the highest of God's exalted and heavenly gifts) that God has confirmed upon the person He made. To see with the eyes of the soul, that is what the painter does. He paints what his soul feels and sees. The great English painter, Turner, was famed throughout the world for his gorgeous sunsets. A woman came up to him one time and said, "Mr. Turner, I never saw a sunset like that." And the artist replied, "Ah, but you must wish you could?"

To see with the eyes of the soul—that is what the architect does. I have been in some of the great cathedrals of Europe such as Saint Isaac's in Leningrad. What incomparable expressions of the human spirit! The architect saw it first with the eyes of the soul before it became a reality.

Seeing with the eyes of the soul—that is what an engineer does. While I was down in Panama, the man who built the Pan-American Bridge across the canal took me to his office and showed me a little model of it. Before a span was swung, that great engineer had seen it with the eyes of his soul. For you see, facts and things are meaningless in themselves. It is the principle of meaning and purpose that is all pervasive and significant.

October 6

Ephesians 2:1–10

AN UNDERSTANDING OF LOSTNESS

For by grace are ye saved through faith; and that not of yourselves: it is the gift of God (2:8).

When I was a young fellow, Dr. Lee R. Scarborough was the President of Southwestern Baptist Theological Seminary. He told the story of a junior boy who came down the aisle in a service. Dr. Scarborough sat down by the boy, and the boy's Sunday school teacher came and sat on the other side. When Dr. Scarborough began to talk to the boy about being a sinner and about his need of the Savior, the Sunday school teacher broke in and said, "Dr. Scarborough, excuse me, you are a stranger here, I know, and you are not acquainted with our people, but this boy is the best boy in my Sunday school class and he is one of the finest boys in this community."

The preacher ignored the Sunday school teacher and continued to talk to the boy about his need for the Savior. The teacher broke in again and said, "But Dr. Scarborough, this is a fine boy, the best boy in my class, and one of the finest I have ever known." Dr. Scarborough then told the boy, "You move over here." And he sat down between the Sunday school teacher and the boy. Then, turning to the boy, he said, "Son, do you realize that you are a sinner? Do you realize that you are lost? Do you realize that you need a Savior?" In just a few minutes, he led that boy into the kingdom of Christ.

There is no need for Christ if we can save ourselves. There is no need for Jesus if we can be righteous enough to walk with the redeemed into glory. It is because we are lost, because we are sinners, that we must cast ourselves upon the grace and mercy of Christ, and without that understanding of lostness there is no desire for a Savior.

October 7

Ephesians 2:11–17

WITHOUT HOPE

That at that time ye were without Christ, being aliens from the commonwealth of Israel, and strangers from the covenants of promise, having no hope, and without God in the world: But now in Christ Jesus ye who sometimes were far off are made nigh by the blood of Christ (2:12–13).

If you have read Dante's *Divine Comedy,* you have seen hell described as having a giant door that leads down into the pit to the abyss. Above this door are inscribed these words, "Despair of hope all ye who enter here." That is a description of all outside the Lord. They are without hope. Our lives without God are like a shipwrecked mariner thirsting to death in a sea of brine, looking up to a burning sun, looking down to the bottomless pit, and looking around to barren decay. Our lives are like that without Christ; we are without hope.

Sometimes I think of life as a race with death on a great track. When one is young, the grim, skeleton monster of death seems to be far behind. But as the days go on and the race continues, he approaches closer and closer until finally, if one looks over his shoulder, he can see him breathing down his neck. I do not need to speculate who wins. Death always wins, like a stag-hound that drags down the deer. Ultimately, inexorably, and inevitably, death drags us down without hope. You are not going to win. Some day it will be with you as it has been with those who have preceded us. Only in Jesus Christ is there victory from death and hope for eternity.

October 8

Ephesians 2:18–22

THE WALL OF PARTITION

Now therefore ye are no more strangers and foreigners, but fellowcitizens with the saints, and of the household of God (2:19).

Had one gone to the holy city to worship God in biblical times, he would have found as he entered the city and approached the holy temple a gigantic wall of partition. Had he passed through that wall into the Court of Gentiles, he would have found again a gigantic wall of partition. Had he gone beyond that wall in the Court of Gentiles into the Court of Women, there again he would have found another wall of partition. Had he gone beyond that wall from the Court of Women into the Court of Israel, there again he would have found a wall of partition. Had he gone through the wall of the Court of Israel into the Court of the Priests, there he would have found again a wall of partition. Had he gone beyond the Court of the Priests and approached the Sanctuary itself, there he would have found another wall. Had he entered the Sanctuary itself, as only the priests could do, there again he would have found a veil separating him from God.

But in Christ all of these partitions are broken down. There are no walls with Jesus. The whole concourse is broken down. In Christ we can walk directly into the presence of God Himself—just stand in His presence and talk to Him face to face as a person would talk to his best friend. Christ has broken down those walls of partition.

October 9

Ephesians 3:1–13

LESS THAN THE LEAST

Unto me, who am less than the least of all saints, is this grace given, that I should preach among the Gentiles the unsearchable riches of Christ (3:8).

The deeper the vessel and the more laden it is, the further down in the water it will sink. Empty cans clatter and jostle on the surface of the sea. Those individuals who are self-conceited are loud, cheap, and empty. But the true man of God is like Paul, "less than the least."

In the nineteenth century two famous preachers, Joseph Parker and Charles Haddon Spurgeon, lived in London. One day a man came to Joseph Parker and asked him, "Why did the Lord choose Judas, one of the twelve, who betrayed him?" The humble preacher replied, "I am not able to answer, but the great mystery to me is not why he chose Judas, but why should the Lord have chosen me." Charles Haddon Spurgeon one time exclaimed in a sermon, "In the wonder of the elected love and grace of God, my heart cries out, 'Why me, O Lord, why me?'"

October 10

Ephesians 3:14–21

THE FAMILY OF GOD

Of whom the whole family in heaven and earth is named (3:15).

The formation of the family of God is both natural and eternal, not artificial and temporal. Here in this life there are many associations that draw us together. In the ancient day men were organized by guilds—the guild of silversmiths, the guild of weavers, the guild of dyers, the guild of stonemasons. In this modern day men and women are associated together by many common affinities and predilections. There will be political groups, literary societies, and business organizations, but all of these associations are artificial and temporary. Tastes change, society moves on, the national life is recolored, and the combination is broken up. Whatever the association may be, the end is inexorable and inevitable; it ends in dissolution. If for no other reason, it is dissolved by death.

But it is not so in the family of God. The family of God is formed naturally and everlastingly. As I am born into my family, my mother is my mother forever; my father is my father forever; my sisters and brothers are my sisters and brothers forever; my child is my child forever. So it is when we are born into the family of God. Our relationship is not artificial. It belongs to the eternal order of things; it is everlasting.

Ephesians 4:1–6

THE BINDING TIE

There is one body, and one Spirit, even as ye are called in one hope of your calling (4:4).

In 1947 I went to Germany. I made a like journey in 1950 and again in 1955. When I first went through the war-torn and ravaged country in 1947, the cities were rubble, the nation was prostrate, and the people defeated. I went to the Baptist church in Munich. The building was destroyed, the people had been scattered, and the little group that gathered together was composed mostly of refugees. They met in a dark place underground and our light was a coal-oil lamp.

When I preached, the sermon had to be translated into three different languages so that the different refugees could understand. Yet I felt the Spirit of God in that war-ravaged, defeated, and ragged little band. When I went back in 1950, they had built the church. That was the first time where, after having observed the Lord's Supper that morning, I saw God's people join hands and sing, "Blest Be the Tie That Binds." I came back to Dallas and began that beautiful and lovely practice at the end of our Lord's Supper.

> We share our mutual woes,
> Our mutual burdens bear;
> And often for each other flows
> The sympathizing tear.

As I joined hands with that band of Christians in Munich, I felt the quickening, living Spirit and the unity of the church. There is one body.

October 12

Ephesians 4:7–13

BLESSING AND HONOR THROUGH HIM

Wherefore he saith, When he ascended up on high, he led captivity captive, and gave gifts unto men (4:8).

When I began to preach as a seventeen-year-old youth in my little country church, I would stand up in the pulpit before that congregation of eighteen and try my best to deliver the message of Jesus. Yet I failed so miserably. I could not preach. I could not frame the word to pronounce it. I could not put the sentences together. I would try and fail. I would bow my head and weep and weep, every Sunday afternoon.

But the Lord had called me and God soon gave me the ability to do it. And the Lord blessed the services.

It is God who helps with the message; it is the Lord who fills the church; it is God who sanctifies the appeal. It is a grace gift. It is something God does. For each one of us there is a plan, a place, a purpose, and a program. When we give ourselves to it, yielding to God's call for us, He blesses us. He blesses the church and through us He honors His name in the earth.

October 13

Ephesians 4:14–30

THE OFFICIAL SEAL

And grieve not the holy Spirit of God, whereby ye are sealed unto the day of redemption (4:30).

In matters of state a document was closed with soft wax, and the king sealed it with his own seal. In matters of property and estates, papers were sealed with a signet ring. When Jeremiah bought back the inheritance from his father Anathoth, he sealed it in two copies, in two ways. Jeremiah sealed one copy in a public document with the seal down at the bottom. The other was sealed and placed in the archives as a record for future generations.

The same double sealing is done by the Holy Spirit with us. First, He seals openly and publicly where all can see. If you are not a child of God, you cannot hide it. There is a worldliness about you. But if you are sealed by the Holy Spirit of God you cannot hide that either. You have the seal of God upon you. And then there is a secret sealing upon a document up in the archives of heaven. It has your name on it. The Holy Spirit seals us publicly here and secretly there.

Is that document in heaven authentic? How do you know but that the scribe from hell itself, the master of deceit, has written the document? You know because the seal of the Spirit is on the document. It is publicly seen in you. You cannot hide it. It is also written in the archives of God's heaven. The sealing unto the day of redemption is a sign that God owns us.

Out in the west where ranchers have cattle on the ranges, they put their brand on every animal to signify ownership. God has His brand, His seal, upon us. The Holy Spirit is a sign, a seal, that we belong to Him.

October 14

Ephesians 5:1–20

FUEL FROM THE SPIRIT

And be not drunk with wine, wherein is excess; but be filled with the Spirit (5:18).

There is never a command that we be baptized or sealed or indwelled by the Spirit. These actions refer to something God *does* for us, such as the writing of our names in the Book of Life. On the other hand, the command that we be filled with the Spirit relates to our daily service and walk. For a believer can be a carnal, worldly, and unfruitful Christian. The carnal person lives by the power and dictates of the flesh. The truly spiritual person lives by the power and dictates of the Spirit of God (Gal. 5:16–17).

A Christian living a normal life of yieldedness to God experiences a moment-by-moment fullness of the Spirit. Some people experience a spectacular, miraculous, unique fullness that stands out over all other fillings like a mountain peak on a lofty range. Such men of marvelous witness and testimony are John Wesley, Charles G. Finney, Dwight L.

Moody, and R. A. Torrey. They had one great filling of the Spirit that stood out above all others. But most of us experience the filling of the Spirit in repeated succession like a mountain chain of many equal peaks. Each day's work brings its measure of endowment and inspiration.

Under domination of the Holy Spirit, we also are changed persons. We are doing what we never thought of doing. We are saying what we never thought of saying. We are attempting what we never thought of attempting. And the unique glory in this remarakble confidence and praiseworthy achievement is that in God we *are* different, changed people!

October 15

Ephesians 5:21–33

THE DEATH OF CHRIST

This is a great mystery: but I speak concerning Christ and the church (5:32).

It is an astonishing development that out of the persecution and the indescribable suffering of Christ the church should be born. Notice the contrast between the death of Christ and the death of the other philosophers and religionists who have founded great and lasting movements in the earth. Gautama Buddha, "the enlightened one," while traveling, ate a large meal of pork and fell violently ill. He died in 483 B.C. at the age of eighty. Five years later, in 478 B.C., Confucius became ill, went to his bed, and lay there for seven days. Then he died at the age of seventy-two. Neither Buddha nor Confucius believed in God.

In about 400 B.C., the civil war between Sparta and Athens ended. A political reaction followed and in 399 B.C., Socrates, at seventy years of age, died a beautiful and pleasant death. The vote had been 281 against him and 220 for him. He died through the administration of drugs. In A.D. 632, Mohammed became violently ill with headaches and fever. He died unsensationally in his bed.

Look at these deaths: the death of Buddha, the founder of Buddhism; the death of Confucius, the founder of Confucianism; the death of Socrates, the founder of Platonism; and the death of Mohammed, the founder of Islam. No redemption or grace is ever attached to the death of any of them.

But the crucifixion and the agony of our Savior is different. It is unique and set apart. It is unduplicated. In Christ's death was born the redemption and the atonement of His people.

October 16

Ephesians 6:1–9

THE INFLUENCE OF A WOMAN

Honor thy father and mother; which is the first commandment with promise (6:2).

When I was a guest preacher in Jacksonville, Florida, the pastor took me to one of the famous restaurants on the Eastern seaboard. As we walked into the lobby, I saw beyond the cashier's desk a large portrait of a fine-looking woman. The pastor said to me, "When we are seated, remind me to tell you the story of that woman." After we were seated at the table, he related this story.

On a small, unprosperous farm in South Georgia there lived a father, a mother, and their son. The father died, and the mother took the boy to Jacksonsville. They opened a little eating place downtown, God blessed them, and their little restaurant flourished. They then built a spacious, luxurious eating place on the edge of the city. When the restaurant was almost completed, the mother died. Just before her death, she called her boy to her side and said, "Son, when the beautiful restaurant is opened, promise me that you will never sell wine, beer, or liquor in it." The boy promised.

The luxurious restaurant was completed and the customers began to come. There also came the representatives of the brewery, winery, and distillery, saying to that boy, "You cannot run a luxurious restaurant like this unless you sell beer, wine, and liquor." In each instance the boy went to the lobby and pointed to the picture of his mother. He said, "I promised my mother before she died that I would never sell alcoholic beverages in this beautiful place. Before I break that promise, I will go back to the plow handles on that farm in Georgia." He honored his mother, and God blessed her son. One of the finest restaurants on the Eastern seaboard is that restaurant.

October 17

Ephesians 6:10–12

BROTHERS IN ARMS

Put on the whole armor of God, that ye may be able to stand against the wiles of the devil (6:11).

Admiral Nimitz, as he stood on the battleship *Missouri* in Tokyo Bay on September 2, 1945, after Japan capitulated and the war was done, presented a marvelous address. He was the commander of all the naval operations in the Pacific. Nimitz closed that wonderful address with words something like these: "Close to my headquarters in Guam, in a little green valley, there is a military cemetery. I look out my window on that little valley and see those ordered rows of white crosses. I walk among those fallen comrades: soldiers, marines, and sailors; and I read their names." Then he named a long list of men—ordinary American boys. He said finally, "They fought together as comrades in arms. They died together. And now they sleep together in death. This day our victory, our triumph, is the fruit of their dedicated lives."

That is exactly what God calls us to in the warfare of the Lord. We are humble, ordinary people locked together in a common determination—brothers and sisters in Christ.

October 18

Ephesians 6:13–20

THE INSTRUMENT OF PROTECTION

Above all, taking the shield of faith, wherewith ye shall be able to quench all the fiery darts of the wicked (6:16).

In the story of Paris, the prince of Troy who abducted Helen, there is also found the story of the army hero Achilles. Achilles had been dipped by his mother in the sacred river Styx and was invulnerable except for the heel by which she held him. In the Trojan War, which was precipitated over Helen, Paris shot an arrow full of poison. It struck Achilles in the heel and he died. In ancient warfare there were tiers and tiers of archers. An ordinary arrow, when its force was spent, lay dead and harmless, but many of those arrows were tipped with poison. They were fiery darts. Paul refers to the shield which will protect the soldier from the fiery darts of the wicked one. The armor itself is not enough to protect the soldier. He also needs a shield.

Do your remember how King Ahab died? When he went into the war against the Assyrians, he was protected by armor next to his body. On the outside he was dressed in peasant clothes to disguise himself from the enemy. The Scripture says that as the battle raged, an enemy soldier took a bow and drew it back at a venture, that is, without aiming. The arrow, speeding on its way, entered between the joints of Ahab's armor and pierced his heart. His blood ran out in the chariot, and the dogs licked it up when the chariot was washed. Thus Ahab died.

The soldier wears some other instrument of protection in addition to armor. Paul calls that the "shield of faith." Faith protects the head against doubt. Faith protects the heart against the love of the world. Faith protects the hand that wields the sword.

October 19

Philippians 1:1–24

OUR ATTITUDE TOWARD DEATH

For to me to live is Christ, and to die is gain (1:21).

What should be our attitude toward death? Is it something that we cringe before, something we pray against, something we dread, a terrible and awesome sentence in our lives? Is this to be our attitude toward dying? God says to those of us who look in faith to Him that it is better over there than it is here. God says that we will have a new body and a new home. We will have a new resurrected and glorified body in that world beyond the gates of death. There will be no more blind eyes or crippled bodies. There will be no graves on the hillsides of glory. Down the streets paved with gold there will be no processions of those who weep and cry. God has prepared something better for us. We will be with those who have been redeemed from all the ages. We will sit down with Abraham, Isaac, and Jacob, with the apostles and prophets, with the children of God through all the centuries. Best of all, we will break bread at the table of our Lord.

When I was a youth an old pastor said to me, "Son, so often when older people want to talk to young people about heaven and about the land that is yet to come, the young people will turn aside as though it would be something inappropriate. You see, older people have faced a long journey and want to talk about death, heaven, the grave, and the resurrection. Do not turn them away. If you were going on a long journey, would you not be interested in talking to someone who has been there? If older people talk to you about heaven, listen to them, read to them, say things to them that God has revealed in His sacred Book. This will comfort them and strengthen their belief in the glories of the blessedness of eternal life."

October 20

Philippians 2:1–10

A LITTLE THING

That at the name of Jesus every knee should bow, of things in heaven, and things in earth, and things under the earth (2:10).

When you recall experiences of childhood, certain things stay in your memory. Here is an experience from my life when I started school.

We lived on a farm, and I had a little pony named Trixie and a buggy. I drove the horse and buggy four miles to town to go to school. One time I remember that the temperature was nine below zero. I was so cold and my hands hurt so much that I cried. My mother said, "We are going to move to town so you can go to school." So my mother took my brother and me and rented an empty bank building to make a home. What a courageous woman she was!

One day a preacher came to visit us. He was the pastor of the church in the little town. He read the Bible to my mother and me, and he got down on his knees to pray. Although I was barely six years old at the time, I still can see that pastor kneeling down, praying for my mother and me.

Those are the things that build the Christian faith. Ten thousand other things do not matter, but kneeling in prayer is for eternity.

October 21

Philippians 4:1–9

THE TRAGEDY OF BITTERNESS

Rejoice in the Lord always: and again I say, Rejoice (4:4).

My first pastorate after seminary was at Chickasha, Oklahoma. A woman there lived alone in a dilapidated house. I knocked at her door and she finally invited me in. "You say you believe in God?" she asked gruffly. "Yes," I said. "Well, I do not believe in God," she said, and she cursed the Lord.

As I visited with her, the tragic story of her life came out. Her husband had died and her children had left her. She was almost blind and in poverty.

As I continued visiting with her, she read me one of her poems.

I hate Oklahoma!
Not the land of my native birth
But a land by all the gods that be
A scourge on the face of the earth.
I hate Oklahoma!

I hate Oklahoma!
Where the centipede crawls in your bed at night,
And the rattlesnake lifts its fangs to bite,

Where the lizard and the scorpion play on the sly,
And the lonesome vultures sail high in the sky.
Where water and food are an eternal lack,
And a man's best friend sticks a dagger in your back.

All her poetry was bitter like that. I knelt down by her chair and prayed, doing what I could to encourage her. She died not long afterwards, and I buried her. She left a little note expressing appreciation for me: "There is nothing of value in the house but the rug on the living room floor. I give that to the pastor of the First Baptist Church in Chickasha." I took the rug and put it on the floor where our primary children met.

Oh, Lord, as I grow older, may I not become cynical or bitter. But may my love for God and for You be deeper and wider. Let me be sweet and kind, full of faith and full of hope.

October 22

Philippians 4:10–23

THE LITTLE TWIG

I can do all things through Christ which strengtheneth me (4:13).

An agriculturalist will look at a little twig bursting out of the ground and being knowledgeable, he will say, "That is an oak." An oak? To me an oak is a vast, spreading tree with branches and leaves, a tremendous creation. An oak has acorns, and it can withstand the most terrible of winds and storms. That is an oak. But the agriculturalist will look at the little twig and say that it is an oak. What he is doing is this: He is idealizing, for all of the possibilities of the great tree are in that tiny twig. Its incipient development is a harbinger of what is yet to come. He looks upon it in the knowledge of what it ideally can and will be.

God looks upon us in the same way. We are so tiny and so small and so weak. Most any little thing can blow us over. But God looks upon us ideally—what we are going to be in Christ, in glory—and that is justification. He declares us righteous.

Colossians 1:1–22

HOME BY THE CROSS

In whom we have redemption through his blood, even the forgiveness of sins (1:14).

Years ago the beloved wife of a British king died far away from London. As the king tenderly and lovingly brought her body back to the great city, wherever her body rested during the long journey, the king built a little chapel. He named each chapel for some kind of a cross, as the King's Cross, or Charing Cross.

Standing in Charing Cross in London, a fellow minister by my side said, "Let me tell you a story that happened here. A little girl in the city lost her way. She wandered around in the streets of London, crying heartbrokenly, piteously. An English bobby stopped the child and asked about her sobbing. The child answered that she was lost and did not know how to find her way home. The bobby said to her, 'Do not cry. Sit down here by my side and we will find where you live.' So the bobby sat on the curb of the street, and the little broken-hearted girl sat by his side. He said, 'Now I am going to ask you some places in London, and you tell me if your recognize any of them. Piccadilly Circus?' 'No.' 'Westminster?' 'No.' 'Charing Cross?' 'Ah,' said the little girl in her tears, 'Yes, yes. Take me down to the cross and I can find my way home from there!'"

I must needs go home
By the way of the cross,
There's no other way but this;
I shall ne'er get sight
Of the gates of light,
If the way of the cross I miss.

I must needs go on
In the blood-sprinkled way,
The path that our Savior trod,
If I ever climb to the heights sublime,
Where my soul is at rest with God.

October 24

Colossians 1:23–29

TURNING TO THE LORD

Whereunto I also labor, striving according to his working, which worketh in me mightily (1:29).

Sorrow has such deep repercussions in human life! They are as deep as the soul is deep. When the only son of Sir Harry Lauder, the great Scottish singer and entertainer, was killed in World War I, Sir Harry said, "I had three choices. One, I could drown my sorrow in drink. Two, I could drown my sorrow in the grave; I could take my own life. Or three, I could find hope and comfort in God." And the famous singer said, "I turned to the Lord."

Like nothing else in the world, sorrow can warp your soul, your mind, and your life. Or it can bring you close to God. It can bind you with golden chains to the very altar of the Lord. God is able to do exceeding abundantly above all that we ask or think. Oh, God, that sorrow might bind my soul closer to Thee!

October 25

Colossians 2:1–23

THE WONDER BEHIND CHRISTMAS

And you, being dead in your sins and the uncircumcision of your flesh, hath he quickened together with him, having forgiven you all trespasses (2:13).

We stand in awe, amazement, wonder, and gratitude for what God has done to make atonement for our sins.

That is why beyond the sleigh bells ringing—beyond that jolly Santa Claus, beyond all of the Christmas decoration, beyond all of the gifts, and beyond all of the festivity of the Christmas season—there lies the most profound truth in God's world. Jesus came to die for our sins.

> Alas, and did my Savior bleed?
> And did my Sovereign die?
> Would He devote that sacred head
> For such a worm as I?
>
> Was it for crimes that I have done
> He groaned upon the tree?
> Amazing pity! grace unknown!
> And love beyond degree!
>
> But drops of grief can ne'er repay
> The debt of love I owe;
> Here, Lord, I give myself away—
> 'Tis all that I can do.

Lord God, thank You for sending Jesus to die for our sins. Praise You, Lord, for taking pity upon my lost estate. Bless the name of heaven that instead of my certain judgment and death, God has made provision that I might be saved. That is the purpose of the Incarnation and that is the meaning of Christmas.

> Saved by the blood of the Crucified One,
> All praise to the Father,
> All praise to the Son,
> All praise to the Spirit, the Great Three in One.
> Saved by the blood of the Crucified One.

The church of God was purchased with Jesus' own blood!

October 26

Colossians 3:1–25

REFLECTION IN LIFE

And have put on the new man, which is renewed in knowledge after the image of him that created him (3:10).

Sam Jones was a tremendously effective Southern preacher of the last century. Being an evangelist, he went from place to place holding revival services. One day while walking along a street, Sam Jones looked down and saw a drunk in the gutter. A man then said to Sam Jones, "Sam, that's one of your converts." Sam replied, "That's right. He looks like one of mine. God had nothing to do with him."

How true! "If any man be in Christ, he is a new creature: old things are passed away; behold, all things are become new." A new heart, a new love, a new vision, a new dream, a new home, a new life, a new fellowship. If a person has faith, it will reflect itself in the kind of life he lives and the kind of deeds he does.

October 27

Colossians 4:1–18

PRAY AS YOU RUN

Walk in wisdom toward them that are without, redeeming the time (4:5).

A girl and her brother were late for school. They had been playing along the way and forgot the time. Still some way from school, they heard the school bell ring. The little girl said, "Brother, let us kneel down here and pray that God will not let us be late for school." But the brother replied, "No, sister, let us run just as fast as we can and let us pray as we run." Our work must be like that—our effort plus God's blessing.

That is the way a person ought to live before the Lord. He can pray, "O God, give me a house for my home." Then he ought to say "Amen" with a hammer and a saw. He could pray, "O God, give me a job." Then let him say "Amen" by reading all the want-ad columns and knocking at the door of an employer. We may pray, "Lord, save the world." Then we ought to say "Amen" by giving to missions. You may pray, "Lord, strengthen and bless the church." Then say "Amen" by rolling up your sleeves and pouring your life into it.

October 28

1 Thessalonians 2:1–20

THE ATTACK OF SATAN

Wherefore we would have come unto you, even I Paul, once and again; but Satan hindered us (2:18).

Consider the kind of antagonist the Christian faces today. A young American college student who was converted to communism in old Mexico wrote this letter to his fiancée to explain the breaking of their engagement. He wrote:

> We communists have a high casualty rate. We are the ones who get shot and hung and lynched and jailed and fined and fired from our jobs. We live in virtual poverty. We turn back to the party every penny we make above what is absolutely necessary to keep us alive. We are fanatics. Our lives are dominated by one great overshadowing factor, namely, the struggle for world communism. We communists have a philosophy which no amount of money can buy. We have a cause for which to fight, a definite purpose in life. We subordinate our petty personal selves into a great movement of humanity, and if our personal lives seem hard or our egos appear to suffer through subordinations of the party, then we are adequately compensated by the thought that each of us in his small way is contributing to something new and true and better for mankind. There is one thing in which I am in dead earnest and that is the communist cause. It is my life, my business, my religion, my hobby, my sweetheart, my wife, my bread, and my meat. I work at it in the daytime and dream of it at night. Its hold on me grows, not lessens. I cannot carry on a friendship but must follow this course which both drives and guides my life. I evaluate people, books, ideas, and actions according to how they affect the communist cause. I have already been in jail because of my ideas, and if necessary, I am ready to go before a firing squad.

October 29

1 Thessalonians 3:1–13

NONE BUT JESUS

For verily, when we were with you, we told you before that we should suffer tribulation; even as it came to pass, and ye know (3:4).

In the early days of Christianity God's little flock suffered terrible persecution. One young Christian named Blandinia received such strength when she was tortured that it amazed her persecutors. Marcus, Bishop of Arethusa, was smeared with honey, and angered wasps stung him to death. A little band of Christians was covered with pitch and set on fire, and with their flaming, burning hands clapping in the presence of the Lord, they repeated, "None but Jesus—Jesus only." It almost seems as though it pleased God to feed His little flock to the bloodthirsty world.

There has never been an age or generation since that time which has not known tragic suffering on the part of the Christian. Only the Lord knew what was happening to His children in North Korea, in Communist China, and in mad Uganda. God's little flock has always suffered grief unjustly. And the inspired apostle tells us that this is our calling. Christ suffered for us, leaving us an example. Our Lord, in whom was found no sin, neither guile in His mouth, when He was reviled did not revile again. When He suffered, He did not threaten, but committed Himself to God.

October 30

1 Thessalonians 4:1–14

THE KEEPER OF OUR INHERITANCE

But I would not have you to be ignorant, brethren, concerning them which are asleep, that ye sorrow not, even as others which have no hope. For if we believe that Jesus died and rose again, even so them also which sleep in Jesus will God bring with him (4:13–14).

Once a family called me in tears, saying, "Our mother is dying. The doctor says it is just a little while. Will you come and pray with us?" I went to the hospital, gathered the family around, and prayed with them while the mother was in a coma. She did not even know we were there.

Lord, I might not even be awake, I might not even know! How could I cling to my inheritance then? That is why the Lord is in glory. He is the one who holds my hand. He is the one who sees me through. He is the one who keeps the inheritance for us who have placed our trust in Him. He is there to do it. He is on the other side of the river, there to receive us to Himself and to give us our golden crowns.

1 Thessalonians 4:15–18

THE CHURCH TRIUMPHANT

Then we which are alive and remain shall be caught up together with them in the clouds, to meet the Lord in the air: and so shall we ever be with the Lord (4:17).

Savonarola was one of the greatest preachers of all time. When I was in Florence, I wanted to visit the little cell in St. Mark's where Savonarola lived and studied the Bible. I wanted to stand in the pulpit in the great cathedral where he preached the Word of God. I wanted to go to the square in Florence where he was hanged and where his body was burned.

As I went to those places, I relived that day when the people came from Rome and stood before the mighty preacher who was behind bars. They read him the paper of excommunication and execution. It closed with this sentence: "I hereby separate thee from the church militant and from the church triumphant." Savonarola replied, "Sir, you can separate me from the church visible, and from the church militant, but you cannot separate me from the church triumphant, the church in heaven."

By one spirit we are all baptized into the body of Christ. We are joined to our Lord forever.

November 1

1 Thessalonians 5:1–11

ITHOUT ANNOUNCEMENT

For yourselves know perfectly that the day of the Lord so cometh s a thief in the night (5:2).

The Lord comes secretly, clandestinely, furtively, like a thief in the night. le is coming to steal away His jewels, His pearl of price, the souls for hom He gave His life and died. He is coming for us, the redeemed of the ord.

The Lord is coming without announcement. There is no sign, there is o token, there is no harbinger, there is no warning, there is no anything. ny moment, any day, any hour, any time, He can come. There is no rophecy remaining to be fulfilled. There never has been anything beveen the imminence of the appearing of our Lord and His coming for us. lothing! He may come any day, any time.

It may be at midday, it may be at twilight,
It may be, perchance, that the blackness of midnight
Will burst into light in the blaze of His glory
When Jesus comes for His own.

O joy! O delight! should we go without dying,
No sickness, no sadness, no dread and no crying,
Caught up through the clouds with our Lord into glory,
When Jesus comes for his own.

—*H. L. Turner*

November 2

1 Thessalonians 5:12–28

ONGS IN THE NIGHT

In every thing give thanks: for this is the will of God in Christ esus concerning you (5:18).

Whether we suffer, whether we are sick, whether we are in agon whether we are discouraged because of others, whatever—the Christian to be up, singing songs in the night. He is to be happy in the Lord.

Christian psychologists have avowed that martyrs felt no pain when th were burned at the stake because of their glory in dying for Jesus. Think that! Thomas Cranmer, first Protestant Archbishop of Canterbury, w burned at the stake at Oxford. As he was martyred, he put forth his rig hand and held it in the flame and watched it burn to a crisp. He was exalted in the Lord that he apparently felt no pain.

The Christian is forever triumphant. When Paul and Silas were beat and thrust into a dungeon, at midnight they were singing praises to Go That is what it is to be in Christ. It is to be in the heavenlies, blessed with of the blessing of God. As Clement of Alexandria said, "He has turned our sunsets into sunrise."

November 3

1 Timothy 1:1–20

BRINGING A SOUL TO JESUS

This is a faithful saying, and worthy of all acceptation, that Christ Jesus came into the world to save sinners; of whom I am chief (1:15).

The greatest work one could ever do would be to save a soul fro death. If you were on a sinking ship and were able to man the lifeboat, ho blessed it would be to save the passengers. If a house were burning dow and you dashed through the flames to rescue the perishing, how bless the act. What is greater than saving a soul from death!

In the last century someone asked the famous preacher and schola Lyman Beecher, "What is the greatest thing that a man could ever do f someone else?" Mr. Beecher replied, "To bring another to Jesus." An that is according to the Word of the Lord. In the judgment of God, nothin is so marvelously great as to bring someone to Jesus.

November 4

1 Timothy 4:1–16

BACKBONE OF THE FAITH

Take heed unto thyself, and unto the doctrine; continue in them: for in doing this thou shalt both save thyself, and them that hear thee (4:16).

Doctrine is the essence and the substance of the Christian faith. Without doctrine the Christian system is nothing but a sentimental, formless mass of materialistic clichés. We need the great revelation and truths of God in order that we might have a foundation upon which to stand and in order that we might stand ourselves.

One of the greatest systematic theologies was written by A. H. Strong, a mighty theologian. In that systematic theology he wrote this sentence: "A man need not carry his backbone in front of him, but he needs to have one, and a straight one, or else he will be a flexible and humpbacked Christian." Every person needs a backbone, that is, a great stack of truths around which his life is built. Without it he is a sentimentalist or a moralist.

Peter Marshall once prayed, "Lord, help us to stand for something, for if we do not stand for something, we will fall for anything." We need a great doctrinal basis upon which to build our lives, our hopes, and our faith. That truth is revealed to us in the powerful doctrines of the Bible.

These doctrines are the decisive and fundamental characterizations of all of life. They are more real than a stone or a mountain. A stone or a mountain is dead, but an idea, a doctrine is explosive.

November 5

2 Timothy 1:1–18

STRENGTH IN CONVICTION

For the which cause I also suffer these things: nevertheless I am not ashamed: for I know whom I have believed, and am persuaded that he is able to keep that which I have committed unto him against that day (1:12).

When I was a boy, there was a column in the daily newspaper entitled "Today," and it was written by a man named Arthur Brisbain. I remember reading in one column that Mr. Brisbain mentioned he was not a religionist. But, though he was not a follower of God or Christ, he always went to hear Billy Sunday preach. One day a man discussed this with him and Mr. Brisbain wrote about it in his column. The man said, "It is strange that you go to hear Billy Sunday. Why, Billy Sunday believes in a devil that wears a red suit, has a forked tail, and carries in his hand a pitchfork with which he stokes the fires. It is unthinkable. Why do you go to hear Billy Sunday when you do not believe anything he says?" And Arthur Brisbain answered, "I just like to hear him because he believes it. There is strength in that man. He stands up and says what he believes. He knows his own mind and he avows it. He has conviction, and you feel it."

Did the Lord say blessed are those who are always discussing, philosophizing, and speculating? No. Blessed are they who do the will of God. They shall enter into the kingdom of heaven.

November 6

2 Timothy 2:1–15

THE MISSING INGREDIENT

Study to show thyself approved unto God, a workman that needeth not to be ashamed, rightly dividing the word of truth (2:15).

The following poem was written by a black man, and it has the typical imagery of a black preacher. The poem is about Jesus looking at Peter. He sees that Peter is made of sand and that he is unstable. He needs something. This black poet calls the missing ingredient (i.e., the Holy Spirit) "cement." He takes the cement, the sand, and the water and makes out of them a rock.

Dear Lor — (That Jesus Bless God our Savior)
De Lord see his ciples and he sat and think
He's de men I don called to de word.
Matthew and Tholemu, James and John
and every last one of them heard.

There's Andrew and Philip and Thomas and Jude
and each is a pendable man, but Peter is the one
I call out first and Peter is like the shifting sand.
Peter blow dis way and Peter blow dat way.
Oh!!! What I do wid Peter?

Matthew is my staff what I cut from the oak
I leans on him at my will.
Philip is my arrow, shooting straight from the bow.
James is the candle on a hill.
John is my lamp that they can't blow out,
  shinin' just as steady as can be.
But Peter is the one I count on most
  And Peter is like the changing sea.
Peter moves dis way — Peter moves dat way.
Oh!!! What I gonna do wid Peter?

Oh, what a gwana do wid sand and water?
Both of them slipping away.
When dey's mixed like in Peter you can mold and shape,
  but how you gwana make it stay?
Dey needs cement. Dat's the spirit of the Lawd.
And notin' else can hold him fast.
Ifn it's poured in the sand and water now maybe
  Peter gwine to last. Oh, de sand
and the water done make the rock. Dat's what I done wid Peter.

Isn't that something? That is marvelous about the Lord. He sees us now, as we are, but He also sees what we can be. He sees us at our best.

November 7

2 Timothy 3:1–12

STRENGTH FROM STRIVING

Yea, and all that will live godly in Christ Jesus shall suffer persecution (3:12).

God intended that we have strength in our Christian character, and strength comes to us in the trials that we endure. For example, a man grows strong muscles by strength and stress. He does this by lifting great weights. Any anatomical student will testify that it is in stress, in pushing, in straining that our muscles are made. The same thing is true of our minds. It is in the discipline of study and concentration that a person's mind becomes sharp, knowledgeable, gifted. So it is in our spiritual life. The trial that we face is a purpose of God that we might be strong, that we might be enduringly committed, that we might be mature, reaching that purpose for which God made us and saved us.

A man was once watching a butterfly trying to escape from the cocoon in which it was born and imprisoned. The man thought he would help the butterfly; so he took a sharp penknife and slit the silk cocoon. The little butterfly was free. It came out, flapped its wings feebly for a moment, then fell in exhaustion and death to the ground. God intended that the little creature find strength and maturity in striving, and when the striving was taken away it lived weakly and died sadly. There is intent and purpose in what God does when He throws us into the crucible.

November 8

2 Timothy 3:14–17

BOTH DIVINE AND HUMAN

All scripture is given by inspiration of God, and is profitable for doctrine, for reproof, for correction, for instruction in righteousness: That the man of God may be perfect, thoroughly furnished unto all good works (3:16–17).

God has planned for the human and the divine to join together. This can be seen most vividly in the personality of Christ. He is both man and God. This can be experienced in our regeneration. The human and the divine work together in our salvation. There was a part in our salvation we played; there was a part in our salvation that God played. Both divine and human meet in all that God does in this world.

George Eliot wrote a poem about Antonio Stradivarius in which she represents the famous Italian violin-maker as saying,

If my hand slacked
I should rob God
Since He is fullest good,
Leaving a blank
Instead of violins.
God cannot make
Antonio Stradivarius violins
Without Antonio.

God uses the person, breathes upon the person. Yet everyone retains his own personality, his own approach, his own language, his own idiosyncrasies and styles.

Isaiah was a brilliant court-preacher, and he spoke in highflown, glorious alliterations. Amos was a country preacher, and when you read his talks and prophecies, they smell of a newly plowed furrow, of the dirt and the soil. For God to have placed in the mouth of Amos the highflown literary language of Isaiah would have been incongruous. So Amos speaks as a farmer would speak, and Isaiah speaks as a brilliant court-preacher. But both of them are God-breathed, God using their personalities. Thus it is always in God's use of people.

November 9

2 Timothy 4:1–8

THE WITHERING TOUCH

For the time will come when they will not endure sound doctrine; but after their own lusts shall they heap to themselves teachers, having itching ears; And they shall turn away their ears from the truth, and shall be turned unto fables (4:3–4).

The theological liberal has done more to destroy the faith than all other men who have attacked Christianity through the centuries. The liberal looks upon the Bible as an antique collection of myths, legends, and fables. He looks upon Christ as one among many teachers, philosophers, heroes, and martyrs. He looks upon God as the great unknowable First Cause or as one who is dead.

Why is the liberal able to hurt the Christian gospel so deeply? The reason is most plain. If you meet a blaspheming infidel and he says, "God is dead," you are not surprised. If you meet a filthy bum jumping off a freight train in a railroad yard and he says, "God is dead," you are not upset. If you meet a drunken derelict in the gutter on skid rown and he mumbles, "God is dead," you are not confused. If you meet a dirty, bearded Communist revolutionary and he says, "God is dead," you are not troubled.

But when a learned professor teaching in a great Christian institution says, "God does not exist," you, being awed by his scholastic achievements, are therefore doubly confused by his pontifical announcement. You did not expect such an amazing conclusion from a Christian teacher. He is supposed to represent the finest in the faith, and when the faith he represents is depicted as the gospel of an infidel, you are overwhelmed.

The liberals have destroyed, like a fungus, like a dry rot, the witness of one school, one seminary, one denomination after another, one mission field after another. Their predatory outreach seemingly has no limits. And all they touch withers away as before a plague.

November 10

Titus 3:3–11

THE GREAT TEACHER

Not by works of righteousness which we have done, but according to his mercy he saved us, by the washing of regeneration, and renewing of the Holy Ghost (3:5).

In the days of the Greco-Roman Empire, slavery was most extensive. More than half of the population of the Roman Empire was chattel property. Had you walked down the streets of Ephesus, Corinth, or Antioch in the lifetime of Paul, three of the five men you would have met on the street would have been slaves. They were owned by someone else.

In those days noble and affluent Greek and Roman families placed their children in the care and keeping of a *paidagogos* (the child's tutor and leader). The assignment and responsibility of that slave was to watch over and to care for the youngsters. The law is our *paidagogos* to deliver us to the Master Teacher, Christ, that we might be justified and saved by His grace and mercy. After faith has come, after we have been delivered to the teacher, there is no longer any need for the tutor, and we are no longer under the *paidagogos.* We are then in the hands of the Great Teacher.

It was never the intent of the law to save us. Rather, the purpose of the law was to reveal to us our inability to commend ourselves in virtue and holiness to God in order that we might be brought to Christ and be saved through His mercy.

November 11

Hebrews 1:1–14

A MISCALCULATION

God, who at sundry times and in divers manners spake in time past unto the fathers by the prophets, Hath in these last days spoken unto us by his Son, whom he hath appointed heir of all things, by whom also he made the worlds (1:1–2).

Whether the words are spoken by the prophets beholding the future, or whether they are spoken by the voice of the apostles declaring their fulfillment, they are all one—the Word of God. The Old and the New Covenants cannot be separated.

I read of a young fellow who lived in a large city which is built upon tall hills. This young fellow had an old jalopy, a car of ancient vintage. In order to get up one of those high hills, he needed a running start. He got himself ready, and got his contraption all geared up. But when he came to the intersection before the hill, he discovered that to his right was an automobile coming, followed by another. He had barely time to figure it all out in that split moment. By letting the first car go by and then by gunning his pile of junk before the second car came to the intersection, he had just time to go between the two automobiles and scramble up the hill. The only miscalculation was that he had not noticed that the front car was towing the second car. They were fastened together with a steel cable. When the young fellow got out of the hospital and got through paying the bill, he had learned a great theological lesson. It is very difficult to divide things that are bound together!

It is just so in the Word of God. This piece belongs to that piece; this section is inextricably connected with that section; and the whole thing is welded together by the hand of the Lord.

November 12

Hebrews 2:1–18

TRAGEDY OF TRAGEDIES

How shall we escape, if we neglect so great salvation; which at the first began to be spoken by the Lord, and was confirmed unto us by them that heard him (2:3).

There is no tragedy that I know of that is deeper, sadder, or more everlasting than to come close to eternal life and then lose it. Almost, but lost. I came to my pastorate in Dallas in the days of World War II.

After the war was over and the victory won, a mother in our church, whose son had fought through the entire years of the war, received a call from her son in Europe saying, "I am coming home." He returned to the United States, but tragedy of tragedies, while flying between the East Coast and Dallas the plane crashed and the young man was killed. I took one of the businessmen in the church with me to visit that sorrowful mother. The businessman, who was not accustomed to weeping, wept openly like a child as the mother described her great sorrow over the death of her son for whom she had prayed through the years of the war. It heightens the sorrow and the sadness to be almost saved, almost in the kingdom, almost persuaded, and yet finally miss eternal life and heaven.

November 13

Hebrews 3:1–19

THE MOST TRAGIC WORDS

But exhort one another daily, while it is called Today; lest any of you be hardened through the deceitfulness of sin (3:13).

Out of all the tragic words a person can say, I think the most terrible and frightening are these: "Not now, but tomorrow." On the outside they do not seem tragic, but the sentence only hides threat and menace.

The drunk man says, "I am going to change tomorrow." But he continues being a drunkard because he is going to quit some other day, some other time, but not now.

The evil man says, "I am going to reform tomorrow. I do not intend to continue in this iniquity and evil. I am going to change some other day, some other time."

Most lost people do not intend to be damned and fall into hell. They are going to be saved, but they are going to be saved tomorrow, some other time, some more convenient season.

The Christian also says the words, "I am going to rededicate my life tomorrow. I am going to do better for Jesus tomorrow. I am going to work and serve God tomorrow."

> He was going to be all that a mortal should be—tomorrow.
> No one would ever be better than he—tomorrow.
>
> Each morning he stacked up the letters he'd write—tomorrow.
> Every evening he'd recount the battles he'd fight—tomorrow.
>
> He was a man who worked like a fiend—tomorrow.
> The world would have known him had he ever seen—tomorrow.
>
> But the fact is, he died and faded from view,
> And all that was left when living was through
> Was a mountain of things he intended to do—tomorrow.

November 14

Hebrews 4:1–12

MY BIBLE AND I

For the word of God is quick, and powerful, and sharper than any two-edged sword, piercing even to the dividing asunder of soul and spirit, and of the joints and marrow, and is a discerner of the thoughts and intents of the heart (4:12).

When I was in seminary, I pastored a church in which was a godly deacon who could pray the angels down. When he was called upon to pray, he would always kneel, and he would talk to God as though they were the closest of friends. But I remember him even more for his loving respect for God's Word.

> We've traveled together, my Bible and I,
> Through all kinds of weather, with a smile or with sigh!
> In sorrow or sunshine, in tempest or calm!
> Thy friendship unchanging, my lamp and my psalm.
>
> We've traveled together, my Bible and I,
> When life has grown weary, and death e'en was nigh.
> But all through the darkness of mist or of wrong,
> I found there a solace, a prayer, and a song.
>
> So now who shall part us, my Bible and I?
> Shall 'isms,' or schisms, or 'new lights' who try?
> Shall shadow for substance, or stone for good bread,
> Supplant thy sound wisdom, give folly instead?
>
> Ah, no, my dear Bible, exponent of light!
> Thou sword of the Spirit, put error to flight!
> And still through life's journey, until my last sigh,
> We'll travel together, my Bible and I.

November 15

Hebrews 5:1–14

GLORY OUT OF SUFFERING

Though he were a Son, yet learned he obedience by the things which he suffered (5:8).

John Bunyan was an outstanding preacher, a magnificent preacher. But that was all. People loved to hear him preach. Then God allowed him to be put in Bedford Prison for twelve years, and out of that Bedford jail was born a glorious book, *Pilgrim's Progress.* It was born in the tears of incarceration.

The apostle Paul spent most of his ministry in prison, but out of the imprisonment came the letters that form much of our New Testament. The Lord allowed Jesus to be nailed to the cross, and in suffering and agony there to die. But out of death came life, and out of suffering came salvation, and out of His burial in the tomb came our promise of a better resurrection.

This is the purpose of God. What befalls you is not unknown to Him. And the sufferings that you experience are not strange in His eyes. He is just bringing you to glory. Blessed are they who endure, who keep their faith, who look up in prayer, who glorify God in suffering or in tears. Blessed are they who look up in faith, who trust Him through it all.

November 16

Hebrews 7:1–28

A SHINING EXAMPLE

Wherefore he is able also to save them to the uttermost that come unto God by him, seeing he ever liveth to make intercession for them (7:25).

When the Charles A. Sammons Cancer Center at Baylor University Medical Center was dedicated, I was seated next to the speaker, a famous movie and television star. He has a brother who is a movie star and actor even more famous than he. His brother is an alcoholic. But this famous speaker had been marvelously converted, and he witnessed to the grace of the Lord Jesus in his life. Seated there at the dinner preceding the dedication ceremony, the actor was talking to me about the conversion experience of a beautiful actress and singer, who, when she sang about Mary, the mother of Jesus, wept openly and unashamedly. He remarked that her testimony was such a shining example of what the Lord can do in a yielded life. As I looked at the man talking to me, I thought, "And my brother, God has done a wonderful thing in saving you."

God has performed a miracle in saving all of us. He can and does save. His ministry in the earth is to save all who will ask Him into their hearts.

November 17

Hebrews 8:1–13

A CLEAR ILLUSTRATION

But now hath he obtained a more excellent ministry, by how much also he is the mediator of a better covenant, which was established upon better promises (8:6).

My family attended church in a little white crackerbox of a building in northwest Texas. I would sit on the front seat and listen to the pastor. Those old-time preachers often better illustrated the gospel truth for me than the tomes of theology I have poured over in years since. One of them left a special impression on my mind.

The pastor was illustrating how God took our sins and iniquities upon Himself that we might be saved. A little boy had been disobedient. Though the father and mother reproved him, he continued to disobey. One evening, when the little lad refused to obey, he was sent to the attic to stay there until he learned how to obey, even if it took days. So the little fellow went up to the attic to spend the night and to live on bread and water.

That night the father began to turn and to toss in his bed. He finally told his wife that he could not forget his son in the attic. He knew the boy was afraid of the dark. He took some bedding and went up to the attic. The little boy watched as his daddy made a bed by his side. "Daddy, what are you doing?" And the father replied, "Son, you have been disobedient, and I cannot rescind the punishment, but I have decided to bear it with you." So the father stayed with the little boy all that night—the next day—and all the next night. When the two came down the stairway together, it was justice and love. And the little boy never forgot.

This story is not perfect when we compare it to what God has done for us, but the spirit of that love is there. The Lord cannot be just and rescind the punishment. The Lord has come down from heaven to take our punishment. That is the gospel.

November 18

Hebrews 9:1–28

HE DIED IN OUR STEAD

And almost all things are by the law purged with blood; and without shedding of blood is no remission (9:22).

All of the Old Testament sacrificial systems typified substitution. Every lamb that was slain and whose blood was poured out, every offering on flaming, brazen fire, every Day of Atonement, every Yom Kippur, every sprinkling of the blood between the cherubim, every priest who ever sacrificed before God, typified that great revelation of substitution. "He died in our stead."

When the worshiper came with his offering, he took the sacrificial animal, put his hands on its head, and confessed there his sins. The animal was then slain and its blood poured out at the base of the altar. Why? By putting his hands on the head of the animal, he identified himself with the lamb or with the bullock; and when the animal was slain, it was as though he, the worshiper, had been slain. It was a substitutionary sacrifice. That is the Gospel. "Christ hath redeemed us from the curse of the law, being made a curse for us."

There is in Christ an actual substitution. This is not a metaphor or simile. This is not poetry or fiction. This is not imagination. This is an actual substitution. God took Christ, His only begotten Son, and delivered Him to the judgment and death, to the damnation and cursing assigned to us. Christ received in His own body the stab and the curse and the judgment. He died in our stead.

November 19

Hebrews 10:1–18

A BEELINE TO THE CROSS

By the which will we are sanctified through the offering of the body of Jesus Christ once for all (10:10).

The preaching of the atoning death of Christ is the distinctive, determining doctrine of the New Testament. It differentiates our faith from all other religions. The Christian message is distinctively one of redemption. Its fundamental purpose is to recover mankind from the bondage and judgment of sin. Christianity is not in the first place an ethic, although it is ethical. It is not in the first place a theology, although it has a theology. It is not in the first place reformational, although it has social, cultural, and political overtones. It is above all a gospel of redemption, an announcement of the good news that God for Christ's sake has forgiven us.

A critic said to Charles Haddon Spurgeon, "All your sermons sound alike." To which the world-famed London preacher replied, "Yes, I take my text anywhere in the Bible and make a beeline to the cross." There is no pardon without atonement; there is no remission without the shedding of blood; there is no reconciliation without the payment of debt. Not by the beauty of holiness of His life, but by His stripes we are healed. Such events as the birth of Jesus, His temptation, His transfiguration, His institution of the Lord's Supper, even His ascension into heaven are omitted from one or more of the four Gospels. But all of the Gospels, in fullest detail, relate His suffering and death. He came into the world, He was born in a human body conceived by the Holy Spirit, in order that He might offer in His own flesh a sacrifice for our sins.

November 20

Hebrews 10:19–39

THE ASSEMBLY OF BELIEVERS

Not forsaking the assembling of ourselves together, as the manner of some is; but exhorting one another: and so much the more, as ye see the day approaching (10:25).

When I was a boy, I went to church all the time. I went to Sunday school, Training Union, prayer service, and choir practice. One day I said, "This is idiocy. I am going to church all the time. I am going to quit that, and I will start with prayer meeting on Wednesday night. I am not going to prayer meeting any more." So I sat down at home and got a book to read. There was no radio, television, or movie then. All I had was a book.

While I was looking at the book, I heard the people singing down at the church. I tried to keep my head in the book, thinking, "I am not going to church all the time, and certainly I am not going to prayer meeting on Wednesday night." I was trying to read the words in my book, but the sacred music came over the waves in the stillness of the night. Finally, I just closed the book and got up and went to church.

I have been going faithfully ever since. What could a young boy mean to the kingdom of God, or what would it matter whether I was present or not? I do not know, but somehow that is the way God puts it together. Each one of us is a vital part of the church of the Lord. When the church is beautiful, strong, and healthy, it is because the parts of His body are also strong, healthy, and present. We are members of His body, of His flesh, and of His bones. Christ loved the church and gave Himself for it.

November 21

Hebrews 11:1–13

THE CALL FROM HEAVEN

These all died in faith, not having received the promises, but having seen them afar off, and were persuaded of them, and embraced them, and confessed that they were strangers and pilgrims on the earth (11:13).

One time I heard of a farmer in southern Louisiana who captured a mallard duck. He tied it with a cord to a stake at the edge of the pond. Through the winter the mallard swam around with the domestic ducks and ate from the hand of the farmer. When spring came, all of the other wild ducks that had flown south and were wintering in the marshes, ponds, and waters of southern Louisiana began to fly toward the north. When those flocks arose, they saw the mallard duck down below on the pond. They called to him from the sky. The domesticated ducks did not hear, did not see, did not raise their eyes to look. They just swam in complacency on the farmer's pond. But when the mallard heard the call from the skies, he lifted up his face and his wings and sought to rise. The cord which was tied to the stake pulled him back down. Flock after flock arose, circled, and called. Each time the mallard would rise. Finally, he broke the cord and joined the throng and moved toward the north.

People of the world are content here below. Their investments are here; their lives are here; their interests are here; their happiness is here; their dreams are here; their purposes are here. Everything they look forward to is here, for they are not children of God. But the child of God hears the call from heaven. He lifts up his heart, his eyes, his ears, and his hands, for his life is hid with Christ and God in heaven. This is what the Lord has done for us who have looked in faith to Him.

November 22

Hebrews 11:14–40

TRUSTING GOD

By faith Abraham, when he was tried, offered up Isaac: and he that had received the promises offered up his only begotten son (11:17).

In the providence of God, you may have been called upon to give up the joy of your home, the delight of your soul. Oh, the sorrow of those days of separation! You may have been forced to make a choice between earthly and heavenly love, between the human call of the world and the divine call of God. How hard it is! It was so with Abraham. There was no sadder journey than the journey of those three days. Every step of the way was like the slow tolling of a bell, like drops of blood heard falling from a fatal wound.

Abraham trusted God before Isaac was born. For a hundred years God had been his shield and his exceeding great reward. He had trusted God when the laughing, happy boy stood before him, the child of promise. He would trust God if the boy lay still in death on the sacrificial altar. The duty of Abraham was to obey God; it belonged to God to keep His promises.

November 23

Hebrews 12:1–11

GROWING THROUGH DISCIPLINE

And ye have forgotten the exhortation which speaketh unto you as unto children, My son, despise not thou the chastening of the Lord, nor faint when thou art rebuked of him: for whom the Lord loveth he chasteneth, and scourgeth every son whom he receiveth (12:5–6).

I heard of a small boy who was on a play horse, a little rocking horse, in a department store. His mother pleaded with the child to get off the horse, as it was time to go home. The little boy would not do it. She was one of these mothers who had been taught that you must not lay a hand on the boy, you must not discipline him, because you might warp his personality! So she just pleaded with the little boy to get off the horse, "Please, please, pretty please, get off the horse." But he would not get off.

So the manager was called, and he begged the child to get off the horse, but with no results. Then they called the psychologist. He came and whispered something in that little boy's ear, and the boy got off at once. When they arrived home, the mother asked her son, "What did that psychologist say to you?" The little boy replied, "Mama, that psychologist said to me, 'Listen, if you do not get off that horse right this minute I am going to beat the daylights out of you!'"

Discipline is necessary for growth and edification. It is not optional. It should come from a heart of love and not from an attitude of anger.

November 24

Hebrews 13:1–25

THE SAME GUIDE

Jesus Christ the same yesterday, and today, and for ever (13:8).

If you have traveled abroad, you have found that from place to place your guide has been changed. You had one guide in Rome, another in

Athens, another in Israel, and another in Moscow. It is not like that in the Christian pilgrimage. We have one guide and one leader from the beginning to the end.

Moses led the children of Israel into the wilderness, but it was Joshua who led them into the Promised Land. Not so with us. We have one leader who will lead us to our Promised Land. We have our Lord in the springtime of life, in the days of strength and energy. Our Lord is with us also in the noonday of life, bearing the burden in the heat of the day. And we also have our Lord at the eventide of life, when the way grows weary.

Our Lord is with us in affluence that He might crown it. He is ours in poverty that He might console us and cheer us. He stays at our side in dishonor and shame that he might somehow lead us and help us. He is our Lord in fame and honor that He might sanctify us. He encourages us in sickness that He might heal us. He is our Lord always. That is why when a man preaches Jesus, he preaches the gospel. When a missionary stands in a darkened land and lifts up the cross, that is the light of the world.

November 25

James 1:1–17

THE ORIGIN OF THANKSGIVING DAY

Every good gift and every perfect gift is from above, and cometh down from the Father of lights, with whom is no variableness, neither shadow of turning (1:17).

On a streetcar in Prague, Czechoslovakia, I was seated next to a woman who began to extol the virtues of communism. She said, "There are no poor in a communist nation. There are no poor in Czechoslovakia. There are no poor in Prague." I replied, "There are no poor in Prague because all of you are poor. You have the bare necessities of life. Were it not for the Western world, you would starve."

The communists of Russia and China cannot deny their Marxist ideology, and they dare not admit that their system is futile and failing. There is no such thing as prosperity in a socialist country. The people there increasingly fall into debt and despair.

There is no such thing as a successful communist religious enterprise.

Did you know that when the Pilgrims came to America in 1612 they established a communist society? They suffered hunger and nearly starved to death. The Pilgrims were deeply religious, but they were so hungry that they stole food from their starving fellow workers.

In 1623 they turned away from that communist communal property and the common storehouse, and they gave each family a parcel of land for its own use.

> Women went into the fields willingly, taking their children along with them. All women, men, and children planted as much corn as they felt they could possibly work.
>
> People who had formerly complained that they were too weak to dig or hoe, declaring that it was tyranny to make them undertake such work, gladly began to plant and cultivate for themselves.
>
> When the harvest was brought in, instead of famine, there was plenty. So they all gave thanks to God.

They had a day of Thanksgiving and praise to God, which is where our American Thanksgiving celebration originated.

November 26

James 1:19–22

THE REFLECTION OF A MIRROR

But be ye doers of the word, and not hearers only, deceiving your own selves (1:22).

James likens the Word of God to the truth that a mirror will reflect. A mirror does not lie to you. It reflects you exactly as you are. And the Word of God does that, too. We see ourselves as we are in the Word of the Lord. If we do not do anything about it, we are like the man who looks in the mirror and sees what he ought to do, but he just goes on and forgets about it. For example, he looks in the mirror and notices he ought to shave, but he does not shave. He looks in the mirror and sees he needs a haircut, but he does not get his hair cut. Or he notices that his face is dirty, but he does not wash it.

Two boys were talking and one said to the other, "I know what you had for breakfast this morning." The other boy asked, "What?" The first boy replied, "You had eggs for breakfast. I see it on your face." The boy answered, "I did not—that's what I had the morning before last." James uses a similar illustration about the Word of God.

November 27

James 1:23–27

PRAYER AND VISITATION

Pure religion and undefiled before God and the Father is this, To visit the fatherless and widows in their affliction, and to keep himself unspotted from the world (1:27).

When our church built Embree Hall, we invited the finest company we could locate to create six stained-glass windows. The artist came, and I worked with him. Three of the windows on one side represented the old covenant, and the three on the other represented the new covenant. When the artist came to the third one on the side of the new covenant, I asked him if I could design it. He said, "I would love to see it." So I drew it for him. In the center I drew a medallion and in the medallion a picture of a church with a spire pointing toward God. On one side I drew a pair of clasped hands, and on the other side a hand knocking against the door. Underneath the clasped hand I put the word "Prayer" and underneath the hand knocking at the door, the word "Visitation." The church is built up by prayer (intercession) and by visitation (knocking at the door).

Pure religion, downright genuine religion before God and the Father is this—to visit—to knock at the door. This was the ministry of our Lord who from village to village and city to city and house to house invited men and women to the faith, and this was the great ministry of the apostles.

November 28

James 2:1–9

DIFFERING ATTITUDES

But if ye have respect to persons, ye commit sin, and are convinced of the law as transgressors (2:9).

In the days of the Cavaliers under Charles I, there was a permissive society in England. Then the pendulum swung the other direction, and Charles I lost his head. Oliver Cromwell, the Puritan, came to head the Commonwealth. In those days, pleasure of any kind was looked upon with disdain. I read in a history that the Commonwealth was against bear baiting, not because they were particularly compassionate for the bear but because they did not like the pleasure it brought to the bear hunters. After the Commonwealth, the people brought Charles II to the throne, and the Cavaliers were back again. Thus does human society oscillate from one extremity to the other.

If that differing attitude toward fault is true in society and government, think how true it is in our individual lives. Look at how we are. Here is an affluent man, successful and famous. But he also has faults, derelictions, sins, and failures. Because of his position and his wealth we have a tendency to overlook his sins and to look upon them as eccentricities and idiosyncrasies. But if the fellow is ragged and poor and falls into faults and failures, he brings down the wrath of society on his defenseless head. I am just telling you how we in the world react toward fault, failure, sin, and shortcomings.

November 29

James 2:10–26

LAW AND THE CHARACTER OF GOD

For whosoever shall keep the whole law, and yet offend in one point, he is guilty of all (2:10).

Though a person may look upon himself as being righteous and may walk in his own integrity, God knows his heart. There is no person who does not sin. Sin brings with it a separation and an alienation from God.

The whole world (including us in it) is representative of the laws in the character of God. All of these laws—planetary, gravitational, mechanical, thermodynamical, chemical, physical, governmental, anatomical, and civil are grounded in the character of God.

Every law has a penalty for its violation. A person who sneers at gravitational laws and walks off a ten-story building into blank space comes down to death. He does not break the law; he just illustrates it.

Consider an anatomical law. Our body has to follow certain chemical lines, but a man ridicules God's laws of anatomy and asks for a vial of strychnine. He swallows the strychnine and dies in horrible convulsions.

There are governmental laws. The Bible plainly says that government and law are of God. Society is impossible without it. An anarchist actually believes in the destruction of the human race. So a man stands before the judge and says, "I realize I have broken the law, but it is a trifle and I am expecting to be dismissed." The judge sternly replies, "Sir, I must uphold the law and you must obey the law, for without my upholding the law and your obeying the law, we would be swept away by terror, murder, rape, and robbery. For the law is given for the upholding of society."

November 30

James 3:1–12

THE UNCONTROLLABLE TONGUE

But the tongue can no man tame; it is an unruly evil, full of deadly poison (3:8).

Do you remember those three little monkeys? One has his eyes covered—see no evil. One has his mouth covered—speak no evil. And one has his ears covered—hear no evil.

A gossipy tongue is a dangerous thing
If its owner is evil at heart.
He can give whom he chooses many a sting
That will woefully linger and smart.

But the gossipy tongue would be balked in its plan
For causing heartburning and tears,
If it weren't helped out by the misguided man
Who possesses two gossipy ears.

The whole body is involved and the whole body is defiled when we use our tongue and words to hurt and not to bless.

The tongue is uncontrollable. We can tame the birds and the serpents and the animals in the sea. You can tame and train almost anything, but when the tongue gives itself to words of hurt, it is beyond recovery, beyond taming. The tongue is uncontrollable.

December 1

James 3:13–18

AN UNKIND WORD

And the fruit of righteousness is sown in peace of them that make peace (3:18).

Our lives and our destiny are changed by words. A giant horse is turned around with a little bit in the mouth. A tremendous ship is guided by a little rudder. A vast conflagration is set afire by a little spark. Sometimes just by the arching of an eyebrow or a sneer from the lips or by a shrug of the shoulders, we hurt and destroy. All of us have felt the sting of unkind words.

A godly Quaker came up to her pastor and said, "Pastor, I would think, and dost thou not also think, that if one lived beautifully and walked correctly and stayed away from evil that others seeing us would be inclined to love our religion?" And the pastor replied, "Sister, if thee covered thyself with a coat of feathers white as the driven snow, and if thee had a pair of wings as shiny as those of the angel Gabriel, on this footstool of the earth there would be somebody, somewhere so color-blind as to shoot thee for a blackbird."

You cannot get away from the unkind word. All of us have felt it—the sting and the hurt of it. Sometimes it can be disastrous. The same tongue that blesses God can also curse other men.

December 2

James 4:1–10

THE GRACE OF GOD

Humble yourselves in the sight of the Lord, and he shall lift you up (4:10).

In days gone by in Great Britain a flaming preacher named John Bradford was out on the Commons. He was preaching to a throng of villagers about the goodness of God and the saving knowledge of Jesus. During his sermon, the sheriff and the bailiff, with their henchmen, passed by. They were escorting a man who had a rope around his neck. The poor fellow was to be hanged. John Bradford stopped preaching, and with his eye he followed the officials leading that man with the rope around his neck. Then John Bradford lifted his right hand, pointed to them, and said, "My brethren, there, but for the grace of God, go I."

Why is it that we have not fallen into some of the unthinkable sorrows and heartaches that afflict others? It is not because we are any better, though we think we are. It is not because we are superior, though we suppose we are. It is not because they are the dregs of the earth and we are the angelic elect of heaven. It is only because God has mercy upon us. He somehow chose in His sovereign grace to be good to us.

December 3

James 4:11–17

A SHELL OF LIFE

Whereas ye know not what shall be on the morrow. For what is your life? It is even a vapor, that appeareth for a little time, and then vanisheth away (4:14).

A man with a lovely wife and two darling little girls went off into sin and the world and left his family. The wife moved to the edge of town, rented a hovel of a house, and took in washing to support herself and her family. The girls grew up, and she gave them the finest education she could. They became beautiful young women. Some years later her husband came back home. He knocked at the door and the wife went to answer it. At first she didn't recognize him. He was diseased, and his life was ruined. He had come back home and asked her to take him in. She cared for him until he died. We cannot help but admire a woman like that. I doubt if anyone, anywhere, would say, "That man did a noble deed." Something on the inside of us says that the man did a horrible thing.

Are you like that? Are you giving your life to the devil and to sin? At the end of the way will you cast at God's feet a hull and a shell? We must realize that the strength of a person's life, his finest thoughts, and all that he is, belong to God. A person should give his heart to Christ in his greatest strength and serve the Lord all the days of his life.

James 5:1–12

THE CURSING TONGUE

But above all things, my brethren, swear not, neither by heaven, neither by the earth, neither by any other oath: but let your yea be yea; and your nay, nay; lest ye fall into condemnation (5:12).

After driving through Montana where one of the great national forests had burned to the ground, I asked the ranger what caused the destruction. He said that the flick of a cigarette had set it afire and destroyed that great forest. Oh, what a little thing can sometimes do! It is like that with words. The same mouth can be used to praise God or to curse Him.

When I was pastor in a little country church, each man in the assembly was important because there were only six of them. One of those men would always refuse to pray. I ate dinner in his home, and he did not say grace at the table. Being very young and foolish and falling into places that even angels would not dare to enter, I asked him why. He said, "When I get angry, I am volatile in my spirit and I curse. When my plowing team does not do as I want them to do, I curse them. My boy has heard me curse, and, when you ask me to pray in public, my boy is there and I am ashamed. When we eat dinner at the table, I do not say grace because my boy is there, and he has heard me curse and I am ashamed." How sad! The tongue that could praise God used His name in vain and curses.

Once an outstanding leader in America lost the respect of the American people when they learned how he talked if the world was not listening. It was sad. When a person speaks, let his yea be yea and his nay be nay, and he should never curse. Cursing is a sign of mental and moral weakness. When a person speaks in curses, others know that his speech, his tougue, and his heart are morally and intellectually weak. Let your tongue be one of forthright honesty and integrity. Let its language and vocabulary praise God and bless others.

December 5

1 Peter 1:1–12

THE PURPOSE OF GOD

Elect according to the foreknowledge of God the Father, through sanctification of the Spirit, unto obedience and sprinkling of the blood of Jesus Christ: Grace unto you, and peace, be multiplied (1:2).

Before a stone was laid in the construction of St. Paul's Cathedral i London, the idea was born in the mind of Sir Christopher Wren. He sav the cathedral in his mind, and he purposed in his heart to build it. Befor Michelangelo struck a chisel against the heavy rock of marble, he saw th mighty Moses in his mind. Before Raphael, the dedicated young artist, pu brush against canvas, he saw the spectacular picture of the Sistin Madonna in his mind.

It is thus in the perfection of God. God has in His heart and mind a pla and purpose that lies back of the work He does in the universe and i human life. This revelation of the God of purpose, of planning, of activit of expression is found all through the Word. Not just adventitiously o inadvertently; rather it is woven into the very revelation of God.

December 6

1 Peter 1:13–19

RED BECOMES WHITE

Forasmuch as ye know that ye were not redeemed with corruptible things, as silver and gold, from your vain conversation received by tradition from your fathers; but with the precious blood of Christ, as of a lamb without blemish and without spot (1:18–19).

A little boy and his father were in a building in London watching parade through the window. The British soldiers were dressed in brillian red coats. The little boy exclaimed, "What beautiful white uniforms the have!" The father said, "Son, they are not white; they are red, brilliant red. "Oh, no," said the little boy, "they are white, just as white as snow."

With surprise the father looked more closely. Around the window was a border of red glass, which he had not noticed before. When one looks at something red through a red glass, it looks perfectly white. And the little boy, looking at the scarlet coat through the red glass, saw it as pure white. Thus does God look at our sins through the blood of the Crucified One, and we look pure and white.

December 7

1 Peter 1:20–25

A MULTITUDE OF MANUSCRIPTS

But the word of the Lord endureth for ever. And this is the word which by the gospel is preached unto you (1:25).

Printing was not invented until fifteen hundred years after Christ. Men wrote down God's holy Word in manuscript form. There are 4,105 ancient Greek texts of the New Testament, almost 30,000 ancient Latin versions of the New Testament, and more than 1,000 other versions besides the papyri and the quotations from the Fathers.

Fifteen hundred years after Herodotus lived, only one manuscript copy of his history was still in existence. Twelve hundred years after Plato lived, only one manuscript copy of his great classics remained. Just one manuscript of the annals of Tacitus exists today. Only a few more than that exist from Sophocles, Euripides, Thucydides, Virgil, and Cicero. But of the Bible thousands and thousands of ancient manuscripts still exist. God caused many to be written so that if a copyist made an error or if someone tampered with the text, we could easily see the error by comparing it with the other copies.

God made provision to keep His Word infallible, and He continues to provide for the preservation of His Word. If a modernist translation of the Word of God is produced, the Lord will see to it that many other translations are true and faithful to the infallible Word. If a preacher apostasizes, God will raise up a preacher in another pulpit who will be true to the Word of the Lord. That is also true of a church. If a church turns aside from the faith, God will raise up another community of churches which will preach the gospel in faith and power and with the blessing of the Lord.

God's Word cannot be corrupted or written with error. God will see to it that any discrepancies are discovered and corrected or removed.

December 8

1 Peter 2:1–25

THE BEAUTY OF IMITATION

For even hereunto were ye called: because Christ also suffered for us, leaving us an example, that ye should follow his steps (2:21).

One day in the International Airport in New York City, I met the man who was at that time the Governor of Maryland. He is a gifted political leader who delivered the keynote address at the Republican Convention that nominated Richard M. Nixon for president.

Learning that I was a pastor, he began to talk with me about the things of God and about his family, who were Methodists. He spoke of his mother as a devout Christian woman. He said, "My mother had an unusual habit. When she went down to the altar to take the Lord's Supper, she always took off her jewelry and put it in her purse before she knelt." He continued, "As the days passed and I grew up, I found myself taking off my jewelry. I would take off my ring and wristwatch when I knelt to take the Lord's Supper. Last Sunday morning, when I knelt to take the Lord's Supper my teen-age boy was kneeling by my side. To my utter amazement, he took off his jewelry—his ring and his watch."

That is nothing but imitation. There is no special reason for it. The man imitated his mother, and he in turn was imitated by his son. How glorious it is to imitate God!

The sons of old Eli did not imitate their father. The sons of Samuel did not imitate their father. Absalom did not imitate his father David. But our Lord Jesus imitated His Father. He was an exact duplicate. "To see Me," He said, "is to see the Father."

December 9

1 Peter 3:1–15

:EADY TO WITNESS

But sanctify the Lord God in your hearts: and be ready always to ive an answer to every man that asketh you a reason of the hope ıat is in you with meekness and fear (3:15).

When I was preaching at a Bible college in Alabama, the president of the ollege told me a story about one of his students. The student had recently een marvelously converted and was happy in the Lord. The young fellow aid to an older man standing beside him at a bus stop, "Are you a :hristian?"

The older man replied, "Yes, sir, I have been a Christian for over forty ears."

The young fellow said, "If you have been a Christian for over forty years, ıow is it that you did not ask me if I was a Christian?"

Years ago I was talking to a businessman in the city of Dallas, and the ıame of a deacon came up. I said to him, "That man is a deacon in our hurch and one of our finest men. He is a superintendent of one of our ;unday school departments."

The businessman replied, "I did not know that. I have done business vith him for twenty-five years, and I did not even know he was a Christian."

We are not all gifted alike. But when we were converted we were called ɔ witness, and God opens doors for us. We must witness. In some humle, sweet, and precious way, we must say a good word for Jesus. When e are saved, we are saved to be witnesses.

December 10

1 Peter 5:1–14

ı PASTOR'S CROWN

And when the chief Shepherd shall appear, ye shall receive a rown of glory that fadeth not away (5:4).

To pastor a church has been the one and only thing I ever wanted to d I have been asked to be president of a university and of a college. I ha been asked to share in some of the executive places in our denomin tional life. In my younger years, because I was so vigorous a preacher ar so zealous an evangel, everyone thought that I would be an evangelist. B nothing has appealed to me except being pastor of a church.

George W. Truett, my predecessor, was like that. He said, "If anythir happened that I could not be pastor of a church, I would go up to the he of the hollow [he was using a term from his North Carolina heritage], an would organize a church and be its pastor." Hearing him say that, I love the thought, I loved listening to him avow it, and I felt a response to tho words in my own soul. To pastor a church, to tend a flock, to shephe God's redeemed is a beautiful and heavenly assignment.

I can say in truth that if I were to resign from the church and becon President of the United States or Prime Minister of the British Empire would feel that it was a step down. It is a God-given calling to minister the church of God.

December 11

2 Peter 1:1–21

SCIENTIFICALLY ACCURATE

For the prophecy came not in old time by the will of man: but holy men of God spake as they were moved by the Holy Ghost (1:21).

How different from this verse is the popularly accepted idea of th writing of the Holy Scriptures! I shall quote from an eminent theologia who is apologizing for the Bible, and in quoting his testimony, I am givir you the attitude of many in the theological world. As he apologizes for th Bible, he says, "Of course, there are scientific errors in the Bible. Howeve we can excuse such mistakes on the grounds that the Bible is not textbook of science and therefore we do not expect it to be scientifical accurate."

I agree with the theologian that the Bible is not a textbook on scienc The Bible is the Word of God written for the salvation of our souls that w might be delivered from damnation and hell.

However, if the Bible is not also scientifically accurate, it is not, to me at least, the Word of God. I have a very plain reason for that. The Lord God who made this world and all the scientific marvels which we are now discovering in it—that same Lord God knew all these things from the beginning. We do not surprise Him with our discovery of the sound waves on which our church services are broadcast. God made those radio waves in the beginning, and we have just discovered them. Jet propulsion that speeds planes along through the sky is not a surprise to God. He made that force in the beginning. Now if the Bible is the Word of God, and if God inspired it, then it cannot contain any scientific mistakes, because God knew every truth and fact of science from the beginning.

December 12

2 Peter 3:1–18

REPENT OR ELSE

The Lord is not slack concerning his promise, as some men count slackness; but is long-suffering to us-ward, not willing that any should perish, but that all should come to repentance (3:9).

A poignant story in history occurred in the days of the Maccabees when Antiochus Epiphanes sought to destroy the faith. He turned the temple into a house of worship for Jupiter, boiled a sow, and poured its juice all over the holy vessels and altars of the temple. He was trying to make the Jews worship in Greek ceremonial services. In addition, he sought to conquer all of the East.

As long as Antiochus Epiphanes carried out his conquests in the far Middle East, Rome was not aroused. But when he came down to conquer Egypt, he touched the breadbasket of the Roman Empire. Their granary and wheat fields were on the Nile. So the Roman Senate in 165 B.C. sent Gaius Laenus Popilius to confront Antiochus Epiphanes. Gaius stood in front of Antiochus and said, "The Roman Senate demands that you desist from this campaign. Take your army out of here and return to Antioch where you came from, or else face war with the Roman legions." When Antiochus was confronted with that demand, he asked for time to consider the matter. So Gaius took his staff and drew a circle in the sand around

Antiochus. Then Gaius said, "Before you get out of that circle, you will give me your answer for the Roman Senate." Of course, facing war with the Roman legions, Antiochus capitulated. He took his army, left Egypt, and vented his anger upon Judea and Jerusalem.

Facing God is not optional with anyone. God demands it. A person must repent of his sins and give God an answer. Repentance has nothing to do with any kind of experience, nor is it waiting for a marvelous happening from heaven. We have no choice. We are to turn our faces Godward and turn our backs to sin and the world.

December 13

1 John 1:1–10

CALL UPON JESUS

But if we walk in the light, as he is in the light, we have fellowship one with another, and the blood of Jesus Christ his Son cleanseth us from all sin (1:7).

Affirm it for yourself whether Christ be living or not. Try praying to Jupiter, Jove, Juno, Janus, or to any other of the gods of old. Attempting such a thing would make us feel foolish. Try calling on the name of Alexander the Great, Augustus Caesar, Washington, or Lincoln. Such an act of appeal would be ludicrous in the extreme, a travesty in the name of religion. But try calling upon the name of Jesus; try praying in the name of Jesus. There is answer; there is power; there is the presence of God.

We feel like saying with the poet Richard Gilder:

If Jesus Christ is a man,
  And only a man, I say,
That of all mankind I will cleave to him,
  And to him will I cleave alway.

But if Jesus Christ is a God,
  And the only God, I swear
I will follow Him through heaven and hell,
  The earth, the sea, and the air.

1 John 2:1–17

GOD'S INVITING LOVE

And he is the propitiation for our sins: and not for ours only, but also for the sins of the whole world (2:2).

There is a divine meaning in the death of Christ. This is God's plan for our salvation. There is no pardon and peace apart from atonement. There is no remission of sins apart from the shedding of blood, and there is no reconciliation without the payment of death. This is our atonement, our propitiation, our sacrifice for sin. This is our means of reconciliation to God. The cross to the apostle Paul and to us is the same thing as the brazen serpent raised in the wilderness was to Moses and the children of Israel. It is a sign of universal love, mercy, forgiveness, and healing from the hands of God.

Look and live, my brother, live!
Look to Jesus now and live;
'Tis recorded in His Word, hallelujah!
It is only that you "look and live."

The cross is a sign of our atonement. It is a sign of our forgiveness. It is a sign of God's inviting love, His invitation to pardon and forgiveness. It is an invitation to life. The cross has an upraised beam. Raised toward the sky, it points toward God in heaven. It has a lower part that touches the earth. God, reaching out His loving hand, extends it down even to us. It has crossarms and they go in either direction as far as the east goes east and as far as the west goes west. The arms of the cross are extended to the limits of the earth. It is the open invitation to all people everywhere to find life, liberty, forgiveness, mercy, and salvation in the atoning love, sobs, tears, and suffering death of the Son of God. We are all welcome.

December 15

1 John 3:1–24

NO SURPRISES FOR GOD

And he that keepeth his commandments dwelleth in him, and he in him. And hereby we know that he abideth in us, by the Spirit which he hath given us (3:24).

Two men, Jim and Joe, went down the aisle in a revival meeting. Years passed and one day the evangelist again saw the pastor of that church in which he had led the revival. He said to the pastor, "You know, I remember that night when two men, Jim and Joe, came down the aisle and gave their lives to Jesus. How are they?" And the pastor replied, "Jim is a saint. He is a pillar in the church. He has grown in grace and is a strength in the house of God. Joe went back into sin after three weeks."

Did that surprise God? No, for God knew all about it. God looked on the inside of the heart and saw Jim's faith and a commitment that glorified Him, and the angels rejoiced. God also saw that Joe had just made a gesture—an outward profession—and it was not in his heart at all. God knew all of that, but the pastor did not know it. The evangelist did not know it. The people did not know it. It was only in works that Jim proved he was justified by faith. It was only in works that Joe proved he had no regenerated experience at all. The only way you can demonstrate what is in your life is by what you do.

December 16

1 John 4:1–6

FROM BONDAGE TO FREEDOM

Ye are of God, little children, and have overcome them: because greater is he that is in you, than he that is in the world (4:4).

John Newton's mother died when he was a small boy, and his father was a sea captain. Newton also went to sea and fell into the most prodigal and profligate life. After being impressed into the British navy, he became a deserter. He eventually sold himself to a slave trader in Africa and fell as low as a man could descend. Then he found the incomparable grace of God in Christ Jesus. Here is a poem that he wrote of his marvelous conversion:

I saw One hanging on a tree
　　In agony and blood;
He fixed His languid eyes on me
　　As near His cross I stood.

Sure, never, till my latest breath,
　　Can I forget that look:
It seemed to charge me with His death,
　　Tho' not a word He spoke.

My conscience felt and owned the guilt,
　　And plunged me in despair;
I saw my sins His blood had spilt
　　And helped to nail Him there.

Alas! I knew not what I did—
　　But now my tears are vain:
Where shall my trembling soul be hid?
　　For I the Lord have slain.

A second look He gave, which said,
　　"I freely all forgive:
This blood is for thy ransom paid,
　　I die that thou may'st live."

Oh, can it be, upon a tree
　　The Savior died for me?
My soul is thrilled, my heart is filled,
　　To think He died for me.

The inscription on John Newton's grave in the little English town of Olney reads: "John Newton; once an infidel and libertine, a servant of laves in Africa, was by the rich mercy of our Lord and Savior Jesus Christ reserved, restored, pardoned, and appointed to preach the faith he had ong labored to destroy." There is power in the gospel.

December 17

1 John 4:7–21

THE FOUNTAIN SPRINGS OF LIFE

We love him, because he first loved us (4:19).

One cannot be a Christian without loving the Christ. Sometimes th love is expressed in adoring silence—just being quiet in His presenc Sometimes that love is expressed by irrepressible tears that are like show ers of rain—tears falling from our faces in His presence. Sometimes th love is expressed by deeds of mercy done in His name. Sometimes th love is expressed by the confession of His faith at the peril of life. Howev it may be, it will always express itself if you love the Lord.

I once read a psychology book in which the thesis of the author was th the fountain springs of life are our emotions. And he discussed them: lov hate, jealousy, fear, ambition, and so on. It is like that in religion, also. Tak feeling or emotion out of religion and it turns to dust and ashes. Think of person's patriotism or love of country. A person is born with an emotion feeling for his country.

So we are bound to our Lord by emotions and by love.

December 18

1 John 5:1–12

HELP SOMEONE HELP HIMSELF

He that hath the Son hath life; and he that hath not the Son of God hath not life (5:12).

Once I was in a drug store looking for something among all tho counters. A big fellow came up to me and asked, "Aren't you Dr. Criswell" I told him that I was. He commented that he had been to our church c occasion and had listened to me every Sunday on television.

The man then told me his story. He was a drunkard—an alcoholic. H said that alcoholism was ruining his life and asked if I could help hir There are thousands of people who need help.

What if someone came to your church to find strength and encouragement, and you treated him as a stranger? Or what if someone came to find strength and help and encouragement, and the spirit of your church was full of divisiveness and quarrelsomeness?

Here are some steps by which you can help someone help himself. (1) He must admit that he is a sinner. The wages of sin is death. (2) He must admit that he cannot help himself. Can he forgive his own sins? No, he must find help outside himself. (3) That help is found in Jesus. When we were without strength, in due time, Christ died for us. (4) He must associate himself with the people of God. He can find strength in their presence.

Personal religion is something that ought to live in me. It is the way I ought to be and it is something other people ought to feel in my presence. They should be constrained to love our blessed Lord.

December 19

1 John 5:13–21

YOU CHOOSE, LORD

And this is the confidence that we have in him, that, if we ask any thing according to his will, he heareth us (5:14).

When we pray, we should pray, "Lord God, I do not know what is best. But You know what is best. I do not understand sometimes, and I cannot see the end of the way; so, Lord, I am not trying to impose my will on yours. You choose, Lord. This is how I would like for it to be done; however Lord, not my will, but Thine be done."

I remember a mother who prayed over her dying son. The Lord answered her prayer and the boy lived. But years later he was electrocuted in the state penitentiary for murder and robbery. How much better if that mother had prayed, "Lord, if the boy can live and honor You, or if it is God's will that he be translated to heaven, Your will be done."

We should pray, "Lord, am I to die? If You can give me length of days, help me to honor You in every breath I breathe. But Lord, if it honors You that I die, then Master, give me dying grace. Your will be done."

Some things we know are God's will. It is God's will that all people be saved. It is God's will that all people come to repentance. Therefore, when I pray for a person to be saved, I am praying according to God's will.

December 20

3 John 1–12

NO GREATER JOY

I have no greater joy than to hear that my children walk in truth (v. 4).

Once I conducted a revival meeting in a strategic church in one of the greatest cities east of the Mississippi River. The pastor of that church was a gifted man. Sometime before that I had gone to a Southern Baptist Convention and listened to that pastor preach the convention sermon. He did it in power, and in the true spirit of Christ he blessed the thousands who were there. In a plane, riding back to Dallas, a Methodist businessman was seated next to me. We began to talk. He found out that I was a Baptist minister and proceeded to tell me a story.

In the little town where he grew up, a young girl gave birth to an illegitimate child. Everyone knew about it, and she was covered with shame and disgrace. She moved to the edge of town, and there, in a humble cottage, she took in washing and reared that little boy. The mother worked hard to rear her son, giving him music lessons and speaking lessons and anything else she could do for him. She sent him through high school and then through college. He also went to seminary and became a minister.

The businessman then told me that the young man had become one of the great preachers in the Southern Baptist denomination. He asked me if I had ever heard of him. When he told me his name, it was the person who had just delivered that powerful sermon at the Southern Baptist Convention. I have since heard of the reverence and love with which he took care of his mother all the days of her life. That man is in heaven now, and I believe that he shares with that wonderful mother the shepherd's crown given to those who minister to the flock.

December 21

Jude 1–25

HE DANGER OF IDOLATRY

Now unto him that is able to keep you from falling, and to present ou faultless before the presence of his glory with exceeding joy, To he only wise God our Saviour, be glory and majesty, dominion and ower, both now and ever. Amen (vv. 24–25).

For seven hundred years the brazen serpent that Moses lifted up in the nidst of the camp was an idolatrous snare to the people of God. When ood King Hezekiah came to the throne, he broke it to pieces.

How strange people are. The Russians say they do not believe in God, ut everyone seems to have to worship something. One day I stood in line o walk by and look on the pale face of Nikolai Lenin. Since 1924, housands of people gather every day to pay obeisance to the dead form f Lenin.

What a snare it would have been had Satan seized the body of Moses, rought it before the people, and let them bow before the great lawgiver! lichael the archangel, when contending with Satan, dared not accuse im but said, "The Lord rebuke thee."

December 22

Revelation 1:1–18

HE LIVING JESUS

I am he that liveth, and was dead; and, behold, I am alive for vermore, Amen; and have the keys of hell and of death (1:18).

Once when I was flying home from a preaching assignment, I sat next to young man who extended his hand to me and asked, "Are you W. A. riswell, Pastor of the First Baptist Church in Dallas?" I nodded.

He said, "My name is Charles Cox. I am returning to Dallas from a ilgrimage to the Holy Land. I listened to you preach on radio Sunday norning at the 8:15 service. In the university, I was studying to be a rofessor of religion. We studied the higher critical approaches to the gospel, the lower critical approaches to the text, and all of the divisive destructive things that are written in the scholastic world about religion Then one day during the Lord's Supper, something happened to me Suddenly it came to my heart. 'This is real! He actually died. He paid the atoning price for my sins. He was raised for my justification. He lives. Jesus is real!' Jesus came into my heart. I asked to be ordained and was then assigned to be Assistant Pastor of the Highland Park Methodist Church Now I have been given a little congregation that meets in a school in Grand Prairie. I go from door to door, witnessing about the Lord Jesus. am so happy talking to people about the Lord, inviting them to church asking them to believe on the Lord Jesus for their salvation."

There is not a fact in human life or history more identifiable and confirmable than the fact that Jesus lives. He was raised from the dead. He is in session at the right hand of God. He is living in His churches.

December 23

Revelation 2:1–29

THE BURDEN OF WEALTH

And I will give unto every one of you according to your works (2:23).

At a meeting in 1923 at the Edgewater Beach Hotel in Chicago nine famous men met. They were the richest men in the world. An author writes of them twenty-five years later:

1. Charles Schwab, president of the world's largest steel company, died in bankruptcy, living his last five years on borrowed money.
2. Samuel Insell, president of the world's largest utility empire, died penniless in a foreign land, a fugitive from the law.
3. Howard Hopson, president of the world's largest gas company, went insane.
4. Arthur Cutten, the world's greatest wheat speculator, died abroad in bankruptcy.
5. Richard Whitney, president of the New York Stock exchange, ruined by the years, was sentenced to Sing Sing Penitentiary in the state of New York.

6. Albert Fall, member of the President's cabinet, was pardoned from prison to allow him to go home to die.
7. Jesse Livermore, the greatest trader on Wall Street, committed suicide.
8. Ivan Krueger, head of the world's greatest monopoly, committed suicide.
9. Leon Frazier, president of the Bank of International Settlements, committed suicide.

When you look at life, even casually, you see that there is a truth in what esus says: "It is more blessed to give than to receive."

That man may last, but never lives,
Who much receives, but nothing gives.
Whom none can love, whom none can thank,
Creation's blot, Creation's blank.

December 24

Revelation 5:1–14

SCENDING PRAYERS

And when he had taken the book, the four beasts and four and venty elders fell down before the Lamb, having every one of them arps, and golden vials full of odors, which are the prayers of saints 5:8).

There is an old Talmudic legend about Sandalfond, the angel of prayer. nd the story of his assignment has been written in verse.

Standing erect at the outermost gates
Of the city celestial he waits
With his feet on the ladder of light.
Listening breathless to the sounds that ascend from below.

From the spirits on earth that adore,
From the souls that entreat and implore
In the fervor and passion of prayer.
From the hearts that are broken with losses
And weary with dragging their crosses
Too heavy for mortals to bear.

And he gathers the prayers as he stands
And they change to flowers in his hands.
Into garlands of purple and red.
And beneath the great arch of the portal,
Through the streets of the City Immortal
Is wafted the fragrance they shed.

That is a beautiful and biblical sentiment. Our prayers ascend up t heaven, and as the angel presents them before God, they are turned int fragrances like beautiful flowers. And there they come up before God i precious intercession.

December 25

Revelation 7:1–17

THE MEANING OF CHRISTMAS

Saying, Amen: Blessing, and glory, and wisdom, and thanksgiving, and honor, and power, and might, be unto our God for ever and ever. Amen (7:12).

Once when I stayed at a hotel in Jerusalem I visited a Jewess who had gallery of paintings. She had on display there in her shop a painting of th Wailing Wall. If one visits there, he will see soldiers with their guns, fatigu uniforms, and belts of cartridges, mingling with those old orthodox rabbi in their felt hats with the little fur bells that mark them as being faithfu worshipers of Jehovah. After the Six Day War there was such incompar able jubilation on the part of God's people that the orthodox rabbis an those armed soldiers joined hands and danced together in the presence c God at the Western Wall. I purchased the painting of that scene.

The Jewish woman, Maria Nura Sonis, was born in Moscow and reare in Budapest. This gifted, intellectually perceptive, and discerning lady is Jewess who has found the Lord. Every Sunday she drives to Tel Aviv an teaches a Sunday school class. She told me about a dinner during whic she sat beside the general who led the Israeli Army to victory in the Six Da War and who later served as Minister of Defense for Israel. When h inquired of her what she was doing, she answered that she was preparin to rejoice in the Christmas festivities honoring the birth of Christ. She witnessed that Jesus is the Messiah of God, the King of the Jews, the King of the Gentiles, the King of the nations, and King of all kings.

As she spoke so victoriously of the meaning of Christmas, she testified that the man bowed his head and put his face in his hands. Lifting up his face after a long, meditative period, he said to her, "My dear, you do not know how much I envy you." There never has been, there never shall be a gift from God that approaches the incomparable preciousness of the gift of Christ Jesus.

December 26

Revelation 12:1–11

THE INFLUENCE OF A FRIEND

And they overcame him by the blood of the Lamb, and by the word of their testimony; and they loved not their lives unto the death (12:11).

There were two lawyers who were partners, one named Will and the other Tom. One night, during a tabernacle revival meeting, down the aisle went the lawyer Will, confessing Christ as his Savior publicly. Early the next morning Will got up to go to his office and gather together his personal belongings. He wanted to dissolve the partnership, thinking in his heart, "My partner, Tom, is a bitter critic of the church and of Christ and of God. I do not think I can stand his ridicule, sarcasm, and all of those bitter things he says about God."

On the way down the street he met the last man in the world he wanted to see, his partner Tom. Tom looked at him and said, "Will, why are you up so early, and where are you going?" Will replied, "Tom, last night I gave my heart to Christ. I know how you feel about God and Christ and the church. I just do not think I can live under your bitter and sarcastic criticism. So I got up early this morning, before you would be down, to gather my things and dissolve the partnership."

Tom replied, "Will, you did not know it nor did anyone know it. But last night I went to that meeting and stood outside the tabernacle. I saw you go down the aisle, give your hand to the preacher, stand before the people, and confess your faith in God. You and I have been partners all these years. We have always stood side by side. We have been through numerous cases, trials, and difficulties. Will, when I saw you standing up there by yourself last night, it just seemed to me that I ought to be standing by your side. The reason I have come early this morning is that I thought maybe you would teach me how to become a Christian."

December 27

Revelation 16:1–21

ONLY TODAY

Behold, I come as a thief. Blessed is he that watcheth, and keepeth his garments, lest he walk naked, and they see his shame (16:15).

There is no yesterday with God. Nor is there tomorrow with Him. Always there is just now with God. He sees the end from the beginning, and all of life is present before His infinite eyes. To us things happen a day at a time, but not with God. The whole panorama of human history is open before Him, and He sees it as if it were the present.

Once when I was a boy I went to Soldier's Field in Chicago on Labor Day to see a parade that extended many miles. All of the different labor unions were marching with bands, flags, banners, and personnel. The arena is built in the shape of a horseshoe, and at the end of the field the marchers came in, one at a time. I sat there for a long period watching them enter, and I finally became bored. So I climbed to the top of the stadium, and from that vantage point I could see the entire parade moving by. Far up Michigan Avenue I could see the final contingent, and down below I could see them come to their places in the stadium.

We are as if we were in the stadium. We see events happen one at a time each day, each hour. But the Lord God stands in His heavenly place and sees all history. All mankind is present before Him.

To some extent our lives are also like that. Yesterday is gone forever. Tomorrow we do not yet possess. We only have now, this moment, and that is all. The difference between us and God would be that we are here in a moment, whereas He is forever. The difference is that we are finite like a speck—like a moth—living in a moment. In His infinitude, God is eternal.

Revelation 19:1–21

THE FINAL DAY

And the beast was taken, and with him the false prophet that wrought miracles before him, with which he deceived them that had received the mark of the beast, and them that worshiped his image. These both were cast alive into a lake of fire burning with brimstone (19:20).

There are about one hundred different elements, all of which can be reduced to liquid and finally to gas. The ocean is an example, for it is made of hydrogen and oxygen, which are both highly combustible.

My high school chemistry teacher illustrated this by placing a vial of hydrogen in a beaker and then putting a match to it. It made a great explosion, and when we opened the container, only a drop of water was left. Our world is covered with oceans and seas of water made of highly combustible material. When we see something burning, it is not on fire. Rather it is oxidizing. The union of oxygen with whatever elements are in that article is what is on fire. All God has to do is to speak the word, and His elements become a flame of fire.

Geologists say that we literally live our days upon a burning mass of molten lava. God would have only to break the crust of the earth and all would burst into a molten mass.

The astronomer also adds his picture. He looks up into the heavens and finds exploding stars and burned-out spheres through great galaxies. The Scriptures tell us that when that awesome day comes, the moon will turn to blood red and the sun will be shot out in darkness like sackcloth of ashes. When the moon turns blood red, it will be a reflection of the burning of the earth. The shadows of the burning fire will make the moon look red; and when it says the sun is darkened like sackcloth of ashes, I think the fire and the smoke of the burning air will shut out the very sun itself and it will be dark. What a day that will be, when God makes His final intervention in human history!

December 29

Revelation 20:1–15

COMING HOME

Blessed and holy is he that hath part in the first resurrection: on such the second death hath no power, but they shall be priests of God and of Christ, and shall reign with him a thousand years (20:6).

To the Christian, what the world calls death is but a sounding of the trumpets on the other side of the river to announce the coming home of God's chosen children. What the world calls death is to us nothing but the angels coming to take us up into Abraham's bosom. What some call death is nothing but the sailor coming home from the sea and the hunter from the hills. Robert Louis Stevenson wrote a little poem to be inscribed on his tomb, and it is there to this day:

> Under the wide and starry sky,
> Dig the grave and let me lie.
> Glad did I live and gladly die
> And I laid me down with a will.
>
> This be the verse you gave for me:
> Here he lies where he longed to be;
> Home is the sailor, home from the sea,
> And the hunter home from the hill.

That is death to the child of God—coming into port, the pilgrim's coming home. If for me to live is Christ, to die is a gain. If for me to live is the world, to die is a loss. If for me to live is money, to die is a loss. If for me to live is sinful pleasure, to die is a loss. If for me to live is self, to die is a loss. But if for me to live is Christ, to die is a gain. Oh, blessed hope, precious comfort.

Revelation 21:1–27

GOD'S UNCHANGING GRACE

And he that sat upon the throne said, Behold, I make all things new. And he said unto me, Write: for these words are true and faithful (21:5).

At a national convocation of prison chaplains in Arlington, Virginia, the chairman of their board was as fine looking a man as you could ever see. Earlier he had been convicted of embezzling from a bank and was sent to prison, but there the grace of God changed his life. Now he is not only a fine businessman but also a deacon and the treasurer of his church. Another man had been convicted for writing more than $40,000 in bogus checks. He is now a fine officer in a national corporation. Another speaker had been a murderer, but in prison God's grace had so changed his heart and life that the governor had given him a full pardon.

Another speaker had been a hit man for the Mafia. He had been sentenced to live in the penitentiary. But the grace of God cleansed his soul, and he, too, had been given a full pardon.

Still another speaker had become deranged because of a tragedy that overwhelmed the world, the Second World War. During the Nuremberg Trials for the Nazi war criminals in Germany, he was the American representative assigned to carry out the executions. He had hanged twenty-two men. The oppression of that assignment had unbalanced his mind, and he turned to alcohol and finally to drugs. Because of this he was sent to the penitentiary, but through a prison chaplain the Lord Jesus Christ healed his mind and soul and made him a new man. Now he is a stalwart defender of the faith.

As I listened to testimonies of the marvelous grace of God, I could hardly imagine how such a thing could be. I thought of the marvelous, incomparable, indescribable blessings that God has shed upon us in the atoning grace of our blessed Lord.

December 31

Revelation 22:1–17

A GLORIOUS GOSPEL

And the Spirit and the bride say, Come. And let him that heareth say, Come. And let him that is athirst come. And whosoever will, let him take water of life freely (22:17).

One Sunday morning in a church of which I was pastor, God gave us a wonderful harvest of souls. We were not in a special series of meetings; it was one of those morning hours when God's Spirit works mightily. As I pressed the appeal, down the aisle came a ten-year-old boy. He gave me his hand and said, "I take Jesus as my Savior; I will follow Him in baptism and be a member of His church." I welcomed the boy, and he was seated.

When I looked up, down the same aisle was coming the most notorious gambler and outlaw of Indian Territory days, seventy-four years old. Deeply moved, he said to me, "I repent of my sins; I give my heart to Jesus; I want to be baptized and become a member of this church."

When I lifted up my eyes again, I saw coming down the same aisle a feeble, tottering old man. He was a full-blooded Cherokee Indian, one hundred and three years old. When he came to me, he said, "I take Jesus as my Savior; I want to be baptized and become a member of His church." Among the others who came, these three sat together, the boy, the notorious outlaw, the aged Indian. All alike were repenting of their sins, trusting Jesus as their Savior, entering the kingdom of Jesus through the one door of hope.

What a glorious gospel! What a wonderful Savior! Oh, my friend, the door is open to you, wide as the world is wide, high and broad as God's infinite heaven. While there is hope, while days of grace are given us, heed the call of the Spirit. While our hearts are strangely moved toward heaven, come, let us walk in to safety, to life, to heaven, and to home.

Acknowledgments

These devotional messages have been adapted from books written by Dr. W. A. Criswell.

Acts: An Exposition, Volume I, © 1976
Acts: An Exposition, Volume III, © 1980
The Baptism, Filling & Gifts of the Holy Spirit, © 1973
The Bible for Today's World, © 1965
Ephesians: An Exposition, © 1974
Expository Sermons on Galatians, © 1973
Expository Sermons on the Epistle of James, © 1975
Expository Sermons on the Epistles of Peter, © 1976
Five Great Affirmations of the Bible, © 1959
The Gospel According to Moses, © 1960
In Defense of the Faith, © 1967
Isaiah: An Exposition, © 1977

All of the above books were published by The Zondervan Corporation and are used by permission.

Did Man Just Happen? (Chicago: Moody Press, 1980)
Used by permission.

Look Up, Brother! (Nashville: Broadman Press, 1970)
All rights reserved. Used by permission.

The Scarlet Thread Through the Bible (Nashville: Broadman Press, 1970)
Used by permission of the Criswell Center for Biblical Studies.

Sources for Devotional Messages

See Acknowledgments, page 307, for complete book titles. Devotional titles were prepared especially for *Abiding Hope*.

January

1 / The Mystery of the Human Body — pp. 116–117, *Did Man Just Happen?*
2 / The Hoax of Evolution — pp. 27–28, *Did Man Just Happen?*
3 / The Certainty of Judgment — pp. 141–142, *Acts,* Vol. I
4 / The Foundation of All Values — pp. 89–90, *Acts,* Vol. III
5 / These Are My People — pp. 49–50, *Acts,* Vol. III
6 / How to Please the Devil — p. 51, *The Gospel According to Moses*
7 / The God of Healing — pp. 86–87, *The Baptism, Filling & Gifts*
8 / The First Bright Spot — pp. 101–102, *The Gospel According to Moses*
9 / Equality for All — pp. 39–40, *James*
10 / A Bent to Sinning — pp. 149–150, *The Gospel According to Moses*
11 / The Weeds in Your Garden — pp. 279–280, *Ephesians*
12 / Lent to the Lord — p. 104, *Acts,* Vol. I
13 / A Mandate From God — p. 54, *Acts,* Vol. I
14 / Through the Eyes of God — pp. 127–128, *Galatians*
15 / Gaining Through Loss — p. 282, *Acts,* Vol. III
16 / The Measure of Devotion — pp. 212–213, *Galatians*
17 / The Gift of Faith — p. 74, *The Baptism, Filling & Gifts*
18 / A Prophet's Great Need — pp. 17–18, *Look Up, Brother!*
19 / A Chariot of Fire — p. 235, *Acts,* Vol. III
20 / The Great Encourager — pp. 206–207, *Isaiah*
21 / Fighting the Battle — pp. 24–25, *Look Up, Brother!*
22 / Who Is the Missionary? — p. 234, *Acts,* Vol. I
23 / What Is Life? — pp. 84–85, *James*
24 / Satan's Boundaries — pp. 104–105, *Peter*
25 / The Emptiness of Infidelity — pp. 236–237, *Acts,* Vol. I
26 / The Entire Picture — pp. 153–154, *Peter*
27 / Who Knows the Future? — p. 55, *Peter*
28 / The Bible and Science — pp. 20–21, 24, *The Bible for Today's World*
29 / Life Is Fleeting — p. 197, *Galatians*
30 / Prosperity for a Partner — p. 101, *Peter*
31 / The Downfall of a Nation — p. 69, *Peter*

February

1 / Comfort in Affliction — p. 115, *James*
2 / The Insignificant — pp. 154–155, *Peter*
3 / The Inadequacy of Reason — pp. 55–56, *Ephesians*
4 / God's Tracks in the Sky — pp. 10–11, *Five Great Affirmations*
5 / The World's Need — pp. 178–179, *Acts,* Vol. I
6 / Trust and Commitment — p. 277, *Acts,* Vol. I
7 / From Mourning to Rejoicing — pp. 114–115, *Ephesians*
8 / We Trust in Thee — pp. 263–264, *Acts,* Vol. III
9 / Rejoice in the Lord — pp. 23–24, *Look Up, Brother!*
10 / Christ—The Answer — pp. 179–180, *Acts,* Vol. I

March

April

1 /	The Original Evolutionists	pp. 18–19, *The Bible for Today's World*
2 /	The Pilgrimage	pp. 189–190, *Isaiah*
3 /	In Your Own Strength	p. 199, *Isaiah*
4 /	What Is Prophecy?	pp. 34–35, *The Bible for Today's World*
5 /	The Fruit of Infidelity	pp. 156–157, *Acts*, Vol. I
6 /	When the Spiritual Mercury Is Low	p. 60, *Acts*, Vol. I
7 /	Right Is Forever Right	pp. 16–17, *In Defense of the Faith*
8 /	Look and Live	p. 216, *Isaiah*
9 /	God Has a Plan	p. 225, *Isaiah*
10 /	The Mercy of God	p. 26, *James*
11 /	The Tragedy of Disfigurement	pp. 229–230, *Isaiah*
12 /	The Heartbreak of Rejection	p. 237, *Isaiah*
13 /	The Paradox of Prophecy	pp. 57–58, *The Bible for Today's World*
14 /	Death of the Lamb	p. 251, *Isaiah*
15 /	The Abundance of Divine Wares	p. 255, *Isaiah*
16 /	Change Wrought by the Word	p. 75, *Isaiah*
17 /	The Eternality of God	p. 270, *Isaiah*
18 /	Sharing the Word	pp. 94–95, *James*
19 /	Rise and Shine	pp. 62–63, *Isaiah*
20 /	The Noblest Calling	p. 238, *Acts*, Vol. III
21 /	The Lighting of a Fire	pp. 194–195, *Isaiah*
22 /	The Human and the Divine	pp. 52–53, *The Bible for Today's World*
23 /	The Tragedy of Delay	pp. 160–162, *The Gospel According to Moses*
24 /	The Deceitfulness of the Human Heart	p. 128, *Acts*, Vol. I
25 /	The Clothing of the Soul	pp. 84–85, *Galatians*
26 /	Who Does the Changing?	pp. 55–56, *James*
27 /	Prerequisite for Pardon	pp. 88–89, *Peter*
28 /	Fire That Liberates	p. 211, *Isaiah*
29 /	A Non-Compromising Faith	pp. 28–29, *Galatians*
30 /	A Gethsemane Experience	pp. 214–216, *Galatians*

May

1 /	The Monument to a Slave	pp. 249–250, *Ephesians*
2 /	How to Empty a Church	pp. 34–35, *Peter*
3 /	Healing in His Wings	pp. 58–59, *Ephesians*
4 /	The Greatest Conflict	pp. 18–19, *The Scarlet Thread*
5 /	The Great Physician	p. 110, *James*
6 /	Let the Bible Speak for Itself	pp. 27–28, *The Bible for Today's World*
7 /	The Consequence of Worldliness	p. 185, *Acts*, Vol. I
8 /	Empty-Handed	pp. 197–198, *Galatians*
9 /	The Narrow Way	pp. 171–172, *Acts*, Vol. I
10 /	The Gnat on Mt. Everest	pp. 17–18, *In Defense of the Faith*
11 /	The Reality of Suffering	pp. 113–114, *James*
12 /	The Appeal for Pardon	p. 107, *Galatians*
13 /	Delivering the Truth	p. 55, *Acts*, Vol. III
14 /	The Faithful Witness	pp. 33–34, *Peter*
15 /	The Gift of Miracles	pp. 83–84, *The Baptism, Filling & Gifts*
16 /	Come Unto Me	p. 94, *Peter*
17 /	The Master's Hand	pp. 205–206, *Isaiah*
18 /	Breaking the Bonds	pp. 105–106, *Peter*
19 /	The Seed of Life	pp. 113–114, *Peter*
20 /	The Size of Faith	p. 117, *Peter*

June

July

August